33 on Sunday

Two Friends Struggle to Advance to the Pinnacle of American Auto Racing

Rich Gilberg

illustrations by Todd Buschur

Copyright © 2023 by Rich Gilberg. All rights reserved.

Illustrations by Todd Buschur

This is a work of fiction. Names, characters, businesses, places, events, locales, and incidents are either the products of the author's imagination or used in a fictitious manner. Any resemblance to actual persons, living or dead, or actual events is purely coincidental.

This book or any portion thereof may not be reproduced or used in any manner whatsoever without the express written permission of the publisher except for the use of brief quotations in a scholarly work or book review. For permissions or further information contact Braughler Books LLC at:

   info@braughlerbooks.com

Printed in the United States of America
Published by Braughler Books LLC., Springboro, Ohio

First printing, 2023

ISBN: 978-1-955791-84-7

Library of Congress Control Number: 2023919640

Ordering information: Special discounts are available on quantity purchases by bookstores, corporations, associations, and others. For details, contact the publisher at:

   sales@braughlerbooks.com
   or at 937-58-BOOKS

For questions or comments about this book, please write to:
   info@braughlerbooks.com

Dedication

This book is dedicated to Fred and Delight Gilberg.

Credits

I have many people to thank for their contributions to the creation of this book. The late "Mutt" Anderson and his sons Mike and Phil were a rich source of stories and details of car preparation. Jim Simon provided technical explanations. Steve Stapp was generous with his time, knowledge, and experiences in this sport. Rosemay Stapp was just as important, providing another point of view of 60's racing. Drivers Tom Bigelow, Larry Dickson, Buzz Rose, Bruce Walkup, and Johnny Rutherford provided first-person perspectives. Phil Reilly helped explain chassis adjustments. Bob McConnell was generous with his time and collection of cars.

Medical issues and treatments were explained by Dr. Mark Hess. Elaine Rosier and Meredith Matheny shared insights into horsemanship. Dave Kramer's vast collection of memorabilia from the New Bremen Speedway was an important source of detail. Danny Dicke, son of New Bremen promoter Frank Dicke, provided important track information. John Mahoney shared some of his many photographs.

The wonderful illustrations were by my good friend, Todd Buschur.

Michael Moeller read and critiqued the manuscript. Jane Ann Vest helped prepare the final copy.

Indianapolis programs, Floyd Clymer's annual books, Open Wheel magazines, other motor sports periodicals, and countless books were all important background.

There may be others who helped create this fictional portrayal that were inadvertently omitted, an oversight for which I apologize.

Preface

This story is fiction, but what happens is not impossible. I am an enthusiast, not an "insider." I was never a helper in the pits. I never drove a race car (except for two fan experiences). When I was young, my interactions with drivers were simple. "Sir, can I have an autograph?" Or perhaps, "May I take your picture?"

The events in this book are my creations, but they could have occurred. The people are not actual people that have been renamed. Their creation was informed by years of watching racing from the stands, reading books and magazine articles, watching race films, and listening to men (and women) who experienced auto racing in the 1960's. I knew years ago that I wanted to write about racing as I had seen it but understood that mere enthusiasm for the subject could never be enough to create a factual book. That has been done by writers such as Joe Scalzo, John Sawyer, and L. Spencer Riggs. Those men had experiences and connections that enabled them to write with great authority. That could never be me. However, I had sufficient knowledge of the cars, tracks, drivers, mechanics, and owners that allowed me to imagine characters and events that could represent that time which I, to this day, consider to be the "best of times." Though I am realistic enough to say that it was also in some ways the "worst of times."

In 2016, I set out to write my first book, *17 Minutes on Sunday*. Books, memories, and magazines weren't enough. I knew that from the start. My credits page lists the people with whom I spoke about their involvement and experiences in sprint car racing in the 1960's. I could not have started with better participants than Steve Stapp and Clarence "Mutt" Anderson. Steve's father raced at Indianapolis in the 1920's and 1930's. Steve built and raced his own cars, and after his retirement from driving, an impressive list of men drove his cars, resulting in two national championships. Mutt's involvement began in the late 30's and continued with great success for four decades. Roger McCluskey won the 1966 National Sprint Car Championship in his car. Had I started my project earlier, I could have included many other individuals. Sadly, their generation is passing on, along with their knowledge and experiences. Such discussion would have enriched this book, which is a sequel to the book mentioned above.

My goal was to create a "rounded" depiction of drivers and related individuals. One incident that I observed in the pits at the Dayton Speedway in the mid 60's became the germ of an idea that stayed with me for over fifty years. It was not a dramatic racing incident, no argument between drivers and officials, no mechanic throwing tools, no accident. Nothing of that sort. Just as a driver was preparing to qualify, his distraught wife ran to him, saying their son had been playing on the race car trailer, had fallen and was badly hurt. I have not used that event, but it motivated me to portray the "human" side of this sport. I feel comfortable with these imagined events. Those men and women were average people. They were not wealthy. They dealt with the stresses and rewards of family life and worked forty-hour jobs. They had those responsibilities AND drove dangerous cars on dangerous tracks. Most came from humble beginnings.

It was common then that a man might race in the 500 and two days later be back at work in an auto body repair chop, as a deputy sheriff, or manager of a motel. After winning the 1953 and 1954 Indianapolis 500, Bill Vukovich often could be seen working in his Fresno service station.

At the very outset of my project, I told Steve Stapp that I wanted to create a work that would honor all the men like him (a dedicated family man) who made auto racing, for me, an incredible spectacle. It is for the reader to decide if I have achieved that goal.

Chapter 1

Tom Lawton walked out on the porch of his old farmhouse on a gray, wet Sunday morning in February. His well-used Ford pickup was reluctant to start on damp days, and today would probably be no exception. Tom followed his usual routine—pump the accelerator two times, hold it down halfway, then turn the key. The engine turned over easily. Then it turned over and over and over without firing. Soon he could smell gasoline, and he knew the engine was flooded. He cussed the old truck half-heartedly, went back into the house, got another cup of coffee, another doughnut, then sat on the porch swing for a few minutes, killing time till the truck would be more cooperative.

He was not a tall man—a little over five feet eight inches—nor in perfect physical condition. He was soft and pudgy in the middle and his upper body and arms did not impress one as muscular. His thinning, brown hair was cut in a short crew style and was sparse. His daughter, Tina, teased him, saying, "My horse's brush has more hair than you, Dad." His doctor was concerned about his chronically low blood pressure. Tom self-medicated: vitamins, a lot of them. His thirty-five-year-old body did not handle the hot and humid months of July and August well, leaving him flushed, sweaty, and weak.

He walked out to the barn to check on his daughter's horse. The filly had caught her right flank on a fence nail which had ripped through its skin. The vet had been out yesterday and prescribed an antibiotic ointment. The horse heard Tom walk into the barn, looked at him, snorted, and ambled to the other side of the stall. "Yeah, I know, you're disappointed to see me, so you couldn't be hurtin' too much." The horse was his sixteen-year-old daughter's pride and joy and anyone else was just second best. Second best would be good for Tom. He and "the old hayburner"—just one of his many names for Candy—did not relate. "Well, old Paint, your mistress will be out soon, I'm sure. I gotta go see a man about…horsepower! Ain't I so-o-o damn funny this morning!"

The next time the truck started like a new one, and Tom put it in reverse, let the clutch out—it chattered and grabbed, shaking his left foot—then backed out of the barnyard and headed down the long lane. He'd take Ohio Route 127 south till he hit Route 47 where he'd turn west and drive on to Muncie, Indiana.

The drive would take around an hour and a half. It wasn't a good day to be alone for an hour—a guy can think too much, and Tom had a lot to think about. There were the normal concerns of family and money, but Tom had a number of uncertainties to face. His car-owner/mechanic, Chuck Williams, had agreed to take on a new sponsor for the upcoming racing season and field two sprint cars. Chuck had built a new car for Billy Wallace, a young Arizona hotshot. Tom had been guaranteed Chuck's older car, the red number eleven that he'd driven last year a few times. Fair enough, but Chuck had delegated the maintenance of number eleven to his young nephew, Donny. Donny knew his way around a race car well, but he'd be responsible and on his own. Chuck had said, "Hell, Tom, I'll be there! He can ask anything! We'll be pitted next to each other!"

But Tom knew Chuck's attention would be on the new car. There were always many issues to be sorted out with a new car, and they'd occupy Chuck. Donny was not Chuck, despite his considerable experience. He was so young. Tom had to stop this train of thought. He knew he was lucky to be assured of that car for the entire season, unlike the last few years when he was jumping from car to car, seldom advancing to better ones.

Currently, there was an issue looming over Tom, one that was seldom far from his thoughts. The service station that he owned was supplied by a major oil company. Rumors had reached Tom about corporate plans to build a new station on the main highway through Barton. That meant they would no longer supply Tom's little station. In order to stay in the local market, they'd treated him well, enabling him to operate at a decent profit. Losing that advantage meant he'd have to get another supplier, and he could hardly hope to get that kind of deal again. Those rumors had not so far included the name of Tom Lawton as manager of this prospective new station. What would he do? Sell the station? It really wasn't in the best location now, since the new highway went through another part of town and bypassed his "antique" station. What other oil company would want to provide their products to him? That unknown oil company could never match his current supplier's price per gallon. His deal had been an indulgence from a sympathetic regional director.

So, what *would* Tom Lawton do if he lost his station? That income was a bit more than half of the family's earnings. Janet still had her job at the farm store, but by itself that would not support his family. And Tom had no single, marketable skill. He could do some basic auto maintenance. Maybe Wally would take him on, but that would be like starting over, like a kid. He'd being doing oil changes, mounting new tires, replacing batteries: grunt work, school-boy work. Factory work?

Well, yeah, there was that, but he'd lose the flexibility of being his own boss. He might have to start on the night shift. If he had a race on a Friday night, or had a long drive for a Saturday race—how would he work that all out? Should he just give up his racing dream?

Crap! Gotta get your mind off that stuff! I don't even remember stopping in that last town! Red lights? Tom pushed in the lighter on the dashboard and got a Camel out of the glove box. *Janet won't know. I'll chew some gum on the way home.* Tom turned on the radio to occupy and distract his thoughts. He drove on for another thirty minutes with the "Top Forty Countdown" on the Fort Wayne radio station playing hits of the day—the louder the better, even though he didn't like the music.

As he neared Muncie, he passed a garage that entered cars in local modified stock car races. It was an awful-looking business. When the overhead doors were up, it looked like a black hole. How could anyone work in there and come out alive? One could imagine a great fiery hearth far in the back and sweaty men beating glowing iron with giant hammers. There were junk cars scattered all around the shabby, Quonset hut shop. The odd thing was…that guy turned out some of the best looking and fastest cars Tom had ever seen at that level of competition. *Sure, ain't Chuck's way! But it works for that guy.*

Tom drove another two miles and arrived at Chuck's garage. The contrast was jarring. Chuck's cement block shop was painted white, and even though there were some junk cars around, they were at least in rows and parked so far back they were barely noticeable. There were two gas pumps out front and a tall Sinclair Oil sign, the one with the green dinosaur, near the road. Identification was simple and direct: **Chuck's Garage** was painted above the front windows and office door. When he bought it, it was called **Chandler's Garage**. He quickly painted over the **andler's** part, kept the

Ch and added the **uck's** in front of garage. But Chuck's was shorter than Chandler's, so there was a large gap between Chuck's and Garage. *Big deal. I'm known as a good mechanic, not a sign painter!* Chuck thought. It stayed that way and was the source of many good-natured jokes and pranks.

Chuck Williams was sixty years old, tall and stooped, deliberate and measured in his movements and speech. He wore his full, dark hair in the style of Clark Gable, parted on the left and combed back. His mechanical skills had won him a contract to maintain the buses for his local community school. In the morning, he drove a bus route, and the rest of his day was spent on auto and truck repair work for farmers and residents. He was gifted with an uncanny ability to toggle between a kind, welcoming expression that greeted his youngest bus riders, to a dark and baleful demeanor that immediately put high school boys on guard.

A few old, scrap school buses were parked to the right of the shop. Fifty yards to the left was Chuck and Ernestine's ranch-style house, with a neat lawn and cement sidewalk extending from the front door to the sea of limestone gravel that surrounded the entire house-shop-parking lot. That gravel showed the effects of Chuck's efforts to control weeds. He had his own special mixture that he called "weed-away", a mixture of old engine oil, kerosene, and gasoline, to stop unsightly growth around his shop. It was cheap and effective—what it did to the soil never crossed his mind.

Tom drove to the right side of the building and parked near the back. This was the part of the shop that Chuck reserved for his race car, or more accurately now, three cars. Donny Housman, Chuck's nephew (his sister's son), was the first to notice Tom when he walked in.

"Well, if it ain't my race car driver! Still remember how to drive these things?" Donny laughed and got off the floor in front of the red number eleven that Tom would drive this season. "I was just putting new radiator hoses on. Cheap way to avoid an unfortunate experience, ya know."

"Are those fast hoses, Donny?" Tom asked.

"Uh…I think…oh I get it! You do have a sense of humor, don't you?"

"Occasionally I can make a joke, Donny, but it's not my usual way. You workin' on this buggy enough? Ain't gonna wait till the second week of April to get serious, are you?" Tom lit a cigarette and sat on a shop stool. "Your boss, old Chuck over there, looks like he's got his hands full."

"He's about got Olsen's car all done. He had some guy over in Indy repair the nose piece and tail. I don't know how any guy could beat that aluminum back in shape, but it looks like new," Donny arched his eyebrows and slowly shook his head. "Fiberglass is easier, but Olsen wanted it done the old way."

Last year, that car had gone over the turn two guardrail at the high-banked Dayton half-mile speedway, taking the life of Rex "Smitty" Smith. The car-owner, Cal Olsen, hired Chuck to rebuild it. Chuck agreed with the understanding that he could make a copy of the car. Olsen's car was nearly done, lacking a few minor details.

Nearby, on jackstands, was the car that Chuck was building—his copy of Olsen's number seven. It looked like two steel ladders propped up on their sides with pieces of steel tubing tying them together. Chuck was putting tabs on the frame members, lost in the glow and crackle of his welder and didn't even notice when Tom walked in. Tom didn't say a word, just stood with his head turned to avoid the hot blue-white glow of the welding. Chuck pulled his welding rod back, flipped up his helmet, and looked at what he'd just done. Then he nodded his head to flip his helmet down, stopped, and pulled it back up—like a movie actor's second take.

"Tom! I'll be damned! Bet you just happened to be driving around—sixty or so miles from home—and thought, 'Guess I'll gas up here,' right?"

"Sure, Chuck, you know why I'm here. This time of year comes around, well, we're all thinking same thing," Tom said.

"Yeah, we're about, what…six or seven weeks till the Midwest opening race—Eldora. I'm doin' double time on Olsen's car and my new one. Ain't even driving my morning bus route now. Ernie's takin' that and the afternoon route. Gives me a good two hours or so to work here. Donny handles a lot of the routine work now. Billy might not be too happy, but I think I'm gonna skip that Reading race in March. That's a long haul in iffy spring weather."

Tom interrupted, "Speakin' of Billy, where is he? Still sellin' cars over in Indy? That's a challenge when all them used cars are covered with snow. I don't see Billy brushin' cars off every morning."

"That kid is always workin' some deal, can't say that's all bad. Some owners like a 'floater' like Billy. They don't like a guy with a steady job, say they like a hungry driver. You know, a driver that needs money drives harder."

"So…what's that say about me, Chuck?"

"Nothin'. You're different than most drivers. I know you got family to take care of, but in the car you're a hundred percent. I never worried about you that way, Tom," Chuck said matter-of-factly.

"Yeah, I might be one of those hungry racers soon, I don't know. They're talkin' about puttin' the screws to my station. Might lose my supplier, so who knows?"

"Oh," was all Chuck said.

"I suppose I can find something if I have to, but things are kind of unsettled for us now."

"I could help some, but you ain't gonna drive sixty miles a day for garage work."

"Barton's got some little factories. I'll find something, if I have to. Anyway—back to Billy. What's up with Hot Shot?"

"Olsen was here a few weeks ago, and he told me Billy drove some indoor midget races—Ft. Wayne and Cincinnati. Won one of those, not sure which one, and wrecked in the other. That Olsen's got money to burn. He paid the owner of that car to fix it, and then he bought it for Billy! Gave him some money and told him to take it out to California. They're still tryin to keep those midget programs goin' out there, you know—Ascot, the Orange Show, El Cajon, and…I don't know, some others, too. He's always ready to race. That Olsen is gonna be after him to drive *all* his cars. Billy is just burnin' to drive Olsen's Watson at Indianapolis this year. That's Smitty's car from last year's 500."

"What you sayin', Chuck?"

"That yellow number seven there is an Olsen car and Billy ain't drivin' it, yet. We don't sign contracts here, you know. Our arrangements are like Hollywood marriages. Billy can jump ship any time he wants, and Olsen can fire C.J. just as fast. So, you might start the season with Billy as your teammate, but he's goin' where he wants to go. You could have your pick of cars later on, Tom."

"Lot of things up in the air. At least you got one driver for sure, huh?" Tom said.

"Yeah, that's right. And Donny over there, he's lucky to have you. Anyway, look at my new car and Olsen's car. I wanna show you what I think may make that thing handle so damn well."

Chuck and Tom walked over to the yellow car. It was nearly complete, but with the nose cover and fuel tank off the suspension was easier to see. In some ways, it was a slightly

smaller version of an Indianapolis car. Chuck thought that may have been a partial explanation for its success.

Chuck said, "Look up here at the front. No leaf spring like on our red car. 'Course we knew that. It has torsion bars that slide in these chrome-moly frame members. One for each front wheel. That's the spring, if you want to call it that. And over here on the left side, just inside that front wheel, you see that bolt head stickin' up there on that little collar? You turn that down with a wrench, and that jacks weight into the right front. Just like we do with our red car, except we do that on the leaf spring."

"Put weight on the right front and that also transfers some to the left rear, just by twistin' the frame, huh?" Tom said.

"And you can do the same in back, 'course we been doin' that because we got torsion bars back there on number eleven. But this is a four-bar, just like them Indy roadsters. You can adjust them so much easier. And…get this. I'm gonna buy four farm scales. I can put the car on them scales and I can tell how much weight is on each wheel. No more guessin'! Write it in the book, and there it is all accurate for next time!

"Very scientific, Professor Williams!" joked Tom. "Think I'll be happy to drive old reliable here while you and Billy figure out this new buggy. I wonder how patient he'll be."

"You got a point there, for sure," Chuck just nodded his agreement. "And there's Olsen always just waitin' for Billy to get fed up with less than first place. Hey, another thing I want to show you. Come look at the rear axle."

They both walked to the rear of the yellow car. Chuck said, "Look at that bracket. They call that a Jacob's ladder. On the left side. I never seen one like that, they're always on the right, at least as far as I know. Maybe that has something to do with the way that thing handles so well."

"What's that rubber inner tube lookin' thing on the floor?"

"Olsen wants me to put that in the fuel tank—fuel bladder. A new-fangled idea, the way I see it. The way that tank split in that wreck, it's a wonder it didn't turn into a torch. Musta been 'bout empty. Anyway, that thing helps seal the tank in a wreck."

"You gonna put one in your new car, or number eleven, for that matter?"

"Geez, them things are expensive!"

Tom shrugged, "Cheaper than a funeral. I'll let you figure

that out though. You got an engine ready to go for the new car?"

"On that stand over there. I'm not gonna do a lot different, but I am tryin' a new cam this year. I'm keepin' that Wilson that's in number eleven, but I put an Engle roller cam in my new car. Engine is brand new, well you know, new to me. Chevys got that new 327, you know about that, don't you? I got one out of a new Corvette that some guy totaled. Only had six thousand miles on it. I stripped the engine and had Donny take it over to Dell's. He line-bored it and decked the block for me, and here's my new thinking, Tom. I got a 283 crank, from the factory, brand new! I'll machine a few modifications on it, clearances and stuff. Should go right in that 327 block, pretty much. Should give me around 301, 302 cubic inches. I think that thing will really wind up! I ported the heads and put stock valves in it, but some better valve springs. Really, didn't want to change much, you know. You put a bunch of new stuff in and, well, if it don't run good, it's harder to isolate the problem. Changin' that crank and cam will be enough."

Tom listened, nodded his head, and looked at Donny, still working on the other car. Tom lowered his voice and said, "So, our boy-mechanic over there, has he learned enough, you think?"

"I know what you're sayin' Tom. I think so. And he can always ask, but I gotta be honest, he better do his askin' before the car comes off the trailer. It's gonna be hectic with this new car. I can handle a few questions, but he'll be your man. Don't you think you can make it work? The two of you seemed to get the car sorted out at Kokomo last fall in our little dry run."

"Yeah, I guess so."

Just then, Donny asked, "Tom, you like this 'granny' seat that Chuck put in before Langhorne last year? Some guys say they interfere with their right arms, you know."

"Yeah, but I don't want to go back to them Sam Browne belts, Donny." Tom walked over to the red car he would drive this season, climbed in the seat, and twisted the steering wheel slowly through ten or twelve degrees of a circle. He sat there, silent, for a good three or four minutes while Donny went about his work. "You still got that old seat, don't you? I'd like to know we could go back to that."

Donny said, "I keep all the old stuff in the back room."

"That's good. Donny, I'm goin' home soon, after I talk to Ernie for a while. I guess she's in the house, Chuck?" Chuck was focused on his new car and didn't respond. "Ok, guys. I'll see you in about a month or so, let's just stay in contact." Tom walked out of the shop and headed to the little ranch house, hoping to catch Ernestine "Ernie" Williams for a chat, and, if he was lucky, a piece of pie and fresh coffee.

* * * * *

On that same Sunday afternoon, Billy Wallace pulled off the freeway a few miles outside of Gardena, California, with the left rear tire on his trailer smoking and squealing. He managed to get pulled into the first service station he found. He parked in the side lot, away from the pumps, got out and looked at the smoking tire and wondered how and where he could fix this problem. A man—station owner or maybe attendant—walked out.

"Well, I'll be! That is one sweet lookin' race car. You at El Cajon today? You have a good day?"

"Well, good night and a bad day," Billy said flatly. "They tell me this midget racing ain't what it used to be out here, but these guys still know how to race. I ran out of luck or something Friday night at a race over in Arizona. Engine went sour and I thought maybe I could pick up a car and run today at El Cajon, a URA program. But that good night sorta got in the way of racin' today. I need to go up to L.A.

and get the engine goin' again. But first, I gotta fix this tow rig, of all things. That left rear wheel ain't turnin'. Must be a seized bearing."

"Always something, I suppose," the man said and then got distracted by another customer.

Billy went inside the station and got a bottle of Coke. He had a little money left for a few more days on this road trip. A win would help him get by more easily, but now he had a lame trailer to fix, and he was no ace mechanic. Billy stood sipping his Coke and tapping his right foot. He was not a big man—a bit over five and a half feet tall—but made up for that with confidence. His full, blond hair was combed back in long wavy strands. He looked like a surfer—tanned and trim—and had a ready smile. He didn't have to do much to attract attention from the opposite sex.

This problem though couldn't be solved with charm. He walked out to the station wagon, got in and sat thinking, when the man shouted at him. "Hey! Hey! You want to work on that thing here? I ain't got nothing in the shop."

And that's how Billy got the repair started on his trailer. By the time he got the wheel off and bearing out, it was late. And it was Sunday, anyway, so there was no way to get a new part till Monday. Billy Wallace, "up-and-coming", racer slept in his back seat that night behind the gas station. Billy admitted to himself, *This would not be a place for Roxie, that's for damn sure. She made the right decision. But still a pretty companion would be more fun, for me, at least.*

Cal Olsen had given Billy a shot at the big-time last summer at the Milwaukee 200. Cal owned several cars: a Watson Indianapolis car, an upright Kuzma championship dirt car, and that yellow number seven sprint car that Chuck had repaired. Cal was impressed with Billy's race at Milwaukee. In January he watched Billy win an indoor midget race in

Cincinnati. That night he was so taken by Billy's style and aggression that he made an offer to the car's owner that he couldn't turn down. Cal offered to buy the whole rig—race car, trailer, and tow car—but the owner said, "Hey, I gotta get home somehow! I'm keepin' my car. The rest is yours." The owner couldn't make that kind of money with a race car, not in *two* years, *so* there wasn't much for him to think about.

After buying a cheap, used car, Billy pulled the midget race car out to California—after Cal had the race car painted yellow and numbered thirty-seven—in late January. He went alone, but not by choice. He'd asked Roxanne Lytell to go along on this racing trip, a trip that would likely last three or four weeks, including the time it would take to drive out and back. Roxanne was four years older than Billy. She lived in Muncie and worked in the office of a steel products company.

"Billy, I can't do that! I've got a job. I've got to pay my rent. If I'm gone…well…I can't be gone that long. It's not vacation time! I'll get fired! That would be fun, but Billy, I just can't do that."

"Okay, Rox, I'll miss you, but I gotta take this opportunity. You understand?"

"Sure, Billy. Be careful out there. I'll miss you, too. I like you a lot, Billy, really I do, but this trip can't work for me now."

"Yeah, I see, and…I like you. I'll call, probably collect, so I hope you'll take my call," Billy joked.

That was the last time Billy Wallace had talked to Roxie Lytell. He'd been busy. He'd driven long days, seven hundred miles and more at times, just to get to the West Coast. And there was a stop in Tucson to see his dad, who had not heard from his son since last November when he'd driven in the Phoenix Hundred Mile Championship race.

Four days before the trailer issue, late on a Thursday afternoon, Billy pulled into the service station in Tucson where his dad worked. Vernon "Vern" Wallace looked up from the car he was working on, stared to see an unfamiliar midget race car and tow rig, and broke into a wide grin. "Billy boy, I'll be damned! Got your own race car now?" He shook Billy's hand and clapped his shoulder, then stepped back to admire the gleaming, newly painted car. "Really, your car?"

"Well, sorta, Pops. Cal Olsen set me up and told me to come out here for a month or so. Stay busy racin', maybe make a little money."

"Olsen, huh? That's movin' up. Better than that box you drove out here last fall. Olsen lost his ace last year, that Smitty guy, at Dayton, right?"

"Yeah, heck of a way to move up, but that's racing, they say. That time I drove at Milwaukee for Olsen last year helped a lot. He liked what I did, said maybe we could do more this year. I didn't hear anything from him for a while," Billy said.

"Well, you said him and Smitty were pretty close, and he wasn't out here for the two Champ races last fall. Probably kind of hard to deal with, maybe," Vern ventured.

"Could be, Dad. But anyway, I ran an indoor midget race at Cinncinnati in January. Ran really good. After the race, I'm makin' nice with the trophy girl and all, and up comes Cal Olsen, all smiles."

"I don't know the man, but the little I heard—yeah, sounds like him. He's got a big personality, don't he?"

"And plenty of money. Well, he's back to his old self these days. On the spot that night he bought that race car and. He gave me a few hundred bucks and told me to take the car out west, try to make a little money. He said, 'Don't do nothin' stupid, Billy. Just run sanctioned shows, you know, none of that outlaw crap.' And here I am to race that thing for a few weeks before heading back east."

"He's right on that last bit of advice, Billy. You can't mess with those big guys in the office. You gotta play by the rules now. Hey, it's almost closing time. I'm gonna turn out the lights and shut the doors. Let's go get a burger and some beers. Do some catchin' up. You want to work on the car tomorrow? I can help."

"I'm goin' up to Tucson for that race Friday night, so I should get it ready."

"We ain't got the time, but it would be a good idea to get them old shocks off. That's not just a one-hour job, you know. We'd have to change the mounts and all. Most cars don't use them old antique-lookin' things."

Over burgers, fries, and plenty of beer, Billy brought his dad up to the present, from his departure nearly a year ago when he moved to the Midwest. He talked about the accident that broke his arm, the frustration of sitting out for five weeks, fellow drivers, Tom Lawton, his girlfriends—especially Roxanne Lytell—his Milwaukee race, and the race he won at Dayton. He talked about how he was forced to get a part-time job selling used cars—and how little he liked that.

Vern Wallace tried to fill in Billy on his year, but there wasn't much to tell. His ex-wife, Billy's mother, had left with her boyfriend. They'd moved to Florida when he lost his job, and his brother in Miami said he needed help in his construction business. Vern had a "lady-friend", as he called her, but she'd left him last summer. That was about all he could think of to tell Billy. The station owner was mostly retired and had hired Vern as manager. That got him uniform service and a seventy-five cent an hour pay raise. Vern Wallace's life was flat, but he was happy for his son.

Billy spent the next few nights at his dad's bungalow and days at the station, performing the maintenance that he was able to handle, but mostly just tinkering and polishing—Billy drove race cars better than he fixed them. His dad helped him mount new tires, but they spent most of their time talking to old friends, racing buddies, visitors, and curious customers drawn in to look at the bright yellow race car. Vern Wallace was proud of his boy, who seemed to have a promising future.

Late on Friday, Billy towed the race car to the Tucson quarter mile dirt track. Vern had been a helper on his boss's race cars: jalopies, modified stock cars, and his last car, a CAE kit sprint car that he helped build. He had some background in the sport and a fair amount of experience with the Tucson track.

"Billy, I been here plenty of times. The track dries out and gets hard and slick. No rim-ridin' hero likely to win, tryin' to go around the top of the track. I think what you should plan for is the last six or seven laps. What they runnin', a thirty-lap feature?"

"Two twenty-lap features, I believe," Billy said as they unloaded the yellow car. "First twenty-lapper lines up like any race, you know—time trial gets you in a heat, where you finish in your heat gives you your starting place in the feature, like always. But second twenty-lapper starts straight up—whoever wins starts first; second place starts second."

"So, they score the two races separate then? Two winners?" Vern asked.

"No, they average it out. A guy who gets a second and a third could be declared winner. Like maybe the first race winner didn't do good or dropped out of the second race. Second and third is better than first and a tenth. See?"

"Yeah, don't have to win both races to win the whole thing. You could, like you said, get a couple good finishes, and still win overall, depending on where the other guys finished, right?"

"Yep, that's it, Dad. So, you got some ideas about this dustbowl?"

Vern's plan was to set the car up to run the first race like any dirt track. They'd run the rear end loose, so Billy could drive an aggressive race. "Now, Billy, just remember this—this ain't that little indoor hockey rink you drove in a few weeks ago with them hard, concrete floors. And this ain't no four-hundred horsepower sprint car, so don't go blasting into those turns, thinkin' you got lots of power to control that big slide. You gotta use a bit more of a fine touch. Sure, it'll do the dirt-track slide thing, but these cars don't have to be man-handled. Not tons of power in that little engine, you know."

"Hell, Dad, you sound like an old pro, and you never drove!"

"I just remember how some of them drivers talk about handling midgets. Now, how about you do what you can in that first twenty lapper. Just try to get up front as far as you can. Win? Yeah, that's great, but it's the two races combined, remember? They'll water the track during the break, and then that track is gonna turn hard and slick for the second half. So…here's what I thought, if it seems okay to you. During the break, we crank a bunch of weight into that left rear and run a new tire on the right rear, huh? Then you run the bottom of the racetrack. Them other guys lookin' for the fast way around the top will just be spinnin' their tires on that slick clay."

It was a good plan that nearly worked. Billy won the first race and finished fifth in the second race, but a local guy finished second in both races, and he was the overall winner, based on points. His dad had been right, but the track began to dry out even during the first race. The dry conditions didn't suit his car as well in the second of the twin twenties, and then his engine began to misfire in the last two laps. Still, he made enough money to easily finance the next leg of his trip—on to the West Coast.

* * * * *

Billy arrived at the El Cajon Speedway, near San Diego, on a Saturday afternoon. The weekend racing programs were varied. Motorcycle races were scheduled, so Billy figured on just being a spectator. If anybody ever accused him of being crazy, he usually responded saying, "You ever watch flat-track motorcycle racers? *That* is crazy!"

He parked his car and trailer, thinking about how to protect his equipment. Bikers were a rowdier crowd than sprint car fans. *You never can tell,* he thought. Billy walked around the outside of the stands until he saw two men in the press box high above the stands. He shouted up to them.

"Hey, guys, I'm early, I know. I'll introduce myself as Cameron…uh…Cam…uh…Turner! I got to go under the radar here for your race tomorrow, so that's who I'll be. I'm going to that Orange Show race in San Bernardino next and if them USAC guys know I raced this URA race here, they'll bust me for sure. I can't run my car—engine went bad last night. I thought, just maybe, I can get a ride in some car here."

The men looked at each other and grinned. "Sure, Cam. Clever name, but really who are you?" the older man said.

"I'm Cam Turner, guys."

The taller of the two men climbed down from the press box, walked up to Billy with his right hand extended, and said, "Pleased to meet you, Cam. I'm Chet Martin. I'm the promoter here. Got bikes tonight and I'm running a URA race tomorrow, almost like an open program. I'm happy to see any racers. Glad you're here." Martin introduced the other man as the "owner" of the track, Jim Adams. He leased the land from a realty company that was happy to have the land being used productively, at least until they got a better offer. El Cajon was a very active racing venue, racing three, sometimes four nights a week. The promoters offered sprints, midgets, jalopies, motorcycles, even "figure eight" races with junk cars crossing at the X in the middle of the infield. The last category meant crashes—lots of them—and near crashes. Whatever filled the stands, whatever paid the lease.

"So, Chet, I'm here to kill time and get a look at your racetrack. I'd like to put up here tonight, park in your lot, just sleep in my car. Okay with you? But I am a little worried about my car, you know. Any suggestions?"

"Tell ya what. Pull your rig inside the track, park in the infield. You can be an advertisement for tomorrow's race. Car will be right out there in plain sight—who's gonna mess with that? Make yourself to home, walk around, talk to them 'su-i-cycle' racers! Then tonight after everything's done, we lock the gates up, you can sleep there in your car. Even have first class restroom facilities for you. A two-hole outhouse. What more does a man need? I'll leave a few cold beers and left-over hot dogs out! Living the life of a racer, Cam!"

The motorcycle racers started to filter into the infield a little after four that afternoon. Most had a single bike on a trailer behind a tow car. There were a few pick-up trucks pulling a trailer, but many had just a sedan as a tow car. Billy knew that a race car needed more, and of course, bulkier spare parts: tires, wheels, fuel cans, toolboxes. How much extra do you need for a bike race? He wandered around the pits inside the track, small-talking and soaking up the situation.

Billy watched the track crew drive to the outside edge of the turns. Two men on the back of a flatbed truck jumped off, and two other men still onboard threw down hay bales, which they used to line the outside crash wall.

Billy stood next to a rider, chuckled, and said, "I bet them hay bales make for a real soft, easy wall collision, huh?"

The rider stood up from squatting next to his engine and said, "Want to try it out some time?"

"No, thanks, bud, I like four wheels. Anyway, good luck today." Billy walked down the line of racing bikes, noting different brands. There were English bikes: Triumph, BSA, Norton and a few that he hadn't heard of. And there were many American bikes, Harley-Davidsons, in other words, too.

There was much more variety here than in the midgets and sprint cars that he drove. Both of those classes used Offenhauser four-cylinder engines—a purpose-built engine for racing only. Some midgets still used a 1930's era modified Ford flathead passenger car engine, called a "V8 60." Those old Fords were outclassed by the little 110 cubic inch Offenhauser, but occasionally a well-tuned Ford could be competitive with the "Offys."

In sprint car racing, the larger 220 cubic inch Offenhauser—more accurately, Meyer-Drake—was being seriously threatened by a hot rodders' engine, the small-block Chevy. In the late 50's and early 60's, when the Chevy engines first came to USAC in the Midwest, rule enforcement was relatively lax. But those engines soon began to seriously threaten the traditional favorite of many car owners and fans, the powerful, but expensive, Offenhauser. The United States Auto Club (USAC) restricted the "stock-block" to around 300 cubic inches to maintain parity with the venerable Offy. But even that restriction could not stop the adoption of cheaper, American-made V8 engines.

Midget racing had peaked in popularity by the early 1950's, challenged by television, jalopy car racing, and the many other entertainments of post-war America. There was a time when midget car racing at the Los Angeles Coliseum had drawn crowds as high as sixty thousand. Gilmore Stadium in L.A. regularly had sell-out attendance of eighteen thousand fans for races. Balboa Park in San Diego had a popular track, but that was in the past. Midget racing had faded by the time Billy Wallace got involved.

The water truck made a light, quick pass around the track, followed by a few other trucks and cars to "run in" the water. This would help to make a "tackier surface", better for tire grip and more competition.

When all track prep was done, the bikers had some "hot lap" sessions, just like midget and sprint car racers, for practice and diagnostic purposes. It was during the first session that Billy saw a rider enter turn one a bit too fast. The bike skidded out from the rider. He went down and slid into the hay bales inside the crash fence. He lay there for perhaps fifteen seconds, slowly got up, then limped to the inside of the track, waving off help from a few track workers.

Su-i-cycles, Chet calls them. I see why! Think I've seen enough 'up close and personal.' I'll watch from up in the stands. Billy walked across the track, got a beer and hot dog, and picked out what he thought would be a good place to spectate. That location may have been influenced by the two attractive young ladies that he sat to the left of and behind. *Never can tell* he thought to himself.

· · · · ·

As it turned out, sometimes he could tell. Billy woke up on Sunday—race day—beside the brunette from the stands. Try as he might, he couldn't remember her name. He remembered that last night's "enthusiasm" unwisely caused him to leave the race car in the infield and ride with—what's-her-name. A lost race car could cripple a promising opportunity with Cal Olsen. Bright sunlight framed the dark window curtains. He got out of bed, stood unsteadily, waited for his stomach to settle, and looked at the clock-radio.

"Oh, holy Christ! It's ten thirty! Hey…uh, girl! I gotta go! I gotta get to the track and get ready. You can stay and watch, you know…uh, what do you think?"

The girl rolled over and said, "Aw, let's stay a little longer. I'm tired, Billy."

"I *said* I've got to get to the track. Come on…drive me back to the track, okay?"

"Oh, I just wanna sleep…"

"Get up! Get movin'…uh…girl!" Billy jostled the bed and pulled back the covers.

She shot up and glared at him, "You don't even remember my *name,* do you?"

The girl said little as she drove Billy back to El Cajon, or more accurately, *tried* to drive back. It would be an hour drive, in perfect traffic conditions. They did not find the conditions perfect, and she did not have the sense of urgency that Billy did. A back-up caused by an accident on the highway cost an extra forty-five minutes. By the time the girl left Billy in the parking lot, he'd missed any chance of racing on Sunday.

Billy spent Sunday roaming the pits, thinking that perhaps an owner-driver dispute would result in an offer, but that never happened. So, at the end of the day, the phantom driver Cam Turner, aka Billy Wallace, drove his station wagon and race car out of the infield and headed for the freeway. His next race was at the Orange Show on Friday night, but first he had to do something to get the engine in Cal's car repaired.

That shouldn't be a problem. *Hell, they built these Offenhauser engines out here!* He'd have to call Cal to explain about the repair, and he didn't know how that would go. Billy began second-guessing himself, thinking *Maybe this wasn't such a great idea, comin' here alone like this, no helper or anybody.*

* * * * *

Tom Lawton stopped at the mailbox at the end of his long, gravel lane and got Saturday's mail. He went through the usual bills, daily newspaper, what looked like a letter from Janet's sister, and a letter from the regional office of his gasoline supply company. Tom pulled into the lane, stopped the truck, and stared straight ahead. He thought, *This could be the bad news.* He hesitated to open the letter, but to delay only seemed dramatic. He didn't have to read far to confirm his suspicions. "Dear Mr. Lawton, it is with great regret that we must inform you of our decision to supply just one service station in Barton. You have been a loyal and valued part of our company, but your location…" That was enough. Tom folded the letter, put it in his shirt pocket, and drove the rest of the way up to the farmhouse. This would change life for the Lawton family, but Tom couldn't see exactly how—there were so many unknowns. Operating his property as a service station seemed a losing proposition, a long downward slide. Selling it would be a problem: who would want a service station that wasn't located on the main state highway? How would a buyer convert it to another purpose? What about the buried tanks? Just letting it sit idle was no solution; taxes had to be paid, even when the property wasn't earning anything. So many unknowns. He sighed and drove the quarter mile gravel lane up to his house.

He waved to his daughter, Tina, standing inside the open, double barn doors. She had just turned sixteen and looked, Tom thought, well, a little less like a girl—somewhere along that "growing up" path to womanhood. He stopped the truck close to the barn and looked through the open passenger side window.

"Hi, Dad."

"Hey, kid. Have a good day?"

"It was okay. Just hung around here all day after school."

"Mom home?"

"Yeah, she's fixin dinner, I think."

He waved a 'see ya later', went into the screened-in porch, took off his shoes, and sat down on the swing. Too restless to sit, he soon got up and went into the kitchen for a bottle of beer. Janet was on the phone, so he pointed to the porch.

Janet Lawton was about one year younger than her husband. She had brown, naturally wavy hair that did not quite reach her shoulders. She had brown eyes and freckles that oddly, but not unattractively, endured beyond her youth. That feature led a few friends to still call her by an obvious childhood nickname. She was slim but not tall, standing about five and a half feet tall. Her mother often had admonished her, "Stand up straight and use the height that God gave you, Janet!"

He returned to the swing and sat sipping. It was a mild, late winter day and not too cool to sit outside for a while. It was quiet out there on the porch—too early for farmers to be in the field, so no tractors. Janet had the radio turned down while she worked in the kitchen, so there wasn't a lot to disturb him. Their house was on an unpaved country road with little traffic.

Tom sat for ten minutes or so, heard Janet singing along with some popular song, and thought, *That's a nice thing to hear. I should just listen for a bit…don't spoil a good moment.* He debated with himself. *Should I bring it up now or not? Wait till Monday, end of the day? She can read me so easy—she would say, 'You're as easy to read as a book—a children's book,*

Tom Lawton! You're no Shakespeare play.' Bring it up tonight, dinner table? Cause Tina to worry, probably. Before bed? Ain't no good time, is there?

Tom went into the kitchen, crept up behind his wife, put his arms around her, and kissed her neck. "That was a nice serenade to listen to. My own Doris Day! Right here in the kitchen."

"That beer does funny things to you. And how can you kiss that sweaty neck?"

"Come to think of it, you sounded more like Julie London than Doris Day."

"Like I said, that beer does funny things to you. You ready for supper? Call Tina in and drink water with your meal, old man. I can read you—"

Tom put his bottle down, went to the door, "Like a book! I've heard that so many times! Tina! Supper!" Then he turned back to the kitchen and said, "Smells good, Jan. I'm hungry." *I'll just sit on my bad news for a while. Don't want to spoil this now."*

· · · · ·

On Tuesday, Billy stopped at the Meyer-Drake shop in L.A. After a short discussion, a man in the shop said he thought a simple fix would take care of Billy's engine problem. A new magneto would do the job and sent him on to a speed shop. Billy convinced a technician to install one and keep it for a few days, "Do whatever it needs. You know, tune it up, make it sing! It was good till a couple laps from the flag." Then Billy left the race car and trailer at the engine shop and started looking for some of the many race car fabricators in Los Angeles. *Man, it's like speed crazy out here. Dragster builders, engine shops, body men smoothing aluminum panels into curvaceous missiles. It's all out here. Makes the Midwest look like "tractor maintenance!"* Billy soaked it all up for a few days, going from shop to shop. In one garage he asked, "Is anybody doing anything different for the 500 this year or are they all doing the same things—you know, reduce weight, left-side bias. Any new thoughts?"

The shop welder said, "Epperly's workin' on a new one of his laydown ideas. He's layin' his Offy down, horizontal… and…get this, now. He's gonna stick the top of that engine outside the frame rails! Talk about left side weight!"

"Really?" was Billy's only reaction.

The shop welder continued. "But you oughta go over to Glendale, that guy at Kelco Customs is buildin' a rear-engine car. He got all fired up after going to one of them Grand Prix races. He wants to get it to that race in New Jersey first, you know, try it out, before Indianapolis."

"Rear engine. Huh." The idea settled in his mind.

Billy spent a few nights in taverns till "Last Call", then settled for the night on some fellow racer's couch, or the back seat of his car if he ran out of friends. On Friday, he picked up the race car at the shop. He told the shop foreman, "You know the name Cal Olsen, I'm sure. In Indianapolis! If you need more, just call the Speedway. They'll tell you what you need to know. Just send him the bill. Tell him it's for Billy Wallace's car. See ya." Then Billy headed for San Bernardino and a Friday night race on the quarter-mile dirt track there. He had no idea why people simply called it the "Orange Show".

Long ago, citrus growers in the San Bernardino area promoted their industry with a commercial exposition. That initial event in the early twentieth century grew to include a permanent site where industry events could be staged. The supporters of citrus-agriculture built convention facilities for related businesses. The annual fair grew to include much more than first imagined. In time, over one hundred acres was acquired. The property was utilized for events unrelated to the citrus industry: family reunions, swap meets, flea markets, even police and fire training. One of those ventures was an attempt to capitalize on the midget racing craze in California. A quarter mile dirt track was constructed with seating for the throngs of expected fans, and, they hoped, the revenue they would create. The public's interest in midget racing waned in the early 1950's, but the races continued at the speedway, albeit to smaller crowds. It was at this track, simply called the "Orange Show" now, that Billy was hoping to earn some money to make his California trip a bit more profitable.

Last year, Billy broke his left arm in a midget race in Indiana. It was the recuperation period for that broken arm that opened an opportunity for Tom Lawton. Chuck Williams had hired Billy to drive for the Midwest racing season, but a broken arm heals in roughly five to six weeks. Tom drove Chuck's red number eleven car while Billy sat on the sidelines. Tom didn't set the world on fire, but he didn't break anything either. Did Billy learn anything from that experience? Oddly enough, he came to think that more time in the small racers could be good for him. They might teach him skills that could transfer to other divisions, if he were patient enough to learn.

He pulled into the registration line outside the little quarter-mile, dirt speedway. He was third in line and had an awkward moment when a stranger walked by, smiled, and said, "Hi, Cam. Good luck today." Billy didn't say a word. He knew he'd taken a chance at El Cajon, using an assumed name. Had it caught up with him? But he hadn't raced! USAC demanded that a driver commit to their organization. If a driver ran an "outlaw" race (any organization that USAC did not approve) he could have his USAC license revoked. So what? Well, USAC sponsored the Indianapolis 500. No license, no race. Had Billy put his dreams in jeopardy?

The officials processed him and his car, then pointed Billy in the direction of the pit area, outside the track, behind the back straightaway. Keeping cars, trailers, and contestants out of the infield gave fans a clear view of the track, with no visual obstacles. The infield of a quarter-mile racetrack is small and becomes crowded with all that equipment parked inside.

Billy drove around the outside of the track, found a pit stall, unloaded his little yellow car, and set about preparing it for this quarter-mile track. A midget looks very similar to its bigger brother, the sprint car. Typically, midgets have a wheelbase of sixty-six to seventy-six inches. Sprint cars are a bit bigger, with wheelbases around eighty-three to ninety inches. Driver comforts are likewise reduced. Cockpits are cramped and drivers' heads often are above the protective roll bar. What the cars lack in power, they make up in maneuverability. Engines are smaller, but the car is very nimble. A midget car handles more like a go-kart. Tonight, Billy's car would be geared low for quick response on this little quarter-mile, flat, dirt track.

Crowds in the thousands were drawn to these races in the years after World War II, until the racing market reached the saturation point and attendance dwindled. At its peak, the boom years allowed for professional drivers to earn a living by driving race cars, without the need for another job. But Billy and other drivers now found it necessary to drive whenever and whatever they could, if they wanted to be professionals. Midgets one day, sprint cars the next, or sports cars another day. Much depended on the series they were a part of and how willing that organization was to allow drivers to "roam" about.

The Orange Show had a well-prepared track. It had been watered earlier in the day and trucks had "run it in", driving lap after lap to help force the water down into the dirt. The grader pushed a ridge of dirt to mark the inside of the turns and discourage drivers from cutting the corners. That ridge of dirt was substantial enough to present a definite hazard to avoid. The straights were longer and turns sharper than many tracks. The first "hot laps" and qualifications would be in late afternoon light, but racing would be under the lights. There would be no sun to dry out the track, so it should stay damp and tacky.

Each of the twenty-nine cars took two timed laps. The faster of the two was their official time. Billy timed third fastest at 14.73. The two drivers faster than him had times of 14.61 and 14.70. The slowest of the twenty-nine cars had a time of 16.10. The entire field of cars was separated by roughly one and a half seconds. Billy knew he had his work cut out for him.

He finished second in an uneventful heat race, which meant he would start outside the second row in the feature race. The officials "inverted" starts to provide a better race for the fans. Instead of putting the fastest cars up front, where they would run away from the rest of the field, the first six cars were inverted—fastest started sixth, second fastest started fifth, and so on. He was not unhappy with that position. Billy liked to run the outside on a dirt track. He could swing wide, run a bigger arc, and get his speed up. He knew that the engine had been tuned at the shop, so he fueled up and checked tire pressures. He felt good about his chances in the forty-lap feature race.

On the final pace lap of the main event, all eighteen cars were tightly packed, drivers trying not to lag and lose valuable ground. Cars were three to four feet behind those in front of them and steadily accelerating as they entered the front stretch. The starter waved the green flag, and the field charged into the first turn. Billy drifted wide, and the car in front of him did the same. In seconds, his sliding car was on the back stretch and momentarily straightening out.

Just as quickly, the field was in the third turn. The first and second place cars were side by side in front of him, drifting and spraying dirt. Billy was just a few feet behind them, and clear of the car he'd started beside. They entered turn one, and a car suddenly appeared on his left. The two ran side by side as they entered the back stretch, the car beside Billy trying to edge him out farther. Billy gave no ground as he entered turn three a bit lower and allowed his car to slide wider exiting turn four. The car fell back slightly in the front stretch, as Billy pinched inside the first turn. That car then tried to get by him on the outside but got too far out and his tires lost grip in the loose dirt outside the groove. He dropped back. If Billy had looked behind him—something drivers never did—he would have seen that the field was divided into several knots of cars, struggling for position. Billy was in the pack of three at the front, which soon grew to a pack of four as a local favorite in a black car made his way to the front. On the fifth lap, he slipped under Billy, still running his low-to-high approach in the turns. The black car flew by as they entered the back stretch, dropping Billy to fourth place, though he was still close to the lead pack.

Straight—turn—straight—turn. It was all a blur after the first ten laps. It was a moving world that he lived in now. Speed wasn't tremendous, but fifteen second laps on a quarter-mile track worked out to an average speed of sixty miles an hour. Not great speed, but straight—turn—straight—turn. It all ran together after a few laps on a small track like this.

Lap fifteen? Billy had no idea what lap they were on, and he was traveling alone with no helper to flash him hand signs. The only thing he could do was try to get an idea from other helpers as they gave lap signs to cars in front of him. At twenty laps, the starter crossed his flags to indicate the race was half over.

Billy found that his approach to turns three and four—pinch down low in turn three then let the car swing wide exiting turn four to enter the front straight–still worked well, but not so much through turns one and two. The inside of turn one was getting dry and slick, so Billy drove higher into turn one and held that line through turn two.

The black car split the two-car battle in front sometime around lap twenty-six or twenty-seven—that was the best he could figure. That meant the fast qualifier was in second place, and Billy was still in fourth. On the next lap, Billy passed one car entering turn one, giving him third place, just as the black car passed for the lead. The first three cars were still just feet apart. This was so unlike sprint car racing. The close dicing and passing usually lasted perhaps fifteen laps in a sprint car race until the field got sorted out. But these midgets could put on an exciting, close-fought show for the fans.

Last year, Tom Lawton had told him to learn to be more patient in his driving. *How the hell can you be patient in a ten-minute race?* Billy was sweating, and his left arm reminded him of last year's misfortune. On…what lap…he had no idea, but as the first three cars entered turn one, the second- place car in front of Billy unexpectedly slowed, and Billy rammed it from behind. The sudden impact caused the car to spin towards the inside of the track. Billy regained control of his car and watched the black car pull out a greater lead. He was focused now, knowing there could be no more than perhaps eight or nine laps left.

The black car appeared to have a lead of six or seven car lengths. Billy drove with single-minded focus. He changed his approach and drove both turns the same as he had driven turns one and two. He entered turn one high, riding the cushion all the way to the backstretch, then drove through three and four in the same way. The black car chose to run lower, but Billy picked him up bit by bit, and when the two cars drove under the white flag signaling one lap to go, Billy made a near wide open approach to turn one. The right rear got a good bite. Billy carried his speed into the backstretch and passed the black car in turn three, then held the lead to the checkered flag. *Cal Olsen will like this! Not so much the money. He's got plenty, but he does like to win,* Billy thought. *Maybe I'll eat a little better on my way back to Indiana. Maybe even sleep in a motel one night instead of my car.*

After packing up and collecting his winnings, Billy drove until he got sleepy. That first night he slept in a roadside park. Driving long days got him close to home. He treated himself to a steak dinner just inside the Illinois line, thought seriously about staying in a motel, but decided to push on through to Indianapolis where he would check in with Cal Olsen.

Chapter Two

Billy and C.J. (Carl Jones, Junior—people just called him C.J.) drove to the East Coast season opening races. C.J. was lanky and taller than Billy. He had dark and bristly "buzz" cut hair. His head often tipped down as he tried to compensate for his height, attempting to make better contact with others.

Billy drove, and C.J. stretched his long legs out as much as possible. They followed Cal Olsen's mechanic driving the race tow rig with the yellow number seven that Chuck Williams had repaired. Olsen Special was written diagonally in large, elaborate black script across the hood of the car. There was a flourish of black underlining beneath the car name. The hauler was a trailer with a tire rack in front of the race car. It was painted yellow with a similar Olsen Racing in black.

Olsen had told Caldwell, his mechanic, to take the car to Reading, Pennsylvania, for a Saturday night race on the half-mile dirt track. "Take a helper. Maybe you can recruit some young guy from out in the factory. You know who would be most helpful. I'll be a day behind you. Or *we'll* be a day behind, I should say. I'll bring the Watson, and I'll find someone to bring our Kuzma dirt car out. It's gonna be an Olsen armada invading Trenton for that Sunday race. Hey, I got it: Olsen Car-mada! How 'bout that, Caldwell?"

Wilson "Willy" Caldwell was not amused. All he could see ahead of him for the next few days were long drives and three race cars to maintain, for an owner who expected miracles every weekend. Caldwell worked in Olsen's Indianapolis factory part-time—according to Olsen. The original agreement was that Willy would be on the factory payroll for sixteen hours a week of maintenance work. The balance of his forty-hour week was to be devoted to work on Olsen's stable of race cars. But many other jobs seemed to come his way. If Olsen's trucks needed work, Willy would oversee that. Or maybe he wanted a new muffler on his personal car. "Willy will do it" evolved to the simpler "Willy will" and became the fix-all watchword in the shop. Those jobs seemed to increase while Olsen's expectations never changed. He expected winners, and at a bargain rate. Caldwell, a short and lean man, found himself working long hours on race cars after everyone else had clocked out. The sixteen-hour maintenance work/twenty-four hours race car work didn't last long, expanding to more like twenty-eight and thirty-two, not even considering travel time and time at the racetrack. Two packs of Camels a day helped keep him going, and lots of coffee. He may not have been an imposing figure but when irritated, his wordless and dark expression could make even Cal Olsen stop and take notice.

"Tell ya one thing, Cal. I don't want to haul number seven out there with that truck of yours. I'll pull it out there with my car. I'll be workin' my fool head off for three days. That's some weekend! At least my car will be quiet and comfortable," Caldwell had said days ago.

"But it's not yellow, Willy! My pick-up is yellow!"

· · · · ·

Billy drove the first leg through Ohio on US 40, turning the wheel over to C.J. when they got to Wheeling, West Virginia, where they lost sight of Willy Caldwell pulling C.J.'s sprint car. At Washington, Pennsylvania, 40 turned south, so they headed north to hit the Pennsylvania Turnpike. Reading was about thirty miles northwest of Philadelphia. They hoped to stay in a motel after the race Saturday night, *if* they won enough money. If not, they would just sleep in the car. Or maybe some other team might let them sleep on the floor of their motel room. Then on Sunday morning, they would drive the last fifty or sixty miles to the New Jersey Fairgrounds and the paved one-mile speedway.

Foremost in Billy's mind was Sunday's one-hundred-mile race on the Trenton fairgrounds paved, one-mile speedway. Driving at Reading on Saturday night was just an outside opportunity. It all depended on circumstances: did a car show up without a committed driver; was an owner unhappy with his current driver and willing to fire him and put Billy in the car; was a driver not satisfied with a car and eager to turn it over (not a good recommendation for a car's quality)? Chuck had opted not to bring either of his cars out; the new car was not quite ready, and "iffy" early spring weather seemed to discourage a long drive.

. . . . .

Tom Lawton was unable to find an oil company to supply gasoline and products at a rate that would produce a reasonable profit. So, he closed the station, put it up for sale, and took a job on the night shift at a local factory—Maxcell Corporation—running a drill press from 5:00 p.m. till 1:30 a.m. He started at the bottom of the pay scale, making $1.25 an hour, little better than minimum wage. Roger Hicks, a former high school classmate who worked in accounting at Maxcell, took pleasure in telling Tom that he had to start at that rate. "You have no machine shop skills, Tommy. What more can we do? Guess you'll have to work your way up, huh?"

Restraining his wounded pride and anger was difficult, but Tom needed the job. Roger Hicks and Tom had gone to school together for twelve years but took different career paths after graduation. Tom bought a service station, and Roger became an accountant at the local manufacturing facility. He never failed to remind Tom of his position. "I'll be controller here someday soon, Tommy-boy. I'm the assistant now, but when the old guy retires, I'm in line for that. And I'm not ashamed to say that my goal is president here. Roger Hicks, President, Maxcell Corp! Sounds good!"

"That's nice, Roger," was all Tom could say.

Tom had been on the night shift for one week when the shop foreman made the rounds late in the week and announced that he was being "asked" to work overtime on Saturday night. When Tom said he didn't think he could do that, the foreman reminded him he had worked for just one week and asked how long he planned to stay. Tom got the message. He called Chuck to tell him he would be unable to go to the Reading race. Chuck wasn't disappointed. He was still finishing up his new car for Billy and, anyway, Chuck preferred that his nephew Donny not be alone the first time he took charge of Tom's car, the red number eleven. Not just yet. An arrangement had been worked out last fall, at the end of the season. Billy got the new car that Chuck would maintain, and Tom was assured that number eleven—Donny's responsibility—would be his car for the season.

Tom worked Saturday night on the drill press line. Billy went with C.J. to Reading on their way to what Billy considered the main event, the Championship race on Sunday in Trenton. He would drive the same car he drove last summer at Milwaukee for Cal Olsen. It was not the newest car on the track, but it was reliable and well-suited to the demands of the track in New Jersey.

The Reading Fairgrounds speedway was a half-mile dirt track that was used originally for horse races, as were many county fairgrounds tracks. Those facilities have tight turns (horses don't have to slow down for a turn) and long straights, unlike the Eldora and New Bremen dirt tracks, which have longer and wider turns and shorter straightaways. Those long sweeping turns created tracks that were much more circular in overall shape. Reading's sharper turns and unbanked surface made for slower lap times than those two Ohio speedways. But most east coast tracks had dirt surfaces that racers liked. The deep dirt built up a cushion, or ridge that helped provide traction. Racing at night avoided the problem of the track drying out. Dry conditions reduced competition, and many drivers took an inside line through the turns, almost in a follow-the-leader parade. That would not happen this evening. The early spring night was cool, and there had been a fair amount of rain, so the moisture was deep in the track, not as if it had just been watered by truck in the afternoon. And early spring meant there had been less sunlight and less drying. Saturday night could be a very good night for racing.

When the two young men arrived at Reading a little after four o'clock, Billy didn't have a car lined up to drive. C.J. immediately started looking for Caldwell and the yellow number seven. Billy walked along, carrying his helmet and equipment bag. Then he began working his way through the pits, hoping to find an open car.

Caldwell was his usual self—gruff and pessimistic. "C.J., I see you're here. I had plenty of time to worry about everything I could think of. Last thing I needed was a no-show driver. I walked around this place, just to get a look at the dirt. It's tacky and damp. It'll hold up well tonight. I think you're gonna get one hell of a bite. And it's cool now, so dryin' out won't be a problem."

C.J. walked around the car, saying little. He stopped where Caldwell squatted on his haunches, attending to something on the engine. "You done much to this engine since last year?"

"Yeah, I did my usual overhaul, like always. Put new rings and…hell! It's ready to go. Don't you worry about that. Only thing, I'm not sure about is the injector pill. I'll check the plugs, you know, to see if we got the right fuel mix."

"Okay, Willy," C.J. muttered and cleaned his goggles with a shop rag.

Billy chatted his way through the pits, socializing, but also determined to find a car to drive. He talked to Carl Connors, who drove his white number two to a win last year at Winchester, where Tom Lawton introduced Billy to the Midwest's high bank racing and Eddie "Speed" Spencer. Connors said, "Billy, good luck with that car search. I ain't heard about any empty seats though."

Next, Billy introduced himself to the Eastern veteran, Red Allen, who was putting rear wheels on his car. He knew Billy by reputation and was agreeable to give the young man a ride. "I've run a lot of races, and missing one is no problem for me. Suit up! It's yours if you want it! I ain't feelin' so great anyway. Sore from an unfortunate incident last week at Williams Grove."

Twenty minutes later, Billy was in uniform, sitting on a tire, tying up his "racer boots," laced, high-top boxer's shoes. Red Allen's blue number two was fresh out of the shop, gleaming in new paint and chrome work. Red had won a string of east coast season championships and was easing into retirement. He'd had a career that was seldom cursed with bad luck or injury.

Billy ran a 25.13 qualification time that gave him fast time and a shot at pole position in the thirty-lap feature. But then

C.J. ran a lap at 24.87, a time that was not beaten by the remaining drivers. That worked out to around seventy-two or seventy-three miles an hour, a speed that sounded like highway speeds. But that was an average: those sharp, flat turns slowed a car to sixty or sixty-five, but straightaway speeds were ninety-five to a hundred miles per hour.

The remainder of the evening was an unexpected reversal of fortune for C.J. due to misfortune, mechanical issues, and the rules of the sanctioning body. The format of the program called for three heat races with six cars in each race. The first three finishers in each heat then "transferred" to the main event. Fourth, fifth, and sixth places were then added to the second heat and were given another opportunity to earn a starting place in the feature. The third heat race was treated in the same way. The "consolation" race was made up of cars that didn't finish in the top three in the third heat and slow qualifiers who had not been assigned to a heat race.

C.J. stepped into his car, looked at his mechanic, who had a foot on the right front tire, and said, "Caldwell, you seem pretty relaxed tonight."

Caldwell walked to the back of the car, motioned for a truck to approach, and said, "Why wouldn't I be? We got no worry, kid. Fast qualifier, good track, one guy—well, maybe two guys—who might give you a race. Race is ours to win!"

"Easy for you to say!"

"We came to win, right? You got these guys covered."

An official signaled for the pick-up trucks to push start the cars. C.J. pulled his goggles up, flexed his fingers in his gloves, and waved with his left hand for the truck to push him off. He let the engine turn over for seven or eight seconds then switched on the magneto. The expected mule-kick in his back didn't happen.

He switched the magneto off, waited a few seconds, and

tried again with the truck still pushing. The engine momentarily barked to life and just as quickly died. The race car and truck were exiting the second turn and entering the backstretch. After one more unsuccessful try, C.J. signaled for the truck to stop. He let the car coast to a stop and then pulled it out of gear. The remaining five cars began to form up as he was pushed back to the pits.

"What the hell, C.J.?" Caldwell shouted as the car silently glided to a stop.

"My thoughts exactly! I drive! You make it run!"

Caldwell opened the engine cover and checked problematic components. He could smell fuel, so the engine wasn't starving. He checked for loose wires but found none. The five remaining cars on the track and officials waited for two more laps, cars circling in formation. After one more lap, the race started without the fastest car of the night.

The night was not over for C.J. and Caldwell though. He would be assigned to the second heat race. Theoretically, even less challenging because the cars were those that had qualified even slower. During that first heat race, Caldwell discovered that the magneto switch on the dashboard was the problem. He was able to borrow one from an owner whose car had been scratched for the night and would not compete, but he didn't get the repair completed until the second heat was running.

C.J. lined up outside row two in the third heat. His challenge was the same: finish third or better. That would earn him his starting place in the feature. *I'll show Caldwell, and everybody here, that I'm the guy to beat. Shoulda cleaned up in the first race!*

When the starter waved the green flag, C.J. was ready. He stomped the throttle and steered for the outside of turn one, easily leaving third place behind. He found that the high groove worked well. He saw the two cars ahead that were his targets: first and second; though his third place already qualified him for the feature, he was eager to prove a point. *Pass those two and I'm in the main event! Two middle-of-the-pack guys, easy! I'll pass them both the way this is goin'*

The second-place car slewed sideways as C.J. attempted to pass. The cars collided, sending C.J. rebounding into the guardrail. The impact was hard enough to break the tire loose from the wheel and it deflated. The yellow flag slowed the remaining cars, and C.J. waited in his car up against the barrier. *Out again! What the hell? What next?* C.J. angrily tossed his helmet into his car as the wrecker towed it away. He stormed back to his pit.

After Caldwell mounted a fresh wheel and tire, C.J. was assigned to the consolation, the last chance race. The fastest driver of the night was still searching for a starting place in the feature race. It was a rare, but not unheard-of situation. On occasion a driver worked his way through many or all the preliminaries and still did not get in the final race.

"Caldwell, this night has really turned on me," C.J. said. "There's one more race, the consolation race. I know damn well I can win that one. It'll be filled with a bunch of rookies and junk-box cars."

For ten laps, he dominated the field and nearly lapped last place. He raced into his pit, engine barking. He slid to a stop, unhooked his belts, angrily tossed them aside, and stomped off, shouting over his shoulder, "I'm gonna take a leak. I want a lower gear, Caldwell! Get it ready to go! Track is still good and tacky. Lower gear will show these guys what we can do! Show 'em why we had best qualifying time!" He didn't wait for a reply, leaving Caldwell and his helper looking at each other. They had about fifteen minutes.

Willy Caldwell was still adjusting to C.J. He'd worked with Smitty for a few years and came to understand that the rough and sometimes brutal man only responded to similar treatment. He was more indulgent with his new driver, so he did as C.J. demanded. The task took every minute that was available. They were pushing the car out to the front straightaway, C.J. walking alongside, putting his helmet on, when Caldwell said, "We got that gear changed. I put a 5.09 in. Lower, like you wanted. I didn't have a lot of time, but I took time to check the plugs anyway. They look like we're runnin' too lean. If we had time, I'd change that injector pill, richen our fuel up. Last thing I want to do is burn a piston, or worse."

"I know how to take care of an engine. I'll back off once in a while, let it breathe a bit. It'll be okay. Ain't nothing wrong with this car! Once we got that switch fixed, our problems were caused by the other stuff here. Car runs great! I could tell that in the consi."

"Well, I—"

"Caldwell, I'm gonna whip these guys tonight!"

He did "whip them" for *most* of the race, twenty-four laps, to be exact. Billy started right behind him and didn't see C.J. again till he flew by on lap twenty-two to lap him. Caldwell stood near the edge of the track so C.J. could not miss his gestures to indicate a huge lead and pleas to slow down. He had lapped every car except for second place. As C.J. exited turn two and raced down the backstretch, his car was engulfed in steam and blue smoke. He coasted to a stop and steered toward the infield. The last lap saw Billy advance to second place, but C.J. was denied an almost certain win by his misfortune, though Caldwell had a much different interpretation of that "misfortune."

Nearly as many fans were attracted to C.J. as they were to the winner. The adulation of fans impressed by such a dominating performance—for much of the race at least—did soothe his disappointment somewhat. C.J. was distracted by the enthusiastic crowd and did not see Caldwell, throwing tools and fuming behind him as he examined the race car.

* * * * *

Sunday morning was cool, so Billy wore a leather jacket, emblazoned with an oil company logo, borrowed from a mechanic in a neighboring pit. Warm-ups were about to start, and he sat in the cockpit of the yellow number twenty-seven, waiting for the officials to open the track for thirty minutes of practice. This was the same car he'd driven last year at the Milwaukee two-hundred-mile race for Championship cars. In that race, Billy had driven well and finished in tenth place while his teammate settled for second, after leading much of the race. That teammate was Rex Smith, the Smitty who died last year, driving the same car that C.J. drove last night at Reading. Billy's teammate today was C.J., who was driving the other Olsen car, a yellow—no surprise—one-year old Watson roadster, number seventeen.

Caldwell was responsible for both cars today. That was enough to promise a difficult day, but he was still angry about last night's debacle. That was the day-after description. Last night was a different matter. After the autograph seekers and and well-wishers had gone, Caldwell lit into his driver with an angry assault until C.J. walked away. "Damn it, C.J., damn it! First, I told you we should richen that fuel mix. But you said you'd take care of it! Brand new engine! Burned a piston, and who knows what else broke? I was out there tellin' you to take it easy, givin' you hand-signs for seven or eight laps! You had the damn race won after fifteen laps!"

Billy had been around a few racetrack confrontations, but had never seen anything quite like that one, had never seen a mechanic tear into a driver that way. And now Caldwell had to deal with C.J. again, although Cal Olsen, who had arrived with the two cars for Sunday's race, might moderate the atmosphere in the pits. Caldwell was going about preparing the Watson car first, saying little, but gruffly barking commands to his two helpers, who tried not to do anything that would earn Caldwell's wrath. Luckily, he had done most of the prep work several days ago at the shop in Indianapolis. Cal Olsen and C.J. stood behind the pit wall talking quietly, but seriously. Billy watched as C.J. stepped over the pit wall, looked back at Olsen, and nodded when Olsen said something that did not seem to be a joke. C.J. climbed into the yellow number seventeen, pulled up his goggles, and waited for Caldwell to start the car.

Soon, C.J. was pulling out of the pits as two helpers gave the car a boost, pushing on the tail of the Watson racer. It was a car designed to turn left. The engine, transmission, and rear end were all offset to the left. The driver sat on the right side of the car. That configuration, with more left-side weight, worked especially well at Indianapolis and the two other paved tracks that were on the schedule. Both Milwaukee and Trenton were one-mile fairgrounds tracks. Both had been dirt tracks but were paved in the fifties. Billy was driving an older "dirt car", built by the Los Angeles race car fabricator, Eddie Kuzma. It looked like a sprint car, just a bit bigger, with a wheelbase about twelve inches longer and a larger fuel tank. It was the norm at Indianapolis until replaced by the "roadster" style in the 1950's. Sprint car races were commonly thirty laps, fifteen miles long. The larger Championship cars went a hundred miles without a fuel stop. The "dirt championship" car was built to be more robust, to withstand longer races on rough, rutted fairground dirt tracks. The driver sat higher, over the drive line, and the sides of the car were open, whereas in a car like the Watson roadster, the driver sat a bit more "down and in,' *somewhat* more protected.

Caldwell took the electric starter motor and its battery cart up to the front of Billy's car. He inserted a long steel shaft into a hole in the nose of the car and engaged it with the crankshaft of the four-cylinder Meyer-Drake engine. One of the helpers stood with a squirt can beside the four air intakes that led to the fuel injectors. The electric starter motor whined when Willy hit the switch. The helper squirted fuel into the injector horns as the starter motor turned the engine, which chuff-chuffed a few times. Caldwell nodded at Billy to turn the magneto on. The engine barked to life, blowing clouds of noxious fumes out of the long exhaust pipe. Caldwell pulled the starter shaft out and stood off to the left side. Billy engaged the clutch as helpers pushed on the tail of the car. The engine stuttered and then caught. He got the car rolling, then shifted into race gear. There were only two gears: first gear and race gear. The engine bogged down and coughed momentarily, then roared to life as the car gained speed. (It was as if, in a four speed, stick shift passenger car, the driver started in first gear and then shifted into fourth gear, skipping second and third.)

Billy had driven a car with an Offenhauser twice last year, at Milwaukee and at the season- ending race at Phoenix. He had spent the rest of the season driving Chuck Williams' Chevy-powered car. Race car engines were bolted directly to the chassis, with no cushioned motor mounts as in passenger cars. The shock of detonation in each cylinder shuddered through the frame and into the steering gear and wheel. A driver's hands tingled and nearly grew numb during a long race. The displacement of these engines was usually about 252 cu. in. to 255 cubic inches. "Stock-block" engines like the Chevrolet were allowed 302 cubic inches, so one would think they might send even greater shock waves through the chassis. But Offenhausers—Meyer-Drakes—are high compression, four-cylinder engines, and the firing of each cylinder was a explosion that rattled through the car. The memory of that feeling quickly came back to Billy as he accelerated toward turn one.

C.J. was far ahead on the back stretch as Billy entered the first turn, low and out of the racing groove. There was a white line that marked the inside of the track. Left of that were perhaps three or four feet of pavement. Billy kept his left wheels inside the line, staying out of the racing groove in case a faster car was nearing from behind. In practice sessions, drivers were not allowed full racing speed until the starter waved the green flag.

Billy increased his speed as he left turn two and started down the back stretch. He steered right, closer to the guardrail, but was passed by a car still in unpainted, shiny aluminum body panels. The number fifty-six was painted in black, amateurly, and apparently recently finished. *Was that the rear-engine car I heard about in Los Angeles a few weeks ago? Engine?* He couldn't tell because the body panels covered it, but he was sure it was an American V-8, though it had a higher pitch than the 302's he drove. *Smaller displacement? Maybe just different exhaust headers.* He couldn't tell who was driving it. The car quickly drew away from Billy, who was letting the oil and tires warm up. It was a chilly April day and the rock-hard Firestone tires needed some heat before he would lean on them. The screeching "voice of Firestone" wasn't a pleasant sound and often foreshadowed trouble when the tires were pushed beyond adhesion.

This track was similar in some ways to the Milwaukee mile—paved, wide turns, open and grassy infield—but it was banked, unlike the flat Milwaukee turns. The banked turns approximated those at Indianapolis though this track was narrower. The track had an outside guardrail unlike anything Billy had ever seen. It was made of sheets of steel left over from the war, steel that had been used for temporary landing strips on Pacific islands. The steel was punctured with holes eight or nine inches in diameter. It was a crazy looking thing, to Billy's way of thinking. Somebody's creative use of war surplus materials. *Economical and safe? Think I won't try to find out how safe it is,* Billy thought.

The starter waved the green flag to start the practice session, and Billy got what he thought was a good run down the front stretch, making a conservative approach to the first turn. He'd been advised to drive low, two feet or so off that inside white line. Winters were not kind to paved surfaces in the East and Midwest, leaving them bumpy and choppy. A bump on the straightaway might gave a driver a quick jolt, but in the middle of a turn those bumps upset the balance of a car that was already trying to throw itself to the right and into the guardrail. Billy felt the car wiggle to the right on the bumps, and as he followed another car he saw what it looked like from behind, as that car jerked right, and then gripped the pavement again as it rode over the ridges. *Good reason to let those tires warm up!*

Speed here was much greater than that on half-mile tracks, such as Reading. Here cars peaked out on the straights at, perhaps one hundred and fifty miles per hour. Those long straights gave a driver a chance to relax for a few seconds. Half-mile racing demanded constant attention and work. Here each lap had perhaps twenty seconds of straights—time to rest.

C.J., that rear-engine car, and another dozen cars were in this warm-up session. Some stopped at their pit, only to rejoin quickly after a consultation or adjustment. When Billy stopped in his pit after ten laps, he could see that C.J. was still sitting in his car and deep in conversation with Willy Caldwell, who was leaning into the cockpit. C.J. got out and walked back to Billy, still sitting in his car.

C.J. removed his gloves and smacked them on Billy's windscreen, "Did you see that little…car, that rear-engine thing?"

"Yeah, he passed me when I was just getting' warmed up. Why?"

"I was runnin' about as hard as I could, and that damn little roller skate thing went around me on the outside of turn one! So, he's leadin' me as we go down the backstretch, and I'm faster, so I pass him 'bout three-fourths of the way down the straight. And then, he catches me and passes me as we're right between three and four, outside again. Front stretch—again I pass him, just as we go into turn one, but he's faster in the turns, so he passes me again, and we head down the back stretch. And this time I just catch up to him, but ain't got enough track left to pass before the turn. So, I gotta back off. He pulls out a lead on me in the turn, carries it all the way down the front stretch. I start to catch up to him, but not as much! I'm fallin' behind a little more each lap! You know what that means, don't you? Ain't got a chance! I think I'm about as fast as anybody here, faster than most. I told Caldwell we better put some more nitro in the fuel!"

Billy tried to play an unfamiliar role—mediator, "Hey, a few laps of practice ain't the same as a hundred miles of racing. That thing is new and might break,"

"Well, we'll be runnin' for second place at best today." C.J. stepped over the pit wall and looked at a stack of tires. "Ain't we got anything softer than these rock-hard things?"

That "roller skate thing" was the class of the field, turning in a fine 33.71 lap to earn the pole. The driver was an eastern sports car veteran who'd been driving since the early fifties. He'd had a lot of success on courses such as Watkins Glen, Bridgehampton, and Lime Rock Park. He'd driven some of the first rear-engine sports cars in the States, so driving the new car from California was natural for him. C.J. used all he had and turned in second fastest time, 34.21. Billy went out to qualify next to last and shocked many, except for Cal Olsen, when he turned in a best lap of 34.47 in the old Kuzma dirt track car.

At the green flag, Burke Carpenter, in the rear-engine car, jumped into the lead and dominated the race. C.J. was right. He started outside the first row, beside Carpenter, and watched as the little rear-engine car steadily pulled away, lap after lap, easily pulling ahead in the turns. The car sacrificed some top speed to C.J., but the superior cornering of the new car enabled Carpenter to gain more in the turns than he gave up on the straightaway. It seemed a forgone conclusion how it would end.

Billy started fourth and dropped back to fifth place, but a steady pace got him up to third place, right behind his teammate, C.J. Cal Olsen didn't want to encourage a duel between his two drivers and chose not to use pit sign boards to warn C.J. that a car was closing on him. C.J. was caught off guard when Billy passed him entering turn three. There was no doubt that Billy's car wasn't as fast as C.J.'s Watson roadster. CJ. was demoralized by the superior handling of the new car and was cruising, not racing. The two Olsen cars were quite sure to finish second and third, and Cal was already tallying his take for the day—probably around $4, 000, plus or minus a bit.

C.J. decided that getting beaten by a little "roller skate thing" was one thing, but he wouldn't suffer the indignity of getting caught sleeping by Billy, in an old-fashioned dirt track car, of all things. C.J. worked hard to earn second place back—too hard. On lap 62 he drove hard into turn one and slammed the tail of Billy's car. Billy did a half spin and backed into the wall. C.J. had hit Billy so hard that his radiator was punctured, and the resulting loss of coolant ended his day. Three damaged race cars in two days of racing. What looked like a second and third place finish—$4,000 payout—evaporated in that collision. Then on lap 78, Carpenter's day ended when his engine failed. The Olsen cars could have finished one-two, and earned $6,000 and change. Saturday night—a blown engine. Sunday—two wrecked race cars. Cal Olsen was not a happy car-owner. Willy Caldwell was not a happy mechanic. C.J. was not a happy driver.

Billy stood behind the Olsen pit, packing his gear away in his helmet bag, trying to stay out of the way of three very angry men. C.J.'s back was to Billy, so what he said was muffled, but Olsen's reply was audible and angry, "We'll talk Tuesday in Indianapolis, C.J.!" followed by a barely audible, but a determined, "It's either him or me, Cal," from Willy Caldwell. Then C.J. walked away in the direction of the parked rear engine car. Indianapolis was just weeks away.

· · · · ·

Eddie Spencer sat on the couch in his mobile home, late on a Saturday afternoon, getting ready to watch "Wide World of Sports." Supper—a TV dinner, a frozen meal in an aluminum tray—was still in the oven, and Eddie sipped on a Burger beer. A folding, metal TV tray was littered with salt and pretzel crumbs. Eddie was in his mid-sixties. He had thin strands of dark hair combed straight back and a rubbery, slim face and broad smile. Eddie had been a successful racer when he was young, specializing in board track racing in the 1920's, until an accident left him with a stump of a left arm and a left leg that had never healed properly. That brought his promising career to an end. But he stayed close to the sport, working at the Indianapolis speedway in May and doing odd jobs for management at the Dayton, Ohio, half-mile, banked track. One would expect that his trailer would have evidence of his past, but there was just one black and white photograph of Eddie. He was smiling at the camera, surrounded by crew members in white coveralls, men in suits and hats, and one pretty "trophy girl" dressed in 1920's flapper style. All the other framed photos were of his family, including graduation pictures of his two sons. There was a favorite photo of his wife, taken on a rare, non-racetrack trip to Colorado. His wife had passed on after he retired, and this mobile home met his modest needs quite well.

Last year, Eddie helped Billy Wallace advance his driving career. He had introduced the young and green Billy around the Indianapolis Speedway in May, helping him get a minor position as a "go-fer" on one of the "500" race teams. Eddie figured that any contact with the racing fraternity was a positive that would pay off later. And then he introduced Billy to Cal Olsen, who gave him a shot at the "big time" last year at the Milwaukee race for Indianapolis (Championship) cars.

Just as the skier crashed down the slope and Jim McKay said, "the thrill of victory and the agony of defeat," there was a thump on the outside of the mobile home and the sound of feet scratching on gravel. Eddie went to the door, opened it, and saw two boys beside a tree. "Hey, kids! What was that?"

"That's our baseball, mister. Sorry!"

"Ah, hel…heck, that's okay. Just be careful."

The boys were ten or eleven years old and lived in the trailer park. They, their parents, and very few residents in the park knew much about Eddie Spencer and his past. Few knew that thirty-five years ago Eddie was, for a brief time, at the top of the racing world. He drove in a few Indianapolis 500's, but was especially skilled on the board tracks in the 1920's. It was like having a retired Babe Ruth living in a neighborhood that had forgotten what he'd once been.

One boy muttered, "Some people say that guy used to be important a long time ago…boxer or something else. I dunno."

"Aw that don't sound right to me. He's got a bum leg and half an arm. How could he be a boxer, genius? Come on, let's go down to the tracks and watch the trains. Put pennies on the tracks."

The phone rang as Eddie closed the door. He picked it up. "Hello, Eddie Spencer."

"Speed! How ya doin'? This is Fritz Eckhart."

Eddie grinned at the voice and memory of his old friend, who still worked as a supervisor for the race sanctioning body in the Midwest, "I'm good, Fritz, how about you?"

"No problems here. You comin' over to Indy next month? We got work for you."

"Sure. It's a lot easier now, not workin' and all," Eddie answered. It was nice to hear his old newspaper nickname, Speed Spencer.

"Well, I got something that I sure as hell hope isn't going to be an issue, 'cause it's one of our new guys."

"Oh yeah? What's that?"

Fritz went on, "I just got a call from our man out on the West Coast. He says there's some kind of story that Billy Wallace drove a URA midget race out there. You know what that means. Guy gets caught runnin' some race like that and he's out."

"I don't think Billy'd do that. He's got too much to lose," Eddie replied. "He ain't dumb."

"The guy told me he was talkin' to the El Cajon guy, Chet Martin, and he said that Olsen's midget was parked in the infield Saturday night. Didn't run. But some guy who called himself Cam Turner towed it in and planned to race there on Sunday."

"Well, did a Cam Turner drive?" Eddie asked.

"As far as I can tell so far, no. But Billy had Olsen's race car with him and what's a guy gonna do with a car on his trailer? Kid could shorten up a promising career doin' that. Think you can somehow talk to him?"

"Guess I can call out there to…that promoter. That still Martin, you say? I'll try to talk to that guy. That's about all I'd know, Fritz."

"You know the boy, took him around and introduced him to lots of people at Indianapolis, didn't you? Maybe there doesn't have to be a full board meeting thing." Fritz hung up and Eddie went back to ten minutes of figure skating on Wide World of Sports.

* * * * *

Roxanne Lytell was about to get into bed when her phone rang. It was a Tuesday night and she had just returned from a night out with co-workers at SECO, the company in Muncie, Indiana, where she worked as a secretary and "copy girl." She was in her mid-twenties, shapely, and nearly five feet nine inches tall. She had blue eyes and long brown hair framing a pretty face. She ran the copying machine that used original engineers' drawings to make blueprint copies for the machinists on the shop floor. SECO made equipment for the steel industry: coiling, corrugating, and slitting machinery for flat steel. Her appearance on the shop floor to deliver new prints was appreciated by the men, who watched her every move. They would often try to prolong any such delivery with idle and unnecessary small talk. She never failed to brighten the gray world of machine trades.

"Hello, this is Roxie," she said into the phone.

"Hey, Sweetie! It's Billy!"

"Well, stranger. It's been a long time. I thought you…well…I didn't know what to think. I know you were thousands of miles away and all, but I thought you might call sometime, Billy."

"Guess I was kinda not thinkin', huh? But I was thinkin' about you…a lot, really! And I had trouble with my car, and I stopped to see my dad, and that always involves time and…

well, I ain't one to communicate so good." Billy's excuses were met with silence.

"So…what's up, Billy?"

"I'm back in Indy now. I'll be around now, you know. The season is getting started here again so I'll be racing around Ohio, Indiana a lot. Thought maybe we could get together for dinner some night. Maybe Thursday, Friday? You wanna pick out some place up there in Muncie? I got a car now, sorta. It gets me around at least, so I can drive up your way. And I think maybe I got some big news, at least I think something's gonna happen in a few days that'll mean a lot to me. I wanted to talk about that and how it might affect some of your plans for May, if you're interested."

Chapter Three

Janet Lawton worked Friday night at the farm store as a favor for her co-worker and friend, Missy Wilkins. Missy had asked her to take the last four hours of her afternoon at the store. Ray Wiseman had asked her to go out to dinner, and Missy wanted some extra time to get ready.

Ray had said he wanted to go to a "nice" place, as he put it. When she'd asked what "nice" meant, he'd said it wouldn't be a "beer and fried chicken juke box joint." He'd told Missy to "fix yourself up pretty," but it wouldn't be "no city place." So, that probably meant Fort Wayne and Dayton were out. That was Missy's best guess. The last clue she got from Ray was that he would wear a tie.

Ray Wiseman was a few years older than Missy and a "kind-of-steady" date for her. She liked Ray but wasn't sure that she loved him. Ray was reliable for weekend dates. He was the foreman at Quality Machine Tool, a small machine shop in Barton. He'd taken as many shop classes as he could in high school and after graduation began working as an apprentice machinist in that same shop. He learned quickly and soon could skillfully operate all the different machines: lathes, milling machines, grinders, and other metal shapers. He was promoted to shop foreman. His competence secured his job, and his future looked promising. But Missy wasn't sure of his place in her life—in spite of the security he could offer—or *what* she wanted that place to be.

"Okay, Ray, I guess you're going to surprise me. I'll be ready at…?"

"Pick you up at six o'clock. Well, make that six-fifteen. I ain't tied a tie since my sister's wedding two years ago," Ray said, only half-jokingly.

Missy was "friend/sister" to Janet. When she was born to the neighbors, Janet was twelve years old and became the "go-to" babysitter. Janet thought of Missy as her first baby girl. The relationship grew to one of deep fondness. When Janet graduated and married soon after, Missy was an adoring six-year-old, dazzled by the young bride. When Tina was born, Missy was enthralled with the baby girl and her young mother. If Missy's parents had weekend plans, they brought her to Janet and Tom's house. The young Missy learned about babies from her own baby-sitter. And as Missy grew up, Janet became a trusted friend. They were like sisters, in many ways, without the accumulated grudges of siblings.

Now Missy was drifting through her early twenties, living at home and working five or six days a week at the local farm store, forty hours plus or minus a few. She stocked shelves and worked the check-out counter. She earned enough money to do what she wanted. She had no expenses, living at home with her parents, who were in their late sixties. She was an unexpected gift to them when she was born, and they worshipped their one child. Missy had an easy life, though one without direction. In high school she showed an aptitude for bookkeeping but did not pursue it. Occasionally, she thought about telling the store manager that she could help with the books, but never did.

Missy was five feet seven inches tall. "Slim and a little more" or "solid and a little less" is how she described herself—either was accurate. She had dark complexion, light brown hair, and pretty brown eyes—big, dark brown eyes that drew one's attention like a magnet, the kind of eyes that a young man could get lost in. When she walked into the store, Janet could tell that Missy had taken extra care to get ready for this date. Missy wore a dress that seemed crafted for one girl: the dress was yellow and accented with subtly delicate white, stylized flowers. An artist couldn't have more perfectly matched those colors to her complexion and eyes. It was a dress that few women could have worn successfully. And then there were those brown eyes. Missy learned long ago that she didn't have to "work" them to attract a guy. They just seemed to do that without any eye-lash flutter or intentional dramatics. Other girls in high school learned how to employ the magic of a raised eyebrow, a wink and a smile, or lowered sunglasses. Skillfully applied make-up was not necessary—if anything, it was a distraction. Her beauty and appeal were natural, not an applied, part of her.

Janet was stunned when her friend returned. When Missy left the store two hours before, she'd been wearing her everyday slacks, plaid blouse, and penny-loafers. And here she was in that dress, heels, a beautiful necklace, and her hair done so nicely. This wasn't her lifetime "buddy." She'd been transformed.

"Holy cow, Missy! You flyin' to New York? L.A.?"

"What? Is this too much? Ray said we were goin' to a nice place, so I took him at his word."

Janet leaned on the counter. "That boy darn well ought to take you to *nice* at least, if not *more* than nice! If he don't, you tell me, and I'll set him straight."

"He said we're not going to Dayton or Fort Wayne. I figure maybe Lima or around the lake, you know, there are some good restaurants. Some steak places and, I think, one good

Italian place. He said we weren't going to some burger and fries bar."

"What's the occasion? You guys ain't *that* serious are you? If so, you been hidin' that from me."

"That would be a shock. I never gave it a thought. I hope not, 'cause I really don't know how I feel about Ray, and I'm not sure he even feels that way. God! I gotta think about how to handle that, don't I?"

"Missy, you've got good judgment. I think you won't commit to anything that doesn't seem right. But any guy who sees you tonight would certainly have his head swimming. Right now, I'm thinking I might like to be a guy!"

"Oh, shut up, Jan!"

Both ladies blushed but enjoyed the moment. Janet regained her composure. "So you just came in here to remind me that I'm an old married woman, working on Friday night, huh, or why are you here anyway? You've got to get home so he can pick you up."

"Honestly, Jan, I just wanted you to tell me this outfit is okay. Mom is kind of out of the fashion thing, so that's all. I'm not showin' off, am I?"

"I think I already answered that question, don't you think?" Janet came out from behind the counter, hugged her friend, and said, "You look perfect. Now go home before Ray gets there. And have fun!"

Missy smiled, squeezed Janet's hand, backed away from the counter, and rushed out to her car.

Janet smiled and watched her leave, remembering the little girl she had spent so much time with, playing pat-a-cake, helping her walk, riding a bicycle, swimming at the town pool, helping her learn to become a young lady. All the things she did later with her own daughter, Tina. Brown eyes, blue eyes—just eye colors—were unforgettable to Janet for a reason she would carry to her grave, a reason she could share with no one. Ever.

Tom Lawton's first serious high school girlfriend was Janet Richardson. They had a spat and broke up in their senior year. Tom dated Suzy Harmon for a short time, while Janet had a brief relationship with Roger Hicks. Later that school year, Tom and Janet reconciled and have been a couple ever since. In the spring that year, Janet revealed she was pregnant. When she told Tom, there was no question in his mind about what to do. High school sweethearts became husband and wife, and soon, parents of Christina, their only child. It was not a "shotgun wedding" and Tom was satisfied in the life he'd chosen and he thought Janet was as well.

But Janet was haunted by lessons she'd learned in high school biology about heredity and traits passed from parents to children. A first-year biology teacher had taught about dominant and recessive genes and heredity. The young man was fresh out of college and plowed through those lessons, often turning red with embarrassment while boys smirked, and girls looked down at their desks.

Janet sat through the lessons thinking, *Big deal. I know about some of that stuff just from living on a farm! These are just book lessons!*

When Tina was born, she had blue eyes like most babies—blue eyes that most often turn brown. But Janet could not forget the heredity lessons. A mother and father with brown eyes had a slim chance of having a child with blue eyes. But a mother with brown eyes and a father with blue eyes? There was a fifty percent chance that their baby's blue eyes would remain blue. Tom had brown eyes, Janet had brown eyes, Roger Hicks had blue eyes. Baby Tina, like most babies, was born with blue eyes. Janet carried a secret fear that she could not express. That fear was relieved when Tina's eyes turned brown. But that doubt would remain locked inside Janet till her last day. Although it was a doubt that never affected her love for her husband or daughter.

One Saturday afternoon, perhaps two years ago, Janet stopped at Tom's Pine Street Station to get gasoline. The bell rang and Tom came out, surprised to see his wife and daughter. "Why, these are the two best looking customers I've had today! Fill up?"

"Two dollars' worth, Tom. The vet was out this morning and said Tina's horse needed some kind of medicine, so we're going to the farm store."

"Daddy, make that helper-boy of yours get me a Coke," Tina said, joking about James.

"We aim to please here, girls," Tom began, but just then Roger and Suzy Hicks pulled up to the other side of the gas pumps in Suzy's blue Corvette convertible.

And there were the four corners of that high school romance, reunited for one of the few times since graduation—a few friends' weddings and their ten-year reunion. Janet was the only one of the four who invested these relationships with a great, secret emotion. It wasn't fear, because she'd decided long ago the course she would follow. That was a path set in stone for her—the reason for which she could never share… with anyone…ever. Roger, Tom, and Suzy bantered, almost like teenagers again. Janet sat, listened, and smiled—knowing or not knowing.

She reached across the car, squeezed her daughter's hand, and said, "These are some of the people we went to school with, Sweetie. Can you just see us all together, walking those same halls as you now? Can you imagine we were kids once?"

"That must have been, what…forty years ago, Mom?"

"Oh, that is s-o-o funny." Janet's mind wandered. *Whatever, whoever, it makes absolutely no difference, the only one of these four individuals here who knows is me. And maybe even I don't know. Maybe I'm imagining something. But it doesn't make any difference. Tina is my daughter, I love her because she is mine, of that there is no question, and I always will love her—no matter what. Tom is my husband, I love him, and he is…well, he is a father to Tina. This is my life. I am not afraid. I have nothing to be afraid of. This is my story told by me and no one else.*

"Hey, wake up, Janet! You aren't mad at me, are you?" interrupted Suzy Hicks.

"Oh, I'm sorry, Suzy. I was just trying to remember what I wanted to get at the store."

"Jan, I told Roger just a few days ago that we should all go out sometime."

"That would be fun, wouldn't it?" Janet said with hesitation.

That service station encounter soon came to an end with each of the four agreeing to arrange a "double-date, just like the old days," they said, although Roger, as usual, showed even less commitment than Janet had. As did Tom. Roger never let Tom forget that he, Roger, considered himself to be socially and professionally superior.

. . . . .

Eddie "Speed" Spencer left his mobile home in Dayton mid-morning on a Thursday and headed north to the half-mile dirt track in New Bremen. Fritz Eckhart, the Midwest zone supervisor, had called him on Sunday.

"Eddie, Fritz here. Ya know we talked about Billy and that Cam Turner thing last week, remember?

"Sure. You got it solved? I called out to the California guys. Talked to Jim Adams—he's the guy who leases the land the track is on. Said some guy introduced himself as Cam Turner, had a yellow midget that he parked in the infield. The car never ran that Sunday—just sat in the infield, on its trailer. And he doesn't recall any driver named Turner driving there.

Odd thing—yellow midget, number thirty-seven. That sure sounds like an Olsen car, doesn't it? But no Cam Turner or Billy Wallace drove there. That's all I know".

"Well, we gotta settle this. We know he was out there 'cause he won that race in San Bernardino the week after that, in the yellow thirty-seven! I'm getting' some heat from the big guys in the office. And it's damn near May. I think Billy's got a ride for the month, but I can't say too much 'cause it's not a sure thing yet. But if Billy's got a problem, the owner of the car he's *supposed* to drive needs to be able to move on, get some other guy to drive for him."

"So…what? I told you what Adams told me. Seems like there's nothing to it."

"I want to set this kid straight on what, if anything, he's messin' with. I don't know what happened out there, but it sounds kind of odd. Maybe nothing happened. If so, Billy's lucky. But I want him to know *how* lucky."

"Well, tell him!"

"Here's what I'm doin'. Dick Francis in New Bremen is one of them promoters who doesn't just let races happen. He *make*s things happen. He makes sure he gets press releases out to all the local papers and even gets in touch with Dayton, Columbus, Toledo, and Lima sports reporters. He hires some TV sports guy out of Dayton to be his announcer on race day."

"Yeah, I know that guy," Eddie said.

"And that guy—TV sports guy—wants to have a couple drivers on TV for his sports report on the six o'clock news. The promoter, Francis, called me, asking about good candidates. So, here's my thought: I drive over there with Billy and a veteran. I think the sports guy will like that—a hot, up-and-coming driver and a "500" veteran. A race winner would be great, but I'll see who I can get to agree."

"Like I said before. What do I have to do with this?"

"You kinda introduced him around last year, sorta took him under your wing. Helped him get that ride in Olsen's car at Milwaukee. You understand him a bit more. I ain't gonna say a thing about that El Cajon story when we're driving over to New Bremen. Billy might appreciate you being there—friendly face and all. Kill two birds with one stone: TV visit and some kindly advice. See what I'm talkin' about? He might take it better from you."

"Okay, see you there on Thursday, Fritz."

"We'll get to the track around two or so, look things over, and then go do that TV thing. Thanks, Eddie," Fritz Eckhart hung up.

* * * * *

Christina Lawton, Tina, was in the barn with her horse, Candy. Tom and Janet's sixteen-year-old daughter had determined this would be the summer she would enter her horse in a show, a show of some kind, but what kind had not been decided. Gloria Anderson, a trainer in Preble County who had helped Tina last year, advised her to start simple, perhaps in one of Gloria's "practice" shows that she conducted on her own farm for beginners. Gloria structured her show like a county fair show, but all participants understood that it was just practice—no ribbons; no crowd; no judges; no first, second, third place finishes. In other words, less pressure. Just helpful feedback and constructive advice, when necessary. Tina hoped to participate in one of Gloria's shows, and then later in the summer, enter her county fair.

Tina was a pretty girl with an oval face and brown eyes. She had worn her hair in a ponytail since childhood. She told her mother, "It's easy, it's out of my way, and it's not hot!" Janet had advised her to "Fix it nice sometimes, Tina. Boys might notice." She had little interest in her hair, or boys for that matter. She had just reached a height that gave her pleasure to look down, so slightly, at her mother.

When she was in sixth grade she'd seen "National Velvet" and soon after started making comments about horses and how she would like to have her own. Tom and Janet had resisted at first but reconsidered two years ago and purchased a Morgan horse. They had the room and facilities for a horse, but no experience with such an animal and no place in their budget for the expenses that naturally arise. They had even less understanding of how demanding the care of a horse could be. Tina had mild cerebral palsy that left her with a slight limp, but greater issues of self-confidence. A specialist had once advised Janet that caring for an animal could help develop self-esteem and confidence, qualities that she lacked. When Janet suggested a pet, she had hoped Tina would ask for a dog. A dog never entered Tina's mind. She seized on the suggestion as her opportunity to get a horse, even though she had no background for such an animal. Tom and Janet relented, hoping such a project would provide direction for their daughter. It did, but that direction did not come easily. It was a commitment that none of them could then comprehend. There were some private lessons that first summer and visits to Gloria Anderson for help and advice. When Tina was struggling to understand and bond with her horse, Janet and Tom had been advised that Gloria's insight included horses *and* riders. The young girl's relationship with Candy turned around, with Gloria's help. There were minor and unexpected crises but on balance, it had been a good thing, life changing in many ways.

Janet once remarked to Tom, "I understand Gloria's Ten Lessons for Parents so much more now. She had those sayings posted in different places in the barn, so you couldn't miss them. I can't remember all ten of her sayings, but she was right. I remember some: 'Your daughter is learning to control her fears,' and 'She's learning the art of silent communication.' And...um number four, or was that five? The one that said, 'She's learning to be patient.' Then, I kind of forget a lot of them. I'm going to write those down someday, Tom. Oh, there was one about learning to fall and fail but keep trying, and another about learning to be gentle and consistent."

He replied, "She wouldn't be the person she is now without Gloria...and that horse. We didn't have a clue, did we?"

Tina washed her beloved horse, Candy, singing sweetly and quietly, "You are my sunshine, my only sunshine. You make me happy, when skies are gray." Gloria had advised her, "Talk to your horse, Tina. It doesn't make any difference what you say. Talk to her like you would a dear friend, or a baby, or your mom or dad. Just chatter about anything—the weather, what you had for breakfast, what you're doing right now, what you'll do next. Sing or just ramble on about...well, it doesn't make *any* difference. She just likes to hear your voice, like a child likes to hear its mother."

So Tina sang the song that her mother had sung to her when she was young, the song that just meant love and safety. She had never learned more than the first verse, so she sang it over and over to Candy and talked about anything that came to mind.

Tina had a special shampoo she used to wash the horse and a natural sponge because "Gloria said so." Tom had heard such comments many times. He used to mock-growl, "That nag gets better soap than me!" Tina knew he was joking.

"Okay, Girl, let's rinse you off now." She turned on the garden hose, using a gentle spray to rinse the soap off her neck first, avoiding Candy's face—something the horse did not like.

"There. Feels good, don't you agree? Wish somebody would wash my hair like that. You don't know how lucky you are, Candy. And today we're gonna use this special stuff to get the tangles out of your tail and mane, and…who is that in the lane?" Tina heard car tires crunching the gravel in the long lane up to the house. Looking out from the open barn doors, she could see it was James, her father's gas-station helper, at least the high school boy who *had* been Tom's helper at the station.

"What does that boy want, Candy?" she asked in her horse-patter mode. "Ever since he went to that race last year with us…well…we'll see what's going on." She watched James get out of his old Ford coupe, walk up to the porch, and knock on the screen door. He waited a minute, then knocked again. Tina watched him as he waited for an answer, but getting none—both parents were working—he walked back to his car and started to get in.

Tina decided to at least let him know she was home. "James!" She waved from the big open barn doors.

James waved and walked toward the barn. "Hi, Tina," he said as he entered. Candy snorted and turned her ears. "Guess I don't need to ask what you're doing, huh?"

"That's right, all you *upper classmen* know it all," she teased.

"Mom and dad working today?"

"Yeah. How you doin' since Dad closed the station? You got a job yet?"

"For a few more weeks. I'm a clean-up man at Quality Machine. They give me a few hours in the afternoon sometimes, from four to seven o'clock usually, a couple days a week. But that might not last much longer. Maybe they'll take me on for the summer, I don't know. If not, maybe I'll get some farm work. You?"

"Me? Work? Whatever would I do? Mom and dad never said anything about it."

"That sounds good to me, but maybe I should say something to your dad…. "

"Don't you ever, James!"

"Hey, just teasin'! take it easy!"

"You got a way about you, James, you doofus!"

"That's what Mom says about my dad. She says he's got a way—a way that no one else wants!"

Tina chuckled and went back to washing her horse. "Did you want to talk to Dad? He's on the night shift now, you know."

"Oh, yeah, I know. No, uh, I forgot…or something. Well, I worked for your dad almost every day for like…a long time… two years, almost. And it'd be nice to talk to him again. So, you're washing your horse, huh?"

"Well, yeah, that's what I'm *doing*, James."

"Yeah, I wash my car a lot!" James blurted out.

Tina looked at James, looked away and chuckled.

"This is a nice place out here, Tina. Close to town, but kinda in the country, too."

"Yes, it is." Tina finished rinsing the horse and began to towel her off.

James watched Tina tending to the horse. Neither said anything for several minutes and the silence became awkward. Finally, James said, "Well, tell your dad I was out here, and I'll try another time, okay?"

"Sure, James. See you in school, probably."

"Okay, bye."

"See ya."

James walked out of the barn toward his Ford coupe, got in and sat for a minute. Then he got out and walked back to the barn.

"Forget something, James?"

"Tina, prom's comin' up. I'm a junior so I can go. But the girl I wanna ask can't go 'cause she's a sophomore. So, I ain't goin.'"

"That's too bad."

"So, Tina, you're that sophomore girl. Will you go out with me on prom night—someplace else? We can't go to prom, but…I don't know—movie, burgers? Something, but we can figure that out."

"A date? You're asking me to go on a date with you? I never been out on a date with a boy. That could be fun, but you know what has to happen first don't you?" Tina smiled, turned, and continued drying her horse.

"Oh, yeah. Last year your dad told me I had to go through 'channels,' he called them."

"Really? Well, you better do that, then. But I've got to go through those same 'channels', too. So, give me a day, okay? Then call." Tina smiled at James and turned back to her horse.

· · · · ·

About two miles north of New Bremen, Ohio, Eddie Spencer turned right off Ohio Route 66A at a large concrete block sign that announced New Bremen Speedway. He chose one of the many dirt lanes that wound through a grove of trees and drove up to an earthen embankment. That mound of dirt was a few hundred yards long and perhaps twelve feet high. It served as the foundation for the wooden grandstands along the front straightaway. Eddie parked his car and walked past the booth where the ticket seller worked on race days. He could hear the growl of a diesel engine. Holding on to a handrail, Eddie went up the concrete steps built into the earthen bank, pausing halfway up. When he got to the top of the embankment, he saw just two men working. There was what looked like an old oil delivery truck, parked near a large pond in the infield. There were, in fact, two ponds, both located toward the back of the infield, close to the backstretch. The truck had a hose—about the size of a firehose—leading into the pond. A worker was apparently pumping water from the pond into the truck's tank. The other worker was driving a road grader, pushing dirt from the top of the track, near the retaining wall, towards the inside.

Eddie walked down the center row of the stands to a gate in the middle of the front straightaway and waved at the driver of the grader, who stopped at the gate where Eddie stood on the concrete wall.

"Hi, I'm Eddie Spencer. Dick Francis? Or is that Dick out there with the water truck?"

"Nope, I would be Dick Francis. Fritz said you'd be here today. Guess he's comin' over with some drivers, at least I hope so. He said he would, and I got them lined up to do a TV interview in Dayton this afternoon."

"If Fritz said that, you can count on it," Eddie said. "So, what's goin' on here today?"

"We ran a stock car and modified program Saturday night, so we're just tryin' to get this dirt back in shape. I'm pushin' it back down before I cut it up with a disc a little, not too much. Had some rain on Monday, so that was some good luck."

"So, you'll be workin' Friday and Saturday doin what?"

"I'll use the sheepfoot roller, then put some calcium on and water it. Wheel pack it later. With luck and good weather, that should do the job."

"You got a good track. I think the guys like to race here, like the way you treat 'em, Dick."

"We try to run a good program, and we get lots of help from the town. There's a men's social service club that makes fried chicken dinners. Those meals are ready after the races. Free meals to the drivers. They love it! Back there in the parking lot, you'll smell it cookin' about the time they get to the semi-feature. Fans buy meals, mingle with drivers. Kinda keeps them from packin' up and leavin', Eddie. Good all the way around—for fans, drivers, newspaper guys. They can talk to drivers and get stories."

"Yeah, I heard a lot of good things about your show here. Couple years ago, one driver told me only problem he had with this track was the rocks."

"Hey, it's a dirt track, what do you expect? I heard about that, so I talked to a car club in town. I told them I'd give ten dollars to each boy. Must have been twenty teenage boys. They made a side-by-side line and walked around the track, pickin' up rocks. Probably can't get 'em all but it couldn't have hurt anything. But, like I said, it's a dirt track."

"Yeah, drivers know that. It's dirt, and rocks are in dirt. This ain't Indianapolis."

"Bet I know who told you that, too. The guy drove here a few times—Wagner, got killed in practice at Indianapolis. He said he had two problems with this place. The rocks, which we been working on, and he said the guardrail's not high enough—should be higher than your wheels. Next year I want to put another Armco barrier on top of what we got now. That should address the issue."

Eddie looked down and kicked the concrete wall. "You're right. That Wagner could size up a track's character, too. Once he said to me, 'New Bremen—in my mind that place is sort of a Little Horne. Got more banking, but I sort of drive it that way—like the big mile circle at Langhorne. So, I ran that past Connors once, and he paused for a few seconds and said, 'I never thought about it like that, but that's a good way to put it.'"

Dick squinted like he was considering a new thought. "One of the old guys who built this track said it was supposed to be a mile. But the farmer on the south end of the track backed out and refused to sell his land, after they had configured and graded the north turn. That's why it's got those wide, sweeping turns. There were supposed to be long, mile-track length straightaways to connect those turns. So, rather than start from scratch, they configured the south turn to match the north, and put short straights between them. So, they ended up with something similar to a circle, a mini-Langhorne."

"That's one heck of a story, and when I look at it now, I can see how that all came about. And that's still a farm there on the south end. But like I said, Dick, you run a good program here. Most of our drivers like to come here. Some of our other promoters could learn a few things. Hey, there's Fritz now. He's got Billy Wallace with him."

"We got to get goin' for our TV appearance. What you doin' here, Eddie?" Dick asked.

"I told Fritz I'd meet him here and…well, I wanted to talk to Billy."

* * * * *

Dick Francis rode with Fritz Eckhart and the veteran driver Carl Connors, a proven winner and many time Indianapolis 500 racer, with a second-place finish four years ago in the Memorial Day classic. Billy Wallace rode with Eddie Spencer.

Eddie stopped at an ice cream place on Ohio Route 66, just inside the city limits of New Bremen. A cute teenage girl with brown hair was working. He ordered two chocolate shakes. "Can't beat a milkshake, Billy. I'm glad that place is open, early in the season like this. Well, Dayton is what—hour or so away?" As they left New Bremen, Eddie decided to go at the issue straight on, and get it over with. "Billy, I want to say this just once and you don't have to say 'Yes,' 'No,' or 'Go to hell,'" Eddie began as they left New Bremen. "Just accept it as a word to the wise. I hear stuff, usually fairly accurate stuff, too. I heard that some kid who called himself Cam Turner showed up with a yellow midget, numbered thirty-seven, at El Cajon. I also heard that he didn't race a lap at that URA race. Then

I heard that you won a race at the Orange Show in a yellow thirty-seven. And that was a sanctioned race."

"Let me...."

"It's better for you not to say anything. Just listen and think about it. You might be gettin' pissed off with me, but I'm tryin' to keep your career on track. You can go really far in this sport, as long as you don't do something stupid. Them officials can put your career on hold, give you a one-year suspension. I've seen them do it—to a 500 winner once—and there are a lot of other drivers who would be happy to take your place. Lecture over, Billy."

Billy turned his head and looked out the car window, silent for a long time. Eddie just looked straight ahead and drove, sipping his milkshake.

Chapter Four

Janet invited Missy to go along to New Bremen for the early May race. Knowing that the ladies would have each other to talk to, Tina convinced her mother to allow James to go as her guest. "At least I'll have *someone* to talk to, *Mom*," as she put it. They chose seats in the middle of the grandstand, behind the flagman's stand, about halfway down from the top row. Janet wanted to blend in and remain anonymous.

"Mom, can we go get burgers and dogs at the concession stand?" Tina asked soon after they arrived.

"Sure. Here are a few dollars. Oh, and bring me a Coke. Missy, you want anything?"

"No, thanks, Jan, I'm okay for now."

"So, now those two kids are gone for a while. Tell me about Saturday night and that date with Ray, huh, Missy?"

"Well, it was *fine*, I guess. No, it was better than fine. It was good."

"What does that mean—*fine*, and then *good*? You don't sound too sure."

"Well, you know how he went about that whole thing—saying he wanted to go to a special place, a nice place. Sayin' he was gonna have to figure out how to put on a tie, and it wouldn't be no burger joint, and all that. Well, it was a nice place, *really* nice, I mean. You know the place—Luthman's, out by the lake. You remember that place, right? Shoot, they have cloth napkins!"

"Yeah, Tom took me there after he won two races in a row. That's been a while ago! Anyway, you were sorta not sure which way that date was all gonna go, right?"

"Right! I was afraid he was gonna be all serious, you know, and ask a question that I wouldn't know how to answer. Well! Thank God it didn't go that way! He just started talkin' during dinner about how much he liked doing stuff with me—dinners, going to school basketball games, movies, just drivin' around out in the country. Then he sorta got…confused or flustered. And I mean, Janet, I was thinking, 'Uh oh, here we go', but then he looked down at his plate, looked up at me, and just said, 'Missy, I really like you, a whole bunch. I, uh, l-l…like you'."

"And I said, 'Ray, that is so sweet. I like you, too.' I tell you, Jan, I almost laughed, but I got real a serious look on my face, and I reached across the table and squeezed his hand. Then he seemed to relax, got quiet for a minute or so, smiled, and started talking about his machine shop. You know, sweet talk in Ray's book of love!"

"So, what do you think now?" Janet asked, laughing.

"About what I thought before, and what I told him? I like the guy, but I'm sure glad he didn't go where I thought he might. That was a big moment for Ray Wiseman, 'cause he's not good with words and emotions. I have to remember that about him, his actions, and what the evening probably meant to him. That all said a lot about him. But I'm not ready for that step, and I'm not certain Ray is the guy. We ain't high school kids no more, we're at that age, but…Jan, I'm just not sure. Don't we all want more romance, excitement?"

"Glad it worked out that way, Miss, really I am. Tom and I were very young when we got married. I've told you how that all went. I got pregnant when I was a senior, so dating around with different guys ended quickly. I ain't complaining. We've been happy with each other and have a wonderful daughter. But…. " Janet's thoughts hung in the air.

"You dated other guys, though, right?"

"Yeah, a few…Roger Hicks for a while."

"Ick…that guy? I don't know how Suzy puts up with him!"

"Well, you see the car she drives. A new Corvette every year! Money excuses a lot, Missy."

"Hey, Jan, tell me about this boy that's with Tina. He an okay guy?"

"First ever boy she's been out with. He could have gone to prom—he's a junior. He really wanted to take Tina, but sophomores can't go—school rules. So, he said, 'Let's you and me do something on prom night.' They went to a movie. Tina said it was a *long* movie about some English guy in the desert—and *Ay*rabs or something. Then they went to some Italian place for pizza. Out by the lake. That was their prom, in James' limousine, a '46 Ford!"

"Well, that is sweet. She is so cute, Jan. I wish—"

"Here we go, Missy. They call this first part—it's a practice session—hot laps. Ain't that a funny thing to call it?"

"That car broken, or what? How come that truck is goin' to push it, Jan?"

"Tom says that these cars," Janet began to explain, but cars soon began to circulate, and the noise of the cars made conversation impossible. Janet looked at Missy, mouthed words, and gestured as if to indicate, "Wait till later!"

This was the first Sunday in May. The Indianapolis 500 was fast approaching. May 30, Race Day, was four weeks away. That meant little to Janet, because Tom did not race at Indianapolis, although that had seemed a possibility a few years ago. He had not advanced to that level yet, but many of the drivers here today would leave this little dirt track at the end of the day and start preparing for the 500. Tom's teammate, Billy Wallace, had talent and ambition that would take him to that race this year, or so he hoped. Billy had assurance that a deal was about to include him in a first-class car, perhaps when he returned to the Speedway, later this day.

Billy was in the first hot lap session, in Chuck Williams' new car. Tom was strapped into Chuck's old car, the red number eleven he'd subbed in for the injured Billy Wallace last year. Tom felt especially comfortable in it. This year, the car was to be maintained by Chuck's nephew, Donny. Tom's confidence in Donny was a few notches below that of Chuck, the man that Tom considered to be the master of these cars.

There was a field of good cars and drivers for today's event. It would be the Midwest season opener. Last week, the scheduled opener at Eldora had been rained out. So, these cars were bright and shiny-new looking after the winter rebuild they'd all received. The drivers were eager to get the season started, but the day had dawned gray and cool, and the crowd was consequently smaller. This day might be a repeat of last Sunday—another rainout was a distinct possibility. The officials tried to hurry events along as much as possible, avoiding delays and starting a few minutes earlier than advertised times.

The track was in excellent condition, damp and tacky, and not likely to be dried out by sun and wind. If the weather cooperated, the fans might see great racing.

Chuck's new car, painted a brilliant pearl white and highlighted with red and blue striping, did not cooperate for Billy. After being pushed by the pick-up truck for half a lap with just a few sputters, Billy signaled for the push truck driver to stop. Billy stopped the car, pulled it out of gear, and motioned for the driver to push him back to the pits. Chuck and a helper swarmed over the car as Billy sat, waiting for Chuck to do something, anything.

Back in the stands, Tina and James had taken their seats in front of Janet and Missy. Tina said, "Mom, isn't that Billy in that number twenty-two? What's wrong? Why isn't he on the track?"

"Don't know," was all Janet said.

"Oh, look Mom. They're pushin' Daddy out!"

Janet leaned forward and whispered, "Tina, not so loud. I'd rather we be kind of anonymous here. Fans treat you kind of different if they know you're connected with a driver or car."

Tom Lawton and the other drivers in the first hot lap session lapped the half mile track slowly until their impatience began to show. Some drove through turn two, the backstretch, and turn three at near racing speed. Then they would slow on the front stretch.

The flagman waved his green flag and fourteen engines immediately roared. The damp clay gave the cars excellent traction. Several raced side by side, but Tom didn't seem to "race" with any others—he drove around car after car, seemingly passing at will, usually in the middle of the track, then arcing out toward the wall on the straightaways. He steered low in the turns and then allowed the car to drift higher on the straights. He tried to make the track as much of a circle as he could. After ten laps of free-for-all racing, the flagman waved his checkered flag, ending the session. When Tom entered the pits, he gave the engine short bursts with the car in neutral, spewing clouds of dust from the twin exhaust pipes. He stopped at the north end of the pits under a big tree, engine barking. Donny signaled to shut the engine off and stepped closer to Tom, showing something in his hand. Donny slapped Tom on the helmet.

Up in the stands, Missy said, "Janet, that was Tom in that red car, right?"

"Yeah, why?" Janet asked.

"He darn-near passed them all! Then that guy in the pits hit him on the helmet! What was that about? Is that guy mad at Tom? I thought he looked fast! But what do I know?"

"Yes, he did look fast, you're right."

"And why was that one wheel off the track, sorta in the air sometimes? What's wrong with his car? Is it broke?"

"For some reason Tom says that's a good thing—sometimes. He says he likes it when that left front tire is just kind of tapping the track, raising up a couple inches, and then settling back down lightly on the track for a few seconds. I don't know, Missy, but it's good. That's all I can say," Janet tried to explain what she didn't quite understand herself, except that it's okay for a car to do that.

The next hot lap session was about to begin, and Billy was lined up again. Chuck must have found the remedy. When the first car was pushed off, a light mist began to fall. As the other cars entered the track, the light mist turned to sprinkles, and then just rain. The starter waved his red flag.

Janet, Missy, Tina, and James retreated to the covered area of the stands. A steady rain soon turned the track to mud. An hour of rain forced the cancellation of the event. The rain date was Sunday, June 20. Two Sunday rainouts in a row!

· · · · ·

Tom stopped at the Wilkins' farm to drop off Missy and then drove the next few miles back home.

"Mom, can James stay for a while this afternoon?" Tina asked.

"That'll be okay, I guess. You kids got homework though? What do you think, Tom?"

"Uh…sure, fine," Tom replied after a pause.

"I don't know about dinner, kids. I thought we'd eat at the track. That men's club in New Bremen has those chicken dinners after the race, but not today. Burgers and fries—how's that sound to you all?" No one answered. "That's it then, but I'm not cookin'. Kids, go to the Dari King and get take-out for us." Once the kids were out of the car, Janet turned to her husband. "Okay, silent Tom, what's up with you? And what was Donny mad about, slappin' you on the helmet like that?"

"He wasn't mad, Jan. On his stopwatch, he had me turnin' a lap at 19.17. Track record is 19.15! First race! He did not make a single change on the car. Took it off the trailer and fueled it up. Didn't feel like I was even running that hard. Ran like a dream! Handle? Even better than last year!"

"So, why the mood? You should feel good!"

"Well, no money today. And we didn't get to race. That's what we went there to do. That's always a let-down. Now, get this. Billy says he wants to drive Olsen's car at Indianapolis this year and he'll leave Chuck, probably. Says he'll take the first couple of phases of his drivers' test in Olsen's Kuzma dirt car, then finish up in the Watson roadster."

"What about C.J.? I thought he was Olsen's man this year?" Janet furrowed her brow, unsure how this affected her husband.

"C.J. is hot to drive that rear engine car that did a number on everyone at Trenton until it broke. Anyway, Olsen's mechanic had three cars to repair after those east coast races. There was that incident at Reading. That pissed off Caldwell, Olsen's mechanic, so bad. Then the wreck at Trenton the next day. Caldwell gave Olsen a 'him-or-me' choice."

"So, why are you so…moody…mad? I don't get it. This doesn't affect you. You're driving number eleven, guaranteed, right?"

"Billy has a big idea he's gonna talk to Olsen about. Says when he's done with the first couple of phases of his rookie test, he'll lean on Olsen. Try to get him to let me use the Kuzma for a rookie test," Tom looked at his wife, his face expressionless.

"Indianapolis…huh…what do you think about that, Tom?" Janet's face betrayed no emotion, trying neither to encourage nor discourage.

"That's what a driver thinks about, right? I mean, if a guy is a good baseball player, he doesn't say, 'Minor league baseball—man, that's for me! I'm stayin' right here in Columbus, or Peoria, or whatever.' Well, you get the idea."

"Sure, so why are you so…glum? It's what you want."

"Money is the issue. I'd have to be over in Indy for weeks… solid. I'd lose my job. Boss ain't gonna give me that time off. I only been there for what, a month?"

"We can work that all out, Hon. We can."

Can we "work it out" like she says? She's come a long way since, well, ten years ago when I started this. She was not a fan then. I guess she's a reluctant fan now. But…if Billy gets this fixed up, how could I say no? Still It doesn't seem fair to put this on her. Tom stared through the windshield, finally looked at Janet, took her hand, kissed it and said, "You don't have to say that."

Chapter Five

On Monday morning, the day after the New Bremen rain-out, Eddie Spencer sat at the wheel of a new convertible with "Official Pace Car Indianapolis 500" emblazoned in red and black letters on the sides. In the passenger's seat was the winner of last year's big race, Russ Stevens. In the back seat sat Tom Lawton and Billy Wallace. Tom had driven to Indianapolis on Monday after Janet had reluctantly agreed to call Maxcell and say that he was "sick." She understood "sick" could very well turn into unemployed, but Tom assured her this would last just a month, and when he was home more regularly, he'd find another job. But so much was up in the air now, even more than usual it seemed to Janet. Just a few months…a few weeks…of less uncertainty and more consistency would be welcome.

Eddie looked at his two passengers in the back seat. "You guys are lucky, not that I'm here, but to have Russ here. He's gonna talk you through a lap or two. He ain't gonna tell you how to win this race, though."

Russ turned to face Tom and Billy. "That's right guys. Find that out on your own, like me! Just kiddin'. But I do want to tell you a few things that will help you get started—safely! You are all alone in the car, but you're not alone here. If there's something you can't figure out, don't be afraid to ask.

Remember to give yourself some time to adjust to this place. It feels so big compared to those half miles you been drivin'. Even different than the mile tracks. You ain't gonna solve this track in one day. Now, look at the big number signs above the wall, and how they're spaced out." Russ pointed to a large sign with a number three on it as Eddie exited the pit lane and drove the convertible out on the track. The numbers three-two-one, on signs, descended as a driver approached turn one. "You should back off when you get beside that number three. *Do not* go flat out beyond that number three. You back off at three…until you get more experience. You got that? Some young guys learned that lesson the hard way. I'm just gonna explain my way of goin' around here, okay? It's the way it was explained to me, back in the early fifties, so just keep that in mind. Not a bad way to start."

Stevens talked as Eddie drove slowly, trying to follow the path described by the veteran racer. "Now, you understand that my shut-off point—mine, not yours—is beyond that number three marker, ok? When I approach turn one here—you know I'm goin' about one seventy—I'm way out there by the front stretch wall, and I really don't shut off all the way. I come off the power kinda easy and keep it turned on and steer for the white line there on the inside. I've picked out, for myself, a spot on the outside wall between turn one and two. Could be a fence post that looks different than the others or some black mark on the wall, or anything. My mark ain't in the middle of that short stretch wall, but beyond it, almost to the beginning of turn two. I aim for that. That first turn arc is gonna be a bigger arc 'cause you're goin' so fast. You don't want to cramp that first turn. You want a nice big arc. I'm still on the power, just not all the way. So, you get out to that mark, lettin' the car go back up toward the wall in that short chute, lookin' for your mark. Then steer for the bottom of turn two.

This can be a tighter arc 'cause you took some speed off and you can pinch down more. The car's gonna be in a mild four-wheel drift. I said *mild*—we ain't dirt-trackin' here. About in the middle of turn two, you wanna be back on the power all the way so you get a good run down the backstretch."

Eddie interrupted. "You guys, remember now: this is a guy talkin' about *his* way, the way of a guy with a lot of experience. You're gonna work up to this gradually."

"Like I was sayin', back on the power all the way from the middle of turn two. Let your car arc out to the wall, then steer left three or four feet, get away from the wall. These car are fairly light, and strong wind gusts can move your car that much, so allow some room in case the wind gets to you. Then hammer down the back stretch. Turn three and four—handle 'em like one and two. *But*…turn three looks so different than one. Turn one looks like it's gonna swallow you up, them grandstands are all dark and…it's just scary at first, guys. But turn three just seems…open…that might be a way to describe it. You may think it looks like a nice gentle bend in the road, but you gotta remember to lift and aim for a spot on the wall, like I told you. And turn four—that's your setup for the front stretch. So, middle of the turn, back on the power all the way. Now, not every driver agrees with me on this, but here's what I think about comin' out of that turn. There's a little hump that, if you come off that turn too wide, it loosens the car up. Then you got trouble. Oh, and them wind gusts can be worse here on the front stretch 'cause of the gaps in the stands, so get off the wall after you come out of four. Oh, and Eddie, stop here, okay?"

Stevens pointed straight ahead and said, "Look way out there above the turn one stands. See that tall smokestack? That's the Allison factory. The smoke is a good way to see how strong the wind is, and which direction it's blowing. Might help you judge the wind some days. Okay, guys, that's my way. Let's wrap it up, Speed. Take us home!"

Eddie stopped the pace car in the pit area, near the entrance to Gasoline Alley. "That's Indianapolis 101: Introduction to Racing, guys. Thanks, Russ."

"Yeah, Russ. Thanks a lot!" Tom and Billy said, nearly in unison.

Tom wondered how he'd remember all that.

Billy thought *Piece of cake!*

* * * * *

The Indianapolis Speedway had opened for casual on-track activity on May 1, a Saturday. Many teams had not arrived but would soon. The New Bremen rainout was on Sunday, May 2. On Sunday, May 9, there was a race at the Salem, Indiana, high-banked, half-mile speedway, a near clone of the Winchester speedway. It was there that the events of the early spring races began to resolve themselves for Billy, C.J., and Tom.

Willy Caldwell made good on his "it's him or me, Cal" threat on Monday as a result of the debacle at Reading and Trenton in mid-April. Cal Olsen knew he had a rare talent in his chief mechanic. He knew a driver would be easier to find than a mechanic like Caldwell—one who could juggle the demands of his many race cars. Add to that the time he was supposed to work in Olsen's Indianapolis factory. The man who would accept such responsibility was rare, and he knew it.

So, He kept Caldwell and fired C.J., who really was on his way out of Olsen's cars ever since he saw the rear engine car at Trenton. That experience was like a lightning bolt to C.J. It was as if he found religion and life would forever be different. So, getting fired by Olsen back in Indy was just a moment, an afterthought, to C.J. The actual dismissal was not an ugly confrontation. Olsen had asked C.J. to meet him at his factory after the New Jersey race.

In Olsen's office on Tuesday, two days after Trenton, it was C.J. who started the conversation. "Cal, you want me gone, I know. I can't blame you. So, let's not make this any worse than it has to be. I'm gonna look around. You do the same, okay?" And with that he started to walk out, but Olsen stopped him.

"There aren't any 'nevers' or 'forevers' in this sport, C.J. We might get together again some time. I saw that car, too. I know what you're thinkin' about. If that car is the future, I ain't gonna live in the past and get left behind!" He stuck out his hand. C.J. shook it, turned, and walked out. Olsen sat down at his desk, wondering about the best way to find Billy Wallace. He hit the phone button for his secretary and barked, "Hey, Sue, dial up Caldwell at the Speedway. Tell him to put out the word for Billy Wallace."

· · · · ·

Late on Tuesday, May 4, Billy Wallace made a call to Tom Lawton, or more accurately, Janet Lawton. "Hey! Is this the Lawton house?"

Tina answered the phone. "Yes, can I help you?"

"Yeah, this is Billy, uh, Billy Wallace...."

"Mom! Mom! It's Billy Wallace!"

Janet had just gotten home from the farm store and was reading the local newspaper on the porch. "Okay, I'm coming."

She made a nonverbal inquiry as she took the phone from Tina who shrugged her shoulders. "What do you want, Billy? Tom's not here. He's still on the night shift, you know."

"Well, Mrs. Lawton, I took my driver's test this week, but first I had to take a physical, and Tom wanted to know about that. You know, the kind of stuff they checked. Well, it wasn't much. Vision, reaction time, heart rate, blood pressure. I passed okay. What would you expect of a young guy? And then I had to start my rookie test on the track."

"And? That go okay, too, Billy?"

"Sure! Well, on my last phase some observer guy on turn three said I didn't look smooth enough like four laps in a row. Pi...ticked me off! So, they made me repeat that part in the afternoon! I ain't supposed to take it personal. Passed fine, but that put us behind. Olsen wants me to stay here in Indianapolis on Saturday and Sunday and skip the Salem race. He wants to get an early start to get ready for qualifying next weekend. And...he wants to keep me out of sprint cars till the 500 is over...keep me in one piece, he says."

"Okay, I'll tell Tom about this."

"Good—and tell him that I talked to Olsen about Tom using his Kuzma dirt car for his rookie test. He told me, 'Rookie test—that's all right, but that's all we can do for him.' And tell him to come over here Friday. He can take his physical and then get a good look at the car."

Tina stood behind Janet, tapping her shoulder. "Stop, Tina, I've got to listen to Billy!"

"I need a hat and— "

"Not now, hush!" Janet put the phone back to her ear. "Okay, Billy. I'll tell him." She hung up and turned to her daughter. "What kind of hat? You've got a hat!"

Tina said, "A new cowboy hat, a new long-sleeved shirt, and boots, too! Gloria Anderson said I have to look my best for the show."

Janet wondered, Where will that money come from? Tom will be out of work for God knows how long. At least the farm store gives me a discount, if I can even find those things there.

· · · · ·

Maxcell had no role for a "part time" worker or a "part time" racer, and Tom soon found himself without a job—bad for income security but good for time flexibility. He took advantage on Friday and drove to Indianapolis for his physical. He had devised a plan to mask some of his physical liabilities.

After parking his truck, he walked briskly toward the infield medical center. He walked about thirty feet, paused, turned, and went back to his truck to get his hat. For breakfast he'd had eggs—liberally salted—and sausage. Last night, he ate a burger and fries—again, plenty of salt—and two beers. His goal was to ensure that his blood pressure wasn't low. Billy had told Janet what the doctors checked, and Tom knew that low blood pressure might be a red flag. He hoped that salt and a brisk walk might elevate his reading, though not enough exercise to develop a tell-tale sweat.

He walked into the medical building and looked for a man who looked like a doctor, someone in a white lab coat and a stethoscope around his neck. He didn't search long.

"Come over here, young—"The doctor paused mid-sentence. He had expected to see a young, twenty-something driver, but instead looked into the face of pale, pudgy, balding Tom Lawton. "Well, uh, you're here for a driver's physical, I guess."

Tom grasped the doctor's hand and gave it a firm shake. "I'm Tom Lawton, sir. I know you thought, 'Here's another young buck who thinks he's gonna set the Speedway on fire,' but you got me instead."

"You're right, Tom, but this is refreshing. A driver that could be my older brother and not my son! Let's get started. Sit there and look at that eye chart, cover your left eye, and read those letters to me."

The doctor checked the usual—reflexes, lungs, vision—and one surprise, color recognition. When Tom said his mom helped him with his colors, the doctor said, "Hey, there are corner lights, you know—green, yellow, red! And flags!" The check-up seemed to take a long time, so long that Tom began to worry that the effects of his walk would wear off and he'd get a low reading. Those fears were unnecessary—his blood pressure was acceptable for his age.

The doctor took the cuff off Tom's arm, put his stethoscope around his neck, and said, "Tom, you're no spring chicken, but your health seems acceptable, except for one thing."

Oh, crap! It didn't work! Now what will I do? Janet won't be disappointed, that's for sure. "What you talkin' about, Doc? Blood pressure? Something else?"

"Well, when I looked in your ears, I could see straight through to the other side! Course that's true of all race drivers, Tom!"

"Hey, funny man! When you retire, why don't you see if Johnny Carson has a spot for you on The Tonight Show! He's always looking for comedians!"

"Hey, Tom, you look good to me! Let me sign your papers. Good luck and don't come back!"

Tom strode out and headed toward the pit area, hoping to talk to Cal Olsen and look at his car.

· · · · ·

A thirty-lap sprint car race at Salem, Indiana, was the next event on the schedule, one week after the rainout at New Bremen. The Salem Speedway was similar to the track at Winchester, Indiana. It was a half mile, paved, high-banked track. It had a steel guardrail painted in alternate blocks of black and white around the top of the turns and back straightaway, and a concrete wall that separated the covered grandstand from the front stretch. The old wooden grandstand was covered and had the same acoustic characteristics of the one at Winchester. Occupants were treated to the echoing roar of racing engines, a roar that seemed to penetrate and resonate in the chest and body. There was a steel walkover bridge, like the one at Winchester. The speedway had a reputation like its Indiana and Ohio high-banked kin: lightning fast but hazardous. Many men drove their last race at Salem. Some found the track to their liking, appreciating the smoother surface. Some, conversely, found that smoothness oddly disturbing.

Chuck Williams got a call on Monday after the New Bremen rainout. It was a surprise, and it wasn't. He, other owners, and drivers understood that driver-car combinations were often tenuous. There were no written contracts, just verbal agreements that were easily broken. An owner might fire a driver for his performance, or a driver might leave an uncompetitive car. Lack of communication between the important parties might result in dismissal or departure. Billy informed Chuck that he would drive Cal Olsen's cars for the season—at Indianapolis, on the mile tracks, on the sprint car schedule, and—time allowing— midget races, too. Chuck was without a driver for Sunday's race at Salem.

Some early season driver-car combinations were still unsettled, so Chuck's situation wasn't really different from many owners. The winner of a race last year at Winchester, Carl Connors, was between cars. Last year, it was Connor's misfortune that helped Tom earn a fine second place finish at Dayton. In California, Connor's father had died, and in his absence, Tom drove his white number two sprint car at Dayton and New Bremen. Jack Dowty, the owner of that car had hired a new kid, Jimmy McClure, for the new season, leaving Connors without a ride. In Chuck's mind, Connors would be a good man for his new car's first race. An experienced driver could help sort out any teething issues the car might have. Billy Wallace was good, but he thought he could overcome any car problem instead of diagnosing and correcting it. Connors was pleased to drive for Chuck, even in his new, unproven car.

· · · · ·

On Saturday, the day before the Salem race, Tom asked James to help him at his station, preparing for the sale of its contents:

tools, equipment, a few office furnishings. It was a melancholy experience for Tom. He had hung out there when he was in junior high school and had started working there when he was sixteen. In high school he had worked for Jim Deeters, the previous owner, and when he passed on, Tom bought it. Roughly half of his life had been spent working there. Letting go of the past wasn't easy. One item that Tom found in his old desk brought back many memories—not unpleasant, but they added to his sense of wistfulness. He reached down into the bottom of a drawer and found a folding case, with a navy blue, wrinkled finish. He opened one flap that folded up and then a second that folded down. Lying in soft, protective, felt-like recesses were drafting tools: dividers, drafting pencils and pens, small cylinders that held extra pen nibs and leads, an eraser, a compass with extensions. Some of the metal tools were slightly rusted. The drawer also held a slide rule in a leather case.

"Here, James. I want you to take these old things."

"That's a drafting set. Our shop teacher has one of those. He showed the class that stuff last year when we were studying mechanical drawing. He tried to show us how to use a slide rule, too, but most guys didn't get it."

"Deeters, the guy I bought the station from, gave them to me. He told me when I was still in school that maybe I could use them, you know, in college. But that never happened."

"Aw, I couldn't take them. Those are yours and go way back for you, Mr. Lawton."

"I'm never gonna use them, but you might. Go ahead and take 'em, James. Deeters told me that I should get out for a few years, tech school or college, and learn something. Then come back, if I wanted to. I'm just passing on the advice that I got from him, James." Tom put the drafting set and slide rule in James' hands and went back to his work. "I gotta get back to cleanin' this place up for the sale."

He knew he was losing his independence, his livelihood, and a sense of his youth. He wasn't communicative Saturday evening when he got home, and he knew that he wouldn't be a good companion riding along with Donny on Sunday. He called Donny and told him he'd see him at Salem on Sunday morning.

· · · · ·

Tom stopped on the walkover bridge that led to the infield of the Salem Speedway and looked down at the cars, mechanics, drivers, and officials in the pits. The weather seemed to promise a much different day than the two previous weekends. He saw that Chuck and Donny were pitted side-by-side. Donny was in his young twenties but had worked with Chuck on this car for several years and knew it quite well. He knew the car set-ups for each track, and if he had a question, he could consult what Chuck called his "bible", a notebook that contained all the changes and adjustments for each track. Chuck was pitted right beside Donny, but he would be busy with the new car. Tom had absolute faith in Chuck's judgment. Still Tom thought he and Donny could solve most problems that might arise.

He walked down the bridge steps, entered the pit area, exchanged greetings with a few drivers and mechanics, and found Chuck and Donny. Donny had the front end of the red car jacked up and was on his knees at the right front of the car.

Donny rose from his work when he saw Tom. He had round shoulders and a tendency to slump that reduced his six-foot frame. He had a full head of fine, light-brown hair and an oblong face with sunken cheeks, a ready smile and a gentle voice. "My Driver is here, Chuck! How ya doin', Tom?"

"Why wouldn't I be doin' good? Great day for racing, guys. No rain today. How you doin', Chuck? That new buggy ready today?"

"Well, new car, new driver. What can I say, Tom?" Chuck peered at the engine, didn't look up, and said no more.

Donny said, "Tom, I put a half wrap on the right-side front spring, like Chuck would do. But I want to try something else. How about we turn that right front around on the spindle? That'll give us another little offset. Wanna see how it handles in hot laps?"

"If it's no good, that's an easy thing to fix," Tom said as he polished his goggles. "I gotta find a place to change. Back soon. When we hot lap the car, I'll watch for the blue haze on that right front. You remember Chuck's theory, don't you? That'll give us a good idea if we're close on set-up."

・ ・ ・ ・ ・

Five hours later, Tom Lawton stood beside his car parked on the front stretch, surrounded by Donny, Chuck, race officials, and fans with cameras. Tom had driven the red car in a dominating performance to win the thirty-lap race. It had been three long years since he'd won a race. Even last year when he'd subbed for the injured Billy Wallace in this car, he hadn't scored a first place. He'd done well, but still no wins. And he was sorry that Janet wasn't here to enjoy this moment with him. Janet had taken Tina and her horse to Gloria Anderson's farm in Preble County for one of Gloria's "practice" shows, in preparation for county fairs.

When the crowd thinned out, Donny and Chuck loaded the car onto the trailer, folded the ramps up, and locked them down to help hold the car in place.

Donny said, "Tom, during the trophy and congratulations stuff I got to lookin' around the car. That left rear shock mount broke on top."

"You know, I felt somethin' on that last lap, comin' out of turn two. The car just seemed to drop down a bit, and then on the backstretch it was wigglin' around a little. Guess we're lucky that didn't happen on lap twenty or, you know, a lot earlier. And I did back off a little more for those last two turns."

"I'll get on that tomorrow at the shop. But you looked good today, Tom. Nobody even got close to you! And you started lapping cars after what, nine or ten laps? Damn, you were on fire!" Donny's smile seemed to cover his whole face. "Chuck, I got me one heck of a car and driver! And…Tom was creepin' up on your car, too!"

"That's one race, Donny. We got a lot more races to go. You've got to keep this thing running for Tom. It's a long season, so just keep that in mind," Chuck cautioned his nephew as he put tools away. "Anyway, Connors told me about a few changes I can make. Next race might be different, guys."

Tom said, "The kid did a good job today, Chuck. You know, he reversed that right front, gave us another bit of offset. He had that 'haze' on the right front, too. You always want that."

Chuck climbed into his truck. "Be sure to write it down in the book, Donny. Can't remember everything. You are takin' care of that book, ain't you Donny? Hey, ya know, guys, I'm callin' the book on number eleven the *old testament* 'cause I'm startin' the *new testament* on my new car, number twenty-two."

"Well, that's about right, Chuck, 'cause you're gonna need a *savior* and a few miracles to keep up with us now!" Donny joked.

"God dang it, boy! You win one race and think you're king of the racetrack!" Chuck laughed. "We'll talk later this week, guys. One more race—that Eldora rain date is in two weeks—before the 500, so we'll get a little break, a week or so. See ya!" Chuck waved and drove off.

Donny said, "Too bad we can't ride home together, Tom, but you drove over by yourself."

"Yeah, I wasn't in the mood to be chatty Charley this morning. I got fired last week when I told the boss at Maxcell that

I was going to Indianapolis for a couple weeks."

"Oh, sorry Tom."

"And all-day Saturday I was in my old gas station tryin' to get ready to sell most of the contents. Tools mostly, and even stuff that Deeters had up in the attic. Never saw so much junk. Seems he must have kept everything. Like Chuck said, we got a little time off. That rainout at Eldora got rescheduled for two weeks from today. So, get this buggy ready for dirt, Donny." Tom waved to Donny and walked over the pedestrian bridge and to his car. He reached into his trousers pocket to make sure his first-place money was there. He thought about putting it on the kitchen table and saying, "There you are, Jan. All that—for around seventeen, eighteen minutes actual work. That's a good hourly rate!" He considered her possible responses and changed his mind about that approach.

· · · · ·

"Christina, I'm not sure I can help you! What do I know about horses, anyway?"

"Mom, you heard some of what Gloria was saying when we were there. And anyway, you're good at—helping to direct things. You know what I mean, don't you?"

"Bossy, huh?"

"No! I didn't say that. You just…you're smart about a lot of stuff. You can *see* things…"

"But horses, Tina?"

"*All I'd like you to do* is watch when I run her through this routine, okay? You can see where we don't…*flow*…that's Gloria's word. We should smoothly go through the pattern. Candy needs to respond to my cues. You can watch for that, can't you?"

"I'll try, Sweetie, but—I'll do what I can."

Tina had tried to arrange the field to represent what she might experience at the county fair. She would compete in one or perhaps two events. Today she wanted to practice the Western Showmanship routine or a possible pattern in that category. She'd be competing in the fourteen to eighteen-year-old group. Thirty minutes before competition was scheduled to begin, judges would place on a table copies of patterns that horse and handler would follow. Tina was trying to get her horse familiar with one such routine today.

She had opened a fence gate through which she and Candy would enter. Tina walked the horse out, hoping to turn her around, pause, and then pretend to enter the competition corral. Candy was distracted by the novelty of the situation and wanted to run, but Tina redirected her to stand and wait. About fifteen feet from the gate, was a red cone that the handler—there was no riding in the event—and horse were to approach. They were to stop and then walk to the second cone. From there, the rider and horse were to advance, at a brisker trot, to the third cone and make a sharp, nearly hairpin turn, without stopping, and then advance to the last cone where the judge would await them. The girl, or boy, then had to stop in front of the judge, and the horse had to be positioned with its head between handler on the left and judge on the right. The horse's hooves had to be "squared up," the front hooves parallel to each other, the back pair as well, none of them staggered.

The judge would not tell the handler what to do. Behavior at this point was all regimented and unspoken. As the judge, with clip board and score sheet, walked around the horse, clockwise, the rider moved in such a way that she, or he, was never between the horse and the judge. The judge, in this event, ordered the rider to back the horse up and turn the horse in a circle. The judge dismissed the rider and horse to an area where they waited for all others to take their turns. There horse and rider were to stand and wait patiently. When the judges tallied up the results, an announcer called and dismissed each handler and horse by name and place, ending with second runner-up, first runner-up, and champion.

Candy conducted herself acceptably—not spectacularly—but okay in Tina's estimation.

"Well, I'm no expert…" Janet began, but was quickly cut off by her daughter.

"I don't expect that, Mom. Just tell me what you saw."

"Well, she's supposed to pivot on that right rear hoof, correct, without lifting it when she turns? She didn't do that. She was picking it up."

"Yeah, that's a problem I have to work on, I know."

"The only other thing I noticed, when you turned around the cone, Candy kind of dragged behind you, like you were pulling her. You need to…what, adjust your speed to look like you're not doing that—pulling her?"

"Gloria said that, too."

"Your horse seems kind of finicky…and jumpy sometimes. Maybe new things kinda get her off stride. Kinda like a teenage…."

Oh, please, mom!" Tina said mildly rebuking her mother.

"Sorry, just wonderin'! You ever worn that hat around her before? That's a *big* ol' black hat…I don't know, I'm just wonderin'."

"I wore it a few times out here. She's got to get used to it anyway, Mom."

"You've come a long way from that girl who'd never ever been even close to a horse—well, kiddie rides at the fair—to where you are now. You don't have to win, you know."

"Can you watch us one more time, Mom? Then we'll just practice a few things on our own till supper. Daddy coming home today?"

"No, he's at the Speedway all week. He starts his rookie test tomorrow, and then qualifying is this weekend. I'm not sure when he'll be home."

"Well, ain't that something—two rookies being judged!"

"But he'll be going considerably faster than you and this *old nag*, as Dad calls her."

Chapter Six

One day after his win at Salem, Tom sat in Cal Olsen's car that Billy had driven last year at the Milwaukee race and at Trenton in April. It had been built four years ago by Eddie Kuzma, the builder of some of the most successful mile dirt-track race cars at this, the premier level of American oval racing. The car was yellow—no surprise. "That's so they'll always be able to see us!" Olsen said. And all the cars had some variation of seven: his hot Watson Indy roadster was number seventeen, this dirt-track car was number twenty-seven, his rebuilt—thanks to Chuck Williams—sprint car was number seven, and the midget that Billy Wallace took to California in the winter was number thirty-seven. "Seven is a lucky number!" Olsen always said. Cal was his own biggest fan and enjoyed promoting himself and his projects. A good man to be around, usually.

Willy Caldwell stood beside the cockpit, reviewing some basics as Tom sat listening. "The Chief Steward, Ron Porter, will be here in a few minutes to go over the test with you. You ain't no real rookie, except here, Tom, but they treat all first timers the same. A twenty-two-year-old guy is a bit different from a thirty-something like you, though. Few years ago, one of them grand prix champions came here. They even made *him* take the rookie test! Anyway, when we get her started up, me and my helper will get behind you and push to help you get goin'. I don't want you to use that clutch any more than necessary, so, don't ride it or be slippin' it—that'll burn it, for sure. Get the car rollin', shift out of first, up to race gear, and push the lock down. It'll chug and sputter, but it should be okay. Then look behind you to see if any hot dog is in the groove comin' down the straightaway. Stay low, out of the way. Let the oil warm up for a couple laps. Okay, here he comes, Tom. He'll review everything they told you. When he's done, we'll start you up. Oh, and one other thing. When I spin the starter motor, let the engine turn over for three or four seconds so we build up some oil pressure, then hit the magneto switch."

Tom nodded and sat waiting as Caldwell talked with the Chief Steward. An Offenhauser engine started somewhere in the pits behind him. The electric starter motor whined, and there was a sudden exhaust blast followed by a few isolated pops, then silence as the engine stalled. The process repeated, but this time with the driver more assertively punching the throttle, revving the engine up, then letting it run down: hoooo-din! hoooo-din! The Offy had a sound all its own. The driver let the clutch out quickly, drove toward the pit exit, and shifted into race gear. The car chugged and sputtered before the engine evened out. Going down pit lane, the engine would momentarily rev up as the stiffly sprung car bounced over joints in the concrete pit lane.

Chief Steward Ron Porter leaned down to Tom in the cockpit, "Tom, it's good to see you here. You deserve this!"

"Thanks, and thanks to Mr. Olsen for letting me use this car. I got nothing lined up after this test, but I want to be ready in case something comes up," Tom said.

"I see you got your stripes on the tail of the car, and the car's been through tech," Porter said. "You been through the signals that your crew will give you, right? Know about that, huh?"

"Yes, sir."

"Well, we want you to just take around ten or twelve laps to get a bit familiar with the place. It's big and wide and feels really open, except going into turn one. You'll see. Just get out there, run easy laps, stay low in the turns and straights, then come in, like I said after ten or twelve laps. We'll talk a bit and then maybe we can get you started on the first phase of your test." Porter shook Tom's hand and nodded to Caldwell.

Caldwell knelt at the front of the car, inserted a long steel rod into the nose of the car, attached the starter motor, and nodded for his helper to squirt alcohol into the fuel injector intake horns. He signaled for Tom to get ready to switch on the magneto. Then Caldwell hit the starter switch. There was a powerful electric whining sound for several seconds as the starter motor spun and the engine chuffed blasts of air. Then the four-cylinder Offenhauser—more accurately Meyer-Drake—engine exploded to life. That was the best word to describe the sound of the engine. It had a displacement of two hundred and fifty-two cubic inches. Such a large displacement in a high compression four-cylinder engine created a distinct sound…and feel for the driver. Tom had not driven an "Offy" for some time, but the engine vibrations traveling through the frame to the steering mechanism quickly reminded him of that familiar buzz in his hands.

Willy removed the starter motor and steel rod, set them beside the pit wall, and joined his helper, pushing the car as Tom quickly let the clutch out and got the car rolling. It chugged and sputtered as he accelerated and shifted into race gear. The engine lugged in high gear until it evened out with more speed.

Tom made a slight right turn, leaving the pits, and then eased left into the first turn. He hugged the white line at the bottom of the track so as not to interfere with faster, passing cars. The track was smooth and wide, unlike most that Tom had driven on. The turn hardly felt like a turn, though Tom knew that it soon would. That first turn straightened out into a short straightaway that led to turn two. Exiting that turn, Tom stared down more than a half mile of backstretch, wide and clear with a retaining wall on his right, barely higher than his tires. He had fleeting thoughts of the many drivers who had been here, storied events—some tragic, some celebratory. So much history, all on these two and a half miles.

Tom stayed toward the inside of the track, increasing his speed to…what? He had little concept of miles per hour. He never thought that way in a race car. Instrumentation was spartan: oil pressure, water temperature, fuel pressure, engine revolutions per minute on a tachometer. With that last instrument he could roughly estimate miles per hour on the straights, but that would be for later, when he had to try to stay within prescribed ranges for each of the phases of his rookie test. These first laps were meant to get a feel for the track and his car.

Midway down the backstretch—there were trees outside the guardrail, trees of all things—one of the veterans flew by, approaching with such suddenness that Tom flinched. He was in his own world, momentarily forgetful of the fact that there were other cars on the track; not many, but as soon as that first dark blue car flew by, it was followed by another at what seemed an even faster pace. *Tom, you are a rookie, boy! How can you ever drive a car that fast into a turn?* he wondered as he watched the cars approach turn three. The rasp of their engines seemed to tear the air to shreds, despite the muffling effect of his helmet.

Tom remained low, near the white line as he entered turn three, still without any feeling of great speed. The turns were banked more than he expected. This part of the track seemed wide open—no stands outside the track, a few bleachers to his left on the infield. The open sides of the car afforded him little protection, allowing the wind to whip at his uniform, and he made a mental note to add another layer when possible. This mid-May late morning was cool and the chill did not help him relax.

Exiting turn three, he aimed his car for the middle of the track. Any hot dog working on a fast lap would still have room to his right. Tom accelerated steadily through the north short "chute", staring ahead at turn four and the bleachers that rose high on the outside of the track. Again, even with increased speed, Tom had very little "feel" for the car. It was so unlike what he was accustomed to in a sprint car, especially on a dirt track where the G forces and ruts threw him to the right. Of course, he was still far from the upper limit, a speed he was not yet prepared to approach.

As he left turn four, Tom was awed by the sight in front of him: five-eighths of a mile of pavement, hemmed in by bleachers on the left and right, and, farther ahead, tall covered grandstands on the right. They were empty now, but what would they look like, on race day? *If there is a race day for you, Tom. You got a long way to go before that can happen! Don't get ahead of yourself. Remember what you once said to Tina—learn your part, like your lines in a play first. Then…maybe.* And then the sight just got more…incredible, or more something. He gave the car more throttle and picked up his speed to… what—a hundred? He had no idea. The stands and bleachers seemed to hover over him, he passed the entrance to pit row, the five-story control tower rose high on his left where the scorers and officials monitored the race, then there was the tall, thin scoring tower that displayed running order on race day. Straight ahead, as Tom passed the tower, on his right was the first sign, numbered "3", indicating a place to back off the accelerator and let the car slow as it approached the first turn.

Rookies were sometimes stunned by their first approach to turn one. The track seemed to funnel into an impossibly narrow turn; huge, empty grandstands loomed high and dark above. Tom had almost forgotten to look for that sign, not that it mattered—his speed was not so great that going beyond that shut off point would create a problem. But then what seemed to be a sharp turn opened and broadened wide to his left, where a wide, grassy apron and fence provided an open viewing area for fans…and then more trees! He sailed through, so smoothly. *This ain't no half-mile dirt track!*

That was Tom Lawton's first lap at Indianapolis: not fast, not spectacular, just a drive-around, get-to-know-you lap—his easiest lap ever. Now it was time to go a little faster. Tom stayed out of the fast groove as he drove through the short chute between turns one and two and became aware of the sound of a car behind. The car seemed to hang back and not rush by like the two cars on the backstretch before. He could hear engine exhaust barking behind and to his right, but with no mirrors, he couldn't identify the car. As he exited turn two, he again moved left to leave plenty of room on his right for faster cars. A yellow car pulled up beside Tom and matched his speed for perhaps five or six seconds. The driver looked to his left, grinned, and waved. It was Billy Wallace in Cal Olsen's Watson roadster! Tom gaped, recovered and waved, smiling at his young friend. Billy then pointed straight down the backstretch, punched the throttle, and disappeared toward turn three in a slight puff of blue engine smoke.

Billy, I'll be damned! I should have known…I should have known. That's typical Billy Wallace! He might be a hot dog and all cocky, but who couldn't like him? That's just the way Billy does things.

· · · · ·

Eddie Spencer stood in the turn two observer's stand, watching a few rookies prepare for their tests. Eddie, an ex-racer from the twenties, had retired from his warehouse manager's job in Dayton and now spent nearly all of May at the Speedway, working a variety of jobs. This job was his favorite, watching rookies and providing constructive criticism to help accustom them to the big track. Eddie had been known as "Speed" Spencer in his racing days in the 1920's, a name hung on him by sports writers. It wasn't his choice, but it conveniently helped make him famous for a few years. His career was cut short by an accident on one of the super-fast board tracks.

Eddie looked to his right toward the short straight between turns one and two. He saw a sight that had become infrequent in the last five or six years: a dirt-track style, upright racer, slowly motoring along, not even close to racing speed. Eddie thought, *Rookie, hell! Must be grandma goin' to church!* Then a faster yellow car, a number seventeen Watson roadster, caught up to, slowed and matched the speed of the dirt track car. The two cars headed down the back stretch, side by side for a few seconds, then the roadster accelerated away. Eddie watched, then turned back to his right, waiting for the next car. *That was Wallace in the roadster, I know that much.*

Chief Steward Porter's voice spoke on the observers' headsets. "Hey, guys, we got one beginner today. Sprint car driver is gonna take some warm-up laps in that Olsen dirt car. That's Tom Lawton. Good half-mile guy, but just a few mile races. Mostly a short track driver. So, watch him, let us know. We'll give him maybe a dozen or fifteen laps to get warmed up and then try to get him through the first stage, the hundred twenty-mile an hour part. If that's okay, we'll go for phase two today. Then phase three and four tomorrow, assuming all goes well."

Eddie thought, *That explains a lot! Tom Lawton and Billy Wallace, the old and the young, the rookie and the rookie! Just chatting like old buddies, on a racetrack, I guess. I seen worse here. At least they still get along.*

* * * * *

Tom and Billy were pitted north of the control Tower. Their cars were parked nose-to-tail with Billy's car in front of Tom's rookie test car, the one Cal Olsen had provided for just that one purpose. While the car wasn't competitive for the big race, it was surprisingly fast, and capable of turning some laps with average speeds near 141 mph. A four-lap qualifying average like that wouldn't make the race, even with the slowest car in the thirty-third starting spot averaging in the 146-mph range. But the car would be suitable to easily reach the fourth phase of the rookie test, in which drivers were required to complete ten consistent laps at 135 mph under the watchful eyes of observers and veteran drivers.

Billy had passed his test last week, after the New Bremen rainout. Tom had two more phases, the 130 and 135 mph phases, that he hoped to complete this week. The first qualifications would be on the coming Saturday and Sunday. Tom knew that wasn't in the cards for him. He didn't have a permanent ride yet. Most owners without assigned drivers would be reluctant to hire a rookie who hadn't completed his test, especially an unproven thirty-something with very little pavement experience.

The two friends sat on the wall behind Billy's car while Caldwell tinkered with it. "I got through the first three phases just fine, Tom, so you'd think adding just another five miles per hour—how hard could that be, huh?"

"Yeah?" asked Tom.

"Well, I got the speed, but it wasn't easy. Wasn't consistent. They want you to be within one mile an hour, plus or minus, of the target speed. I'd run a 135, a 135, then a 132, then a 138, then a 134. You get the idea—all over the place. And it wasn't easy, either. Felt like I was hangin' on by my fingernails."

"Olsen say anything?"

"Not much, but I could see him and Caldwell were getting a bit concerned. Then later that day I was havin' so much trouble, Olsen said, 'Billy, park it for a while. We'll give that last phase a fresh shot later, okay? I got an idea.' Turned out, that idea was to ride around with a couple old guys. The track was closed for something, inspection or clean up somewhere, I'm not sure, but it lasted about thirty minutes."

"So, like your ride around Langhorne with Smitty last year," Tom said, looking down and kicking at the pavement.

"Right. But I ain't green like last year. So, I had to work on myself a bit, you know how I can get my back up, real quick."

Tom chuckled and said, "Really? I didn't know that, Billy."

"Funny man! Anyway, I went out with two veterans—Connors and Russ Stevens, the guy who won last year. Stevens rode around with us and Eddie Spencer earlier, remember? I thought, 'More old guys tellin' me how!'"

"And?"

"So, we went out in the pace car, Connors driving, me beside him, and Stevens in the back seat. We go around real easy like, and when we came to turn one and them numbered signs, Stevens asked how far I was goin' before I'd back off."

"I said, 'Used to be I couldn't even get to number three and I'd have to get out of the throttle, but I got comfortable and soon was gettin' to the 2 sign. Lift and get on the brakes, not a bunch, but thought I had to take some speed off.'"

"Connors looked back at Stevens in the back seat, turned to me and said, 'That's the problem right there, Billy. You gotta back off at three, stay off the brakes—they just kind of mess with the whole balance of the car. Braking makes the car shift on its suspension, tends to throw the weight forward and right, when you don't want that. You want that car to take a 'set.' Get off the throttle before the number three sign, then practice getting' back on the power—no brakes—back on the power a little sooner, gradually, each lap. Then after a while, you can get to the number two sign before you get off the gas. You'll see.'"

"I thought, 'That's crazy' and 'That's the old man way.' But I'll be damned if it didn't work!"

"Maybe I can learn your lesson, Billy."

"And another thing. Caldwell took the car back to the garage during my 'guided tour' for something. Well, they pushed the car back out, but before I got in, Caldwell said, 'Billy, I want to show you something.' Then he leaned over the cockpit and pointed to a block of wood to the left of the brake. 'That's the Jesus pedal. When you go into turn one, you'll think, Jesus, I gotta slow this thing down! So, step on that when you feel like you gotta slow down. It's just something to stand on instead of the brakes.'"

"It all went pretty much like those guys said it would. That's when I got through the last part of the test. I think I'm ready to qualify on Saturday now. Hey, Caldwell's comin' over here. He said we're gonna work on our set-up for qualifying. Good luck with the last parts of your test, Tom. We took off my rookie stripes yesterday and I'm working on speed today."

Billy "worked on speed" just as he said and started turning averages near 145 mph, so he was on his way to becoming one of the thirty-three starting positions.

That same day, Wednesday, Tom Lawton passed the 130-mph phase of his test and was ready to start the last phase when all the track lights flashed red. An engine had gone bad in turn three, so bad that the driver lost control when engine oil coated his rear tires. He slammed hard into the turn three wall and suffered a broken right arm. There was oil in the racing groove, and clean-up took almost two hours, resulting in down time for all crews. But it also allowed time for a car owner to chat with Tom, a chat that he thought was just a friendly encounter, but in truth was more than that. Lou Turner was the owner of a two-year-old Epperly "lay down" roadster with no assigned driver.

* * * * *

California race car builder Quinn Epperly mostly followed common 1950's thinking about Indianapolis racers. The concept was to shift weight to the left side of the car to improve handling in left-hand turns. Many did this by locating the engine left of the center line of the race car. But Epperly added a twist. The Meyer-Drake engine in most race cars was mounted straight up usually, though some builders had begun to tilt engines, some to the left, some to the right, to help lower the profile of the car, and thus create less frontal area and reduce wind drag. Mercedes-Benz engineers laid the engine horizontally in their Grand Prix cars of 1954-55, creating a lower car with less wind resistance and lower center of gravity. In 1952, a car with a diesel engine competed at Indianapolis with a similar design. Did those cars impact the thinking of Indy builders? Perhaps, but the fact was that laying a Meyer-Drake engine nearly horizontal—as Epperly did—meant that an engine that stood nearly twenty-five inches tall when upright would stand only around thirteen or fourteen inches high when placed on its side. This resulted in a race car with a lower center of gravity, and still provided left side bias with the heavy parts—the engine, transmission, and rear end—shifted to the left side. Epperly cars were sleek and compact but offered challenges in terms of maintenance—things were more difficult to work on when the engine wasn't standing straight up in the engine compartment.

Lou Turner—nicknamed Big Lou because of his girth—owned such a car, one that had finished well two years ago in the 500—a very competitive third place. Lou had arrived at the speedway this year without a driver, but he wasn't ignorant about talent levels and driver personalities. He knew that Tom Lawton was a solid performer who'd had a few lean years. He also thought Tom had the common sense, motivation, and patience to get the best performance out of his car. That's what his friend Chuck Williams had told him in a phone call. Chuck said, "If you're thinking about Tom Lawton, I'll say this. He takes care of the car. Gets a lot out of it without beating it to death." A brief conversation with Cal Olsen was nearly unnecessary. Cal didn't have a lot to offer Lou. "He hasn't broken the car. He's gotten through his first three phases with no drama. Seems okay to me. Billy likes the guy, thinks he can race."

"I want to talk to him, see if he might want to try my car," Lou said.

"Sounds good to me, I don't have a car for him. That dirt miler is just for his test. Matter of fact, I'll be needing it at Langhorne, or maybe I'll take it to Milwaukee, too. Anyway, that'll save the car for me. I have nothing for him after his rookie test is over, so fine, go ahead and talk to him, Lou. Caldwell will be happy with one less car to work on."

That's how Tom Lawton got his own car to attempt to qualify for the big 500. Race day was just a bit over two weeks away. Tom still had to pass the 135 mph phase of his rookie test. And he had to adjust his driving to this new and different car.

• • • • •

By mid-afternoon, the track was cleared for practice. Lou Turner's mechanic leaned over Tom, who was buckled into the red Epperly roadster, called simply the Turner Special. Tom looked down the long front hood to the nose of the car.

The tops of the front tires were six or eight inches higher than the metal hood. Unlike the other roadsters such as Olsen's Watson, this car appeared more slender in profile, due to the horizontal position of the engine. The driver did not seem to be surrounded by the car; here he was more exposed. He imagined Janet's first reaction to the car: "Tom, your head is higher than the roll bar, for God's sake!" He would have to brush that off, somehow. Maybe he could say, "If I wreck, I'll just duck!"

Dutch—the only name Tom ever heard anyone call him—was the chief mechanic. "Tom, the car is like many others out here. But I do have stiff torsion bars in it now, and I have set it up with a bit of push. That way, if you feel like it's getting' wide in the turn, you know, like that wall seems to want to pull you in, you can back off, and she'll come back to you. Hell of a lot better than havin' a loose rear end. You let that get away from you at a hundred and forty—well, that's another story. You know that."

"I'm on the last part of my rookie test, so I shouldn't be hot-doggin' this place today."

"Let's get you used to this thing, okay? I'll take that push out later, when you're more comfortable." The mechanic went through the usual starting procedures and soon the car was rolling down pit road, Tom getting his first feel of a car built with just this one speedway in mind.

The loss of practice time concentrated the attention and efforts of many as they prepared for weekend time trials. Tom made sure to stay low, hugging the white line inside the turns, and stayed toward the middle of the straights, knowing that drivers interested in the best approach to the turns would want to be near the outside wall. He wanted to run some easy laps, perhaps around a hundred and twenty miles per hour, just to get a feel for this car. It wasn't like a dirt car that had open sides, left and right, and pummeled the driver with wind. In this car his left side was protected, but the right side of the car was open. And there was that view up front, the tires standing high above the level of the hood—an odd look, but it soon became just another race car. And Turner's mechanic was right about the feel. The car was so stiff and rigid that it felt almost like a big go kart.

Tom ran fifteen laps, found the car easy to handle, and knew that he could get a lot more out of it…after his rookie test was complete.

An hour later, Tom, Lou Turner, and Chief Steward Porter honored a Speedway tradition. Tom peeled the three tape stripes off the tail of the red car while a newspaper photographer took a picture. He was no longer raw and unproven, but he still was a thirty-four-year-old rookie with much to do. He was faced with the challenge of scoring a four-lap average that was one of the thirty-three fastest. Then he would be a 500 *driver*. Turner, Dutch, and Tom had agreed they would not attempt a qualification run this weekend but wait till the second weekend. Tom had spent only an hour or so in the car and much remained to be done to reach competitive speeds.

· · · · ·

Billy and Roxie sat in the lounge of The Keys restaurant in Indianapolis, waiting for their table. Billy had asked around the Speedway, trusting some advice but not all that he was given. He had learned that there were many practical jokers who liked nothing more than an opportunity to mess with a naïve competitor. He knew he could trust his car owner, but Cal deferred to his wife, Andrea—pronounced *AHN-dree-uh*, as she liked to remind people. Her advice, which Billy took as gospel, was, "The Keys on Meridian! No doubt, Billy!" It was a fine dining establishment, even better than the restaurant where he and Roxie had dinner last year on their way to the Milwaukee race.

Roxie had begged her boss to let her leave a little early on Friday. "Just a little, Mr. Thomas, maybe an hour or so, huh?" She worked him over with her blue eyes and "ways" that were her go-to persuaders. He didn't stand a chance. She was careful to park her '57 blue ("like my eyes" she liked to say) Plymouth Fury behind the office building. Her plan was to advance her departure time as much as possible, just to gain another fifteen minutes or so. She also took care to cover herself with a friend. If someone asked, "Where's Roxie? They need this print out in the shop," the friend was supposed to feign embarrassment and say, "Oh, Roxie's in the ladies' room—she's not feeling so well this week. I'll take it out."

Her ruse worked, and she departed quietly—as quietly as the dual glass packs on her car allowed. Roxie crept the car out of the back lot like a grandmother going to church. An hour and a half later, she picked up Billy at the Speedway Motel on Sixteenth Street, just outside of turn two.

Billy had planned the evening carefully. A car owner owed him a favor. It just so happened that the wealthy car owner had reserved two rooms at the motel for the month of May. Billy said, "Come on. All I want is one night. Your girlfriend doesn't need her own room, does she? Well, unless your wife is in town, and I know for a fact that she isn't. Anyway, I did help you out last year at that Dayton race when you needed that gear set, right? Chuck had an extra and loaned it to you."

He always had his bases covered, on the racetrack and anywhere else. He'd made dinner reservations early in the week, confident that he would need them Friday evening. He had finished his rookie test one week ago and had spent the previous week getting ready for the first two days of qualifications, tomorrow—Saturday—and Sunday. Last week, Cal told Billy he wanted him to stay out of sprint cars until the 500 was over.

"Stuff happens, Billy."

"Not to me, Cal, not to me. That Salem race will be good for me, keep me sharp!"

"Like I said, stuff happens. And you don't have a car for that race, 'cause I told Caldwell not to touch it till June!"

"That's a bunch of crap! Lots of guys want me to drive their sprint cars! Even Chuck would like to take me on for a race or two!"

"You go over there for that race, then you gotta look for a new 500 ride 'cause you ain't drivin' my car!" Olsen knew racing history and knew that owners had lost their drivers just weeks before the 500.

Billy had processed that conversation many times and still hadn't gotten over it. He remembered what Tom Lawton had told him a little over a year ago and decided to back down. He might have to make a stand sometime over another issue, and he knew that the opportunity that this car presented was one he didn't want to lose.

The hostess told Billy his table would be ready in a short while. Billy said, "We'll be at the bar ma'am. We have enough time for a drink, though. I'd like an old fashioned, and this nice young lady would like a…well…screwdriver still good for you?"

"Sure, Billy," Roxie said, "that sounds good."

Race items decorated an otherwise normal cocktail lounge. Lighted glass shelves displayed dozens of liquors and mixers, all reflected by a mirror. Patrons were reminded that this was Indianapolis. Signed pictures of winners festooned the walls. Race programs, even helmets, a large photograph of the race start, and a checkered flag were displayed. Roxie took a seat, looked at the bar, and at Billy then smiled.

"Now, let me tell you about tomorrow, how this will all go, okay? This will be different than those racetrack crowds we saw last year. Multiply those crowds by ten or more. You saw some of those grandstands when you got here, right? Well, the race ain't tomorrow, but those stands will be almost full."

"So, what, twenty thousand people?"

"More like a hundred thousand, or more, depending on weather."

The waiter brought drinks. Roxie looked at her glass and exclaimed, "How cute! The glasses say '500 Cocktails.' Everything is 500 this and 500 that! Oh, I'm sorry, we were talking about the crowd. I can't imagine a crowd like that. I've been to basketball games with hundreds of people, maybe a thousand, but what you're saying is…well, like I said, I can't imagine it."

"You'll see, *and* you're gonna see some characters, too. Though, you do remember Andrea Olsen, don't you?"

"How could I forget *AHN-dree-uh*? Talk about a character!"

"Yeah, you remember. She has some guy get to the Speedway early to mark off a bunch of seats near the big tower for 'her people', as she calls them. So, there will be a seat for you. After breakfast, we can walk there together from the Speedway motel and won't have to mess with a car and traffic. It's not far, maybe a half mile or so, but don't wear heels."

A waiter approached. "Mr. Wallace, your table is ready. Please follow me."

Roxie raised her eyebrows at Billy and made a bemused smirk. When they arrived at their table, the waiter pulled the chair out for Roxie and gently pushed it up when she sat.

"I'll be right back with menus and water, Mr. Wallace. I hope you enjoy your evening here."

Roxie leaned forward. "*Mis*-ter Wallace! I thought you were Billy!"

"That's right, and don't you forget it, girl. *Mis*-ter William Vernon Wallace, racer!"

"Thanks for inviting me over here. You were out West and out of touch so long, I thought maybe I'd never see you again."

"I know I'm not a good communicator, and I'm sorry about all that. But this could be a big weekend, and I wanted you to be part of it, enjoy it with me."

"That's sweet, but it's another race, right? Just a little bigger. My dad used to say, 'Foolishness, that's all that is! Bunch-a-idiots tryin' to git theirselves kilt! And bunch-a-people wantin' to see it happen!' That's the way ol' Pap used to put it."

"It's *not* just another race, Roxie. It is the biggest race in the *world!* The *world!* And there will be more people like Andrea Olsen. That's why I was tellin' you about the stands and all the people who will be here tomorrow, and then on race day there will be even more, maybe three hundred thousand or more! And tomorrow I'll become a part of it, and on race day, well, who knows? I think I can win any race I'm in, especially in Olsen's car. So, it could happen. And I want you to be part of it."

Roxie smiled at Billy. She reached across the table to touch his hand, intending to say something endearing in turn, but the words wouldn't come, so she simply squeezed his hand and smiled. A corner of her mind wondered. *What does he mean, 'be a part of it'?*

The waiter arrived with menus and water. "Would you like your drinks refreshed?"

"That would be good. We'll look over our menus."

"Certainly, Mr. Wallace."

"Perhaps he should call me *Miss* Lytell, don't you think?' She glanced at her menu and her eyes doubled in size. "Billy!" she leaned across the table and whispered, "Did you see these prices?"

"You deserve this and so much more, Rox. Did you see the pictures of some of the celebrities who've been here? That TV guy, Chuck Connors, and the golfer, Arnold Palmer. This ain't no greasy spoon! Well, you just order anything you like."

"I don't even know how to say some of these things. Chat, chatoo-bry…I don't know. And something called Lobster Newberg—$5.50! I'll order what I can *say*."

"Anything, Roxie, anything. We had fun last year on that Milwaukee weekend, and I want to make this better."

"It's Friday, Billy, so I'll have the 'Friday Special.' Golden Brown Walleyed Pike is a bit more reasonable—$3.50. Sounds good!"

That evening introduced Roxie Lytell's to another side of Indianapolis and auto racing, as well as another side Billy Wallace.

· · · · ·

Saturday, May 15, promised to be another day of "Hulman Weather," named for the meteorological good fortune of the current owner of the speedway, Tony Hulman. The wealthy Terre Haute businessman had rescued the track from near oblivion in 1945 after years of neglect during World War II. One inclined to such thoughts might perhaps conclude that some supernatural force had rewarded him with many days of cooperative weather. No matter the cause, today promised to be no exception.

Eddie Spencer arrived early wearing a sweater he knew would be unnecessary by eleven o'clock. Many pretty young ladies showing off pasty-white, Midwestern, untanned legs were uncomfortable now; however, by one o'clock they'd be warmer and on their way to their first sunburn of the season as they tried to quickly acquire a glowing tan. Eddie knew enough to wear that sweater now. Fashion wasn't an issue for him; he wore the same "track stuff"—his words—that his wife had told him to burn years ago.

Eddie walked between two white garage buildings that had changed very little over the last thirty-plus years. They provided room for seventy some cars. One building had suffered a fire in 1941 and been rebuilt. The parallel buildings ran from east to west—one long garage to the north and its double to the south. The double doors for each opened like barn doors, each with horizontal bracing painted dark green. Many teams made this their headquarters for the racing season, not just the month of May. Eddie walked down that center, common lane between the two garages, waving to friends, occasionally stopping in a garage to offer a greeting, joke, encouragement, or small talk. It wasn't uncommon to even see Mr. Hulman, the Speedway owner, walking through. The gentleman was admired by the racing community. He was the man who provided these drivers, mechanics, and owners the world stage of motor racing. He got them off the dirt tracks and county fair dust bowls for a chance at the big time. The race winner often appeared on late-night TV. Even that was probably the work of Mr. Hulman, many thought. He was revered by drivers, owners, and fans.

A line of pay phone booths at the west end of the north garage was empty. There was no one making a call to…whom, about what? A call to an owner for more money, a call to Halibrand or the Meyer-Drake shop in L.A. for parts, a call home to an anxious wife or girlfriend? Who knew, but the booths were there for those purposes and any other issues that arose. On the west end of the south garage was the Magnaflux shop that tested metal components for cracks and wear.

He walked through the gated exit of the garage area, under a banner that read "Gasoline Alley," the name for the two long garages. The passage between Gasoline Alley and the track would soon ring with furious whistle tweeting, as guards shooed fans to the sides to make room for the cars to pass as they were towed out to the pits. At a gap in the front straightaway stands, he showed his ID badge to a security man at a gate and walked onto the pit apron. There were no cars out yet. The tall grandstands directly across from him loomed high and were just now being lit by the low, rising sun. In front of him, slightly to his left, was the tall tower that registered the running order during the race—first at the top, down to position thirty-three. Eddie stood for a few moments and savored it. He thought of all that he'd seen here over the years—the races, the cars, the men. For more than fifty years, men had come here to test themselves. A few had become legends.

He saw a few "stooges" (helpers) moving tools, starters, battery carts, stacks of tires, and other items to their respective pits. No cars or drivers were out yet, but fans were rapidly filling the choice seats. Some knew where their favorite drivers would pit their cars, so a few areas in the bleachers had begun to fill. And the "railbirds" were quickly laying claim to the choicest places to stand—behind the pits of the drivers turning the quickest times.

Eddie looked to his right at the long pit apron and thought about how different it had been in his day—so much more casual then. In those days, the crowds really didn't gather until race day. Motor racing in the twenties—Eddie's day—had been big, but not like this. He could remember sitting in one of Harry Miller's beautiful creations very near this same spot. A front-wheel drive Miller was a work of art, low-slung with the driver sitting far back in the car, almost certainly unbelted and wearing a leather or cloth "helmet"—not even close to the right word. It was more like what a WW I airplane pilot wore. It kept his hair in place and afforded absolutely no protection. *Why, for God's sake, did I wear that?* He wondered now, but never gave it a thought back then. In his day, drivers didn't wear seat belts and shoulder harnesses! There was no wall to protect pit workers from a careening car. *Well, that's the way it was. No roll bars, either! Just think of the lives lost! Friends! We just went along with it because…because that's way it was. Stupid, when you think of it now. But I did love that Miller! What a sound that little engine made. It sang! And that supercharger wailed like a banshee!*

He walked north on pit lane because he knew that's where Billy Wallace would be later, and a bit farther north, he suspected that Tom Lawton's crew and car might take what space remained—if they even made an appearance today. The "big guys", the ones making news now or consistently—the hottest drivers, former winners, wealthy owners—got the choice pit assignments closest to the center of the action: the start-finish line, the scorers' and officials' table. Rookies, also-rans, and struggling teams were relegated to pits farther north. As he walked, Eddie got "Hi" and "Hey, Eddie" and "Good to see you", but those greetings were becoming more infrequent. The old-timers who knew Eddie "Speed" Spencer were becoming fewer. Many participants were just too young to know that he'd been one of those "hot dogs" once. *That's the way it is, boy, the way it is,* he admitted to himself. *You were lucky to be a part of all this once! Lucky to still be a part of it!*

Eddie turned and looked to the south, toward turn one, and saw a yellow race car being pulled backwards by a red lawn tractor. That's what he'd expected and why he'd walked this way. That would be Cal Olsen's car, and Billy Wallace would soon follow.

* * * * *

Billy had changed into his driver's uniform and was carrying his helmet bag, just in case when he and Roxie arrived at the gate an uninformed guard thought he was a gate crasher. *How could anyone NOT know me, Billy Wallace?* He had a pass for a guest—a metal badge—that would allow Roxie to sit with Andrea Olsen and her wealthy girlfriends.

"I don't know, Roxie. Could be a long day. The weather looks good, not hot or windy. But if those two things change, it could go long. Wind can be a problem. If it picks up and gets gusty, that'll discourage a lot of teams. "

"I'm sure! Wind slows you down, at least when you're goin' straight into it, right?"

"Yeah, but the problem is wind gusts come out of the gaps between the stands, and them real strong ones can move a car two or three feet, sideways! Been known to make a driver lose it, crash."

"You're kidding, aren't you, Billy?"

"Not at all. The other thing is, in practice this morning, the fast guys will really turn it on. They might run a lap of one forty-eight or nine. Some of the guys are just about touching a hundred and fifty. This morning, the PA announcer will announce the best times. But if it gets hot, times get slower. They say the heat makes the track ooze a bit, so tires don't get the same bite they did just a few hours earlier."

"That's hard to believe, but if you say so," Roxie said as they reached the end of the pedestrian underpass and emerged into the early morning sun. They walked past a row of cars parked with their trunks open, facing the track. The fans were already grilling hotdogs for breakfast and enjoying their morning "juice"—canned beer. "I don't know how they do that at this hour," she mused.

"Many will be here all day and possibly see three cars. This is more than race cars for them. It's booze, food, girls, booze, girls, food, booze, girls, a few cars, booze, girls. Get it Roxie? Count yourself lucky to have a good seat today."

"Okay. I sure hope it warms up some, though."

They walked through the same gap in the stands that Eddie had walked through. They turned to walk down the row of stands as Billy searched for Andrea Olsen. "There she is. Hey, Andrea! Remember Roxie from Milwaukee last year? Got a seat for her here today?"

"Sure! Send her up!" The flamboyant Andrea Olsen was in her element, surrounded by her "entourage" as the local newspaper society reporters liked to write.

After talking to Andrea for a few minutes, sharing a few "last year" stories, Billy turned to Roxie. "Wish me luck, girl." He kissed her on the cheek and walked toward the entrance to pit row.

· · · · ·

Billy sat in the Olsen race car, listening intently to the Chief Steward as he went through the qualification procedure. He used the same lines for every driver attempting to attain sufficient speed to become one of the thirty-three starters. They were the same lines he'd spoken many times in the past, to veteran and rookie alike.

"You have up to three warm-up laps before your qualification run begins," Porter began as he knelt by Billy. "Three," he repeated, holding up three fingers. "You can begin your qualification run as you exit turn four at the end of that first lap, second lap, or third lap by raising your hand. The starter and his assistant, using binoculars, will watch to see your raised hand. If we don't see a hand up, we assume you aren't attempting a time trial run. You'll see the green flag displayed at the beginning of your first, second, and third qualification laps. As you cross the line to begin your fourth lap, you'll be given the white flag for one lap to go. At the end of your attempt, you'll be given the checkered flag. You and your crew don't have to accept the run. They can wave it off with a yellow flag before you take the checkered flag. The car then has two more tries. Do you have any questions?"

Billy shook his head. The steward gave his okay. Caldwell inserted the long steel rod into the nose of the racer, attached the starter to it, signaled for his helper to prime the engine, engaged the starter motor, and signaled for Billy to turn on the magneto. The engine immediately caught, and Billy revved the engine once to clear it.

The helpers pushed the car to boost Billy's start. The engine revved up quickly in first gear, then dropped a note as he shifted.

The PA announcer said, "Here's our next qualifier. Rookie Billy Wallace from Tucson, Arizona. He's in that beautiful, yellow number seventeen, the Olsen Special! Let's wish this young man good luck, fans." After two warm-up laps, the yellow car came out of turn four, and Billy raised his hand, and the announcer said, "And heeeee's on it!" signaling the beginning of his qualification run.

Roxie sat up on the edge of her seat and clutched her official program. She followed the example of a wife in front of her, writing the lap times and four-lap average for each driver. *This seems to be the thing to do, and it may settle me down a bit. The cars go by SO fast! It scares me,* she thought.

Andrea leaned close. "Here we go, Roxie! I feel good about your boyfriend. He's gonna turn a fast time today!"

Boyfriend. Hmm. Guess that's what it looks like, but is he really? "He's a good driver. Hope he does well today."

But he didn't do so well this day, at least early in the day. He ran two consistent laps right around 147. 500, give or take a few hundredths, but then his third lap slipped to a low 143 mph when he bobbled in turn two, the car wiggling and nearly getting away from him. Billy brought it under control, but backing off caused him to lose momentum on that lap. His crew waved off the run as Billy raced out of turn four on his fourth lap. The likely four lap average might not get him in the race. They knew he could do better, and he wasn't happy when he returned to his pit. He sat in the car for several minutes talking with Cal. Cal walked away and Caldwell slapped Billy on the shoulder.

Up in the stands, Andrea Olsen, Cal's wife, said, "Hmm, Cal expected better today," to no one in particular.

Roxie sat to the left of Andrea and engaged the woman beside her in conversation so she could pretend not to have heard her. She did not want to betray any doubts, nor did she want to offer any opinions that she knew would be uninformed. Roxie said, "Would you just look at that darling little girl," she said to her neighbor. "Down two rows and standing—straight ahead of us—the girl in the blue and white dress."

Billy was out of his car, looking into the stands, trying to make eye contact with Roxie, but she was chatting with the woman beside her, one of "Andrea's Army", as Cal called the fashionable group of women who tagged along with his wife. They were attendants to the queen, not really "race-knowledgeable," but they helped Andrea make her *statement* to the crowd.

When Roxie looked down to the pit area at the yellow

racer, she saw Billy looking up directly at her. He motioned for her to meet him at the pit gate. They both worked their way through crowds of people lining the chain link fence separating pits from stands till they met at the central passage that led to Gasoline Alley.

"Come on, Rox. There's a cafeteria under the stands. It's just for drivers, mechanics, officials, and so forth, so I won't have to deal with fans there. We can get a cola or whatever, burger if you like. You can get out of the sun for a while. It's just gonna get hotter, and we might be here longer than I expected."

They found an empty table in the cafeteria. After putting her purse on the table, Roxie said, "So, tell me what happened. I thought you had some really fast laps."

"Messed up my third lap. In turn two, I musta got back on the power too hard, too soon. I felt the back end slip out, to the right, and I had to back off. So, I didn't get a good run down the backstretch and ran that bad lap. Caldwell said I was barely over 143! Put that with my first two and who knows what my fourth lap would be. That wouldn't guarantee a spot in the race so they waved me off."

"I didn't see anyone wave a flag at you."

"Oh, the guys are way up there, closer to the pit entrance, hard to see unless you know where the crew waits. They're sittin' behind the inside wall."

"You all done now, no 500 for you?"

"No, Rox, that's why I said it could be a long day. Each car has three tries, so we have two left, but we have to try today. The car is good, weather is good. And first day qualifiers get rewarded with the best starting places. Even if I broke the track record tomorrow, I wouldn't start on the pole position, but behind all the first day qualifiers. So, we got to get this car qualified today. Nothing wrong with the car, just the driver right now."

"That's a strange way of doing things. I don't get it."

"Long time ago the powers that be here decided to reward the guys who were ready to go the first day, instead of getting a whole bunch of qualifiers that last day or so. That gives those first day teams more time to prepare for the race. That's another advantage."

"Okay, I see, kind of," she said and took a sip of her cola. "But, you'll be alright, don't you think?"

"Yeah, sure. Caldwell ain't worried, and I ain't either," Billy said and looked absently out the window. "We might wait till late—four or five o'clock. Long day for you, too."

"I have no schedule. I'm not workin' tomorrow—it's Sunday."

They sat in the cafeteria until there was a break in the on-track action and the announcer said that the track would be open for practice till further notice.

"I better get out there so we can run some laps. Olsen will put his watch on me. I'll work on that second turn. Gotta 'get back on the horse' as they say." They walked out of the café and back to the track, the roar of the engines echoing in the canyon of grandstands on the front straight.

Three hours later, Billy had worked out any issue he had with turn two and had found the speed he needed. He qualified with a four-lap average of 147.810 mph, which put him into the middle of row three, eighth fastest of the day. Billy was a happy man, as was Caldwell, but perhaps more importantly, so was Cal Olsen. Billy, satisfied and smiling, sat in the race car for a short interview and waved to the fans standing at the fence. He caught sight of Roxie, sitting with "Andrea's Army" and hoped that she had endured the intense atmosphere up there. He waved and she smiled and waved back. *Time to get back to the motel, clean up, and relax. Roxie has no plans, maybe she can stay. Billy, boy, you are now a 500 driver!*

Bet Dad had his radio tuned in. Then he climbed out of his car and motioned for Roxie to meet him at the gate. As he was about to leave the pit area, a man said, "Nice job, Cam! Good luck on race day!"

Billy didn't reply to, or even acknowledge, the man he recognized out of the corner of his eye as Chet Martin, the El Cajon promoter. A reporter for the Indianapolis Star, standing beside Martin, recognized Billy Wallace and noted the encounter. Minutes later Caldwell came by on a lawn tractor, towing the car that Billy had just qualified for the race. Following the car came Cal Olsen, beaming and waving. As always, Olsen was unmistakable to knowledgeable fans and reporters in his resplendent Hawaiian shirt, standing out even in the sea of colors.

When Olsen went by and turned to the garage area, Martin said, "Hey, Olsen! How did that Cam Turner do out there in California with your midget?"

Olsen looked around, confused by the connection of his midget race car and an unfamiliar name.

"Over here, Cal! I remember a driver with a yellow midget showing up at my place," Martin knew he had just seconds to get Olsen's attention.

"Huh? "Olsen looked around and found the man by the fence. "What the hell? Who are you and what are you talkin' about?"

"I'm the promoter at El Cajon and…"

"Don't know what you're talkin' about!" Olsen turned away and continued to Gasoline Alley. He knew he had to have a chat with Billy.

The reporter, press credentials plainly visible, identified himself and said, "What was that all about?" Chet Martin proceeded to relate the story of a driver—remarkably similar in appearance to Billy Wallace—who had showed up with a yellow midget race car, introducing himself as Cam Turner, an obvious and tortured automotive-inspired pseudonym for a name he hadn't wanted in race results. The reporter listened intently and furiously took notes, smelling scandal and a juicy story that might get his by-line on the front page.

· · · · ·

Janet opened the farm store on Sunday at noon, regular hours, considerate of the church-going habits of most of the residents of Barton. Janet wasn't so faithful recently, since Tom was marginally employed. Losing the station had put a big hole in the family budget, so she'd told her boss she would pick up any available shifts or extra duties. He was glad to oblige her.

She heard a car in the parking lot, looked out and saw Missy Wilkins, her life-long friend and co-worker at the farm store. Their long-lived relationship had evolved in many ways and become deeper with each stage.

Missy went to the front door, pulled, but found it locked. "Okay, guess I'll go home, boss Lady!"

"Hate to say this, Miss, but you look like you should have slept a little longer," Janet said, unlocking the door.

"Thanks, just what a girl likes to hear."

"You go out last night, or just get home this morning?"

"It was a dark and stormy night, Jan. Sure, I got home, but maybe I shoulda just stayed up and come in early. Ray and me, I can't…I don't…know which way we're going or which way I want to go. And he's not…shouldn't there be more spark between us? Sometimes I don't feel that."

Well, you've been going out with him for a long time, and you know them sparks get dimmer even in the best of couples, Missy. I can tell you that from personal experience. But my point is this: you been datin' Ray so long that you're almost in that 'been married' stage, know what I mean? Some of that old mystery is gone."

"I know all that, how that cools and sorta fades. He cares for me, and I do for him, too." Missy's voice trailed off and Janet knew that she was rehashing what she and Ray had been through a few hours ago. "Okay, I'm gonna change the subject. Let's talk about your racer-husband. Is he in that big race now?"

"Tom got a new car Wednesday. Well, new for him. It's two or three years old, but Tom thinks it's a good one. Something different about it, not like most cars. Tom could explain it. He finished his rookie test on Thursday."

"So, he's in the race now?"

"He's got to *qualify* first. He has to be one of the thirty-three fastest cars to get in the race, and they figure that by choosing the thirty-three fastest times run in four lap trials. But the new car he got is just that—*new to him*—and it takes a while for a driver to get comfortable in a car that's new, especially a guy like Tom who has never driven at Indianapolis."

"Oh, guess I got to learn about this stuff."

"They got twenty cars qualified yesterday, and today doesn't look so great. Supposed to rain. That'll change things. Tom might get out to run some practice, but he won't try to take his four-lap run today. They'll work on the car this week, getting it fine-tuned. At least that's what Tom says."

"I think I'd like to see this. Can I go along next time, Jan?"

"We need to get someone to work for both of us. That's not easy."

Just as Janet said, rain hampered qualifying. Only three cars were added to the line-up on Sunday, and Tom did not get out on the track at all that day. Lou, Dutch, and Tom—mostly just Dutch and Tom—had five days to get the car ready and competitive.

· · · · ·

The last two days of qualifications were scheduled for the following Saturday and Sunday. Tom and Dutch had spent the week fine tuning the race car for sheer speed, trying to find the combination that would give Tom the four fastest possible laps. There were no decisions to make regarding tires. All teams used the same style Firestone tires. Some drivers derisively called them "Flintstones"; they were hard, inflated to fifty pounds of air pressure—the manufacturer recommended nitrogen—and an old design. Many thought they were desperately in need of updating. But that was the "way it is and that's what we use because…that's the way it is." On the front were sixteen-inch wheels (tire size 7.60 x 16), and on the rear were eighteen-inch wheels (8.00 x 18). There were some mechanics and drivers who had experience with stock car racing, and they suggested, "How about some of those stock car tires? They're wide and they run those things up to a hundred and sixty on those big old two-ton taxi cabs! These cars here at Indianapolis weigh less than half of those tanks. With tires like that, we'd smoke this place!" But that was not an option for Tom, Dutch, Billy, Caldwell and all teams, at least now.

Tom ran laps all week, but not all day. A driver couldn't run seventy or eighty laps a day for five days. The engine only had so many miles in it before it wore to the point where it would no longer be at peak performance. The goal was to get as fast as possible, with the fewest laps, and not wear the engine out. Dutch's hope was to get the car qualified on Saturday, and then he could tear the engine down, replace any suspect parts, and reassemble it for race day. But he didn't want to run it to ruin before Saturday.

Tom seemed to be stuck running laps in the high 145's and occasionally just touching 146. Those times would not guarantee a starting place on race day. On Wednesday, Billy talked about his "driving lessons" with the veterans, reminding Tom to stay off the brake, lift at the three marker, then get back on the power to get set up for turn two. "Experiment with going slightly beyond the three marker, back off the power a bit, try to stay off the brakes—that's so *damn* hard to do—then pick up the power again. Do that until you get to the second marker before lifting."

"Sounds simple when you put it that way, Billy, but it's not easy to stay off the brake. Dutch put a little push in that front end. I get on the power coming out of one, and them front wheels look a little like snowplows, and it seems like I'm takin' a line that's gonna show me how hard that wall is. I back off a bit, and she comes back in line. You remember Chuck and his theory of setting up a car at Winchester so that the driver can see a slight haze on that right front? He likes just a little push in the front end."

"Yeah, right, So what?"

"Well, you can run a tire like that in a sprint car…in a short race, but that won't work here in this long race. But—I know why Dutch set it up like that. He thinks that's a good way to learn how to drive this place. If it looks like you're headin' for disaster, back off and trouble *should* go away."

That was on Wednesday. On Thursday—two days before qualifying resumed on Saturday—Tom sat with Dutch on the pit wall, waiting for the announcement that the track was open for practice. "How about we put a turn or two on that right front torsion bar, Dutch? I know what your thoughts are about me getting' used to this place, but I think I'm ready to get after it."

"Well, we tighten up the front, you know that makes the back end a little looser."

"Yeah, let's try that. I'd really like to make that right front stick a bit more."

Dutch went to the front of the car, turned the set bolt on the right front torsion bar, and said, "Try that, Tom."

After turning four laps in the mid 146's, Tom returned to the pits and shouted to Dutch, "Give it a bit more, Dutch!"

Tom re-entered the track, got his speed up on the backstretch, ran deep into turn three, picked up the power, and headed for the short chute and turn four. The car felt stable with neither front nor rear end making any movements, wiggles, or wall-bound trajectories. He felt like he made a strong exit from turn four, setting up a good front straightaway run. Tom stayed on the power past the three marker on the front stretch, lifted for the turn, and accelerated into the south short straight, lifted slightly again, then got back into the gas, hard, to exit turn two. As he did, he felt the rear end lighten up and for a moment thought, "Uh-oh, this is it", but the car came out of the turn and seemed to be perfectly lined up for his backstretch run. Tom finished that lap and another. Dutch was sitting on the pit wall, smiling and looking at his stopwatch, when Tom coasted into his pit.

On Saturday, Tom qualified with a four-lap average of 147.024. He was the fastest of seven qualifiers that day. He was faster than six other cars in front of him, but due to the strange rules of the Speedway, he would start behind them because they were ready a week ago.

Lou Turner smacked him on the back saying, "Old rookie man, you did a good job today!"

"That's about the last time you're gonna have a loose rear end in that car. Seventy gallons of fuel on race day will pin that rear axle to the track with all their four hundred pounds. Good goin' today, Tom," Dutch said.

"Guys, I'm goin' home for a few days," Tom said. "I'll be back on Tuesday. Been sleepin' on a couch or the floor over there off Georgetown in some place that Billy lined up for me. Want to sleep in my own bed for a couple days. My back needs it," Tom said to Dutch and Lou as he walked out of the garage.

"Enjoy it, Tom. See you…Tuesday? Oh, hey, I just earlier today realized that we never talked about salary. We'll take care of that when you get back," Lou said, then waved at Tom, who was walking away.

"Yep, see ya!"

* * * * *

A small story buried on the third page of the Indianapolis Star Sport Section on Monday caught the attention of enough of the racing community to set it abuzz. In the past, reporter Val Scott had been known to enjoy "stirring the pot" of the racing establishment. Still, the allegations, if true, had enormous implications, especially for Billy Wallace.

WHO IS CAM TURNER?
Val Scott Sports Reporter

> Did Billy Wallace actually put Cal Olsen's car into row three for the 500, or was it an unknown West Coast midget racer? El Cajon Speedway promoter Chet Martin reports that a "Cameron Turner" brought a yellow number thirty-seven midget to his URA race three months ago. A yellow number thirty-seven raced in two USAC programs, one in Arizona. Wallace in a car with that number and color won an event at San Bernadino. Between those events, did Wallace compete in the URA race? In the past, USAC has suspended any racer who ran in an "outlaw" race. Wallace, Olsen, and USAC have all refused to comment.

* * * * *

Tom qualified on Saturday, May 22. He left that afternoon to go home for a few days, looking forward to spending time with his wife and daughter. He'd been focused on just one thing for so long that it was almost as if that part of his life had been put on hold. Before he left the garage area, he stopped to use one of the pay phones to place two calls: one call to let Janet know he would be back today and another to Chuck's shop, hoping to talk to Donny.

"Donny! It's Tom!"

"What's the story there? You're a 500 racer, I know that. Listened to the time trials on the radio today. I heard your car when you went out, and then they read your times. Congratulations! I hope you remember me now that you're in the big time."

"You're startin' to sound like Chuck now."

"Well, anyway, I been workin' on our car a little, just tinkerin' with this and that."

"You gonna run it tomorrow? That's the rain date for the Eldora race, right? Just tell my sub, whoever that is, that I don't want him to bend anything."

"Naw, I decided to keep it in the shop. I'll just help Chuck with his new car. When you told me that I couldn't count on you for Eldora, that you needed Sunday free in case you didn't get qualified on Saturday, and that I should find a driver—well, I just, I just figured one race won't make or break me, so I ain't takin' it over there."

"I wanted to get home for a few days. I mean, I could drive over to Eldora, it's not that far, but I want to see the girls for a couple days and tell 'em about arrangements for race day. That's just a week from tomorrow."

"This is something, ain't it, Tom? Indianapolis 500! I'm comin' over to watch. Probably can't get a seat, but I can walk around, see what I can. I wanna be there to see you and Billy. I'm not sure about what Chuck's gonna do, if he'll go or not. He was kinda on the 'no' side. But me—I gotta see this!"

"Well, last year I had some serious doubts about ever getting this far, but something just worked out."

"I'm excited, Tom. My guy is an Indianapolis driver!"

On Sunday, Dutch put on an old driver's suit and took the red number thirty-three out on the track. He understood the rules for this disappearing practice. Primary of those was the stipulation that a mechanic could have one "try hard" turn—north or south. The mechanic was not a professional driver and not accustomed to sustained high speeds. He was allowed to build speed on a straightaway and enter the north or south turn at speed, but he couldn't put a whole lap together at speed. He didn't doubt Tom's ability in the car. Dutch had one goal in mind: to try out a device he'd installed over the winter. It was a handle on the right-hand side of the cockpit, near the seat anchors. That handle hadn't been attached for Tom. In fact, Tom knew nothing about it.

The handle connected to a device that could manipulate the left rear torsion bar. Cranking the device manipulated the car's weight. Dutch knew that after a fuel fill up, the rear of the car would have hundreds of pounds that would provide plenty of rear end traction, and thus un-balance the car, perhaps causing the front end to "push." Because the rear had more traction relative to the front, the front wheels had less grip and, therefore, effectiveness. The car seemed to "push" itself to the outside wall. Dutch knew that if he increased the tension on the left rear, the right front tire would have less of a tendency to push; it would steer better because some of that weight would be transferred to the right front. He hadn't mentioned the device to Tom last week. Back then, Dutch just wanted to get the car in the race. He'd figured he could do his fine tuning—of car and driver—later.

He put a heavy load of fuel in the car and ran ten "try hard" laps. He mixed fast front straightaway/south turn with fast back straightaway/north turn laps. Normally stationed behind the pit wall, was his trusted "details" man who was a walking computer. He quizzed Dutch when he returned to the pit area, "So, whatta ya think, make any difference when you used your secret handle?"

"Yeah, a little. Don't know if that 'little' will help on race day, but can't hurt, if Tom doesn't go crazy with it. We'll have to educate him."

* * * * *

On Monday afternoon, Billy, Cal Olsen, Eddie Spencer, Chet Martin, Chief Steward Porter, and Carl Decker, the president of USAC, met in an office under the front straightaway stands.

Decker started the meeting by saying, "This is a simple thing here. Billy, did you race at that El Cajon race? Martin says you were there with Olsen's car."

"I stopped there on my way up to San Bernardino. I parked the car in the infield and watched the motorcycle race on Saturday night. Slept in a motel, picked up the car Sunday and headed up to L.A., till my trailer broke. I did not race at El Cajon."

"Eddie, you got anything on this?" Decker asked.

"I called a newspaper guy out there. He covers motorsports for some local San Diego papers. Usually keeps good notes, reporter you know. He was there for that race and says he never heard of any driver named Cam Turner out there."

Decker turned to the promoter. "So, Martin, what do you have to say?

"This guy introduced himself as Cam Turner at my track. He had a yellow car number thirty-seven. Those are the facts."

"I didn't drive at your track," Billy replied.

"You said you were Cam Turner," Martin said.

"Did not drive," Billy repeated.

Decker narrowed his eyes at Martin. "Tell me, Chet, did Cam Turner *or* Billy Wallace drive at your racetrack? That's the issue."

"No, but...."

"Case closed, gentlemen!" Decker said, got up to walk out, but sat down and said, "Give Billy and me a few minutes. You other guys can go."

Five minutes later, a red-faced Decker walked out of the office with an un-intimidated, smirking Billy Wallace behind. Then Decker went to the public relations office to set the record straight. They would send a "clarification" of Val Scott's story to the Indianapolis Star which would be printed on Tuesday. Billy Wallace had to endure a few days of "Hey, Cam" greetings, but the incident gradually disappeared from the speedway grapevine. By then even he could laugh at the "Cam Turner's Garage" sign taped on Olsen's garage door.

Billy Wallace thought, *Guess when you think about it, that night with the brunette was good for me in the long run. But...I sure can't tell Roxie how oversleeping saved my ass! Lucky I overslept!*

* * * * *

For the first time in weeks, the Lawton family enjoyed a meal together. Janet had asked Missy to close the store so she could get home and make fried chicken, a favorite of Tina and Tom's. When Janet made an off-hand comment at work about wishing she had time to make a pie, Missy called home. Mrs. Wilkins was well-known for her pies and usually made two or three a week, which contributed to Mr. Wilkins' girth.

"Jan, stop at our place on your way home. Mom made a couple pies today. Take your pick!" Missy said as Janet was leaving the store.

"What?"

"I called home and asked Mom if she was making some today. She said, 'Just finished two.'"

"I can't do that. She has plans for them, I'm sure, Missy."

"She loves makin' pie and my dad loves eatin' them, but he…well, he's gonna have to get a bigger belt! Take your pick."

* * * * *

Tom hooked his thumbs into his belt and said, "Fried chicken, mashed potatoes, green beans, and pie! How does a working woman do this?" Then in his corny John Wayne accent, "This purty little young lady here musta helped you, ma'am."

Tina rolled her eyes, glad that none of her friends was present to see that.

"You must be kidding, Tom. I don't think she could boil water," Janet said, but smiled as she passed the potatoes and gravy, hoping that Tina would take her comments as gentle humor. A quick glance at her daughter told her that wasn't the case.

"Well! I was busy! Uhhh! I was going through a few of those commands with Candy. She is *so stubborn* sometimes! Gloria said I should get ready for a county fair, and some fairs start in June. She said I should go to an early one for, like practice, and then it would be easier for our fair…I'd have some experience. She said I should probably try to go to the Paulding County Fair. It starts, I think, sometime in June."

"Sounds reasonable, I'm sure we can get there okay," Janet tried to throw some oil on the waters she had stirred up. "But, you know, we do have an *even*t coming up soon."

"Yes, I wonder what that might be?" Tom teased.

"How is this whole thing going to work, anyway, Tom? Do we have to get tickets, how many of us can go, do we go the day before?"

"There are some seats set aside for family—I don't really know how many. But you for sure." Tom explained as well as he could. He knew he should have found out more before he left Indianapolis.

"Well, I'm sure Tina would like to go, wouldn't you, Sweetie?

I wonder if I could bring Missy along, too. She'd like to see it. Not every woman's husband races in the 500, you know."

"Yeah, Daddy. And how about James? Can you get a ticket for him, too?"

"Not sure. I really got to find out more about this. I wonder if a rookie racer like me can get that many seats, you know. Those guys who won before, and the real hot dogs—management might be more generous with them. But an old first-timer like me…starting way back in row eight? I'll find out and get what I can."

"We have to plan for this, you know. So, I can ask Missy? Maybe she has plans with Ray to go to the lake or something."

"I'm going back to the Speedway Tuesday morning. I'll try to get us a place to stay Saturday night. Right now, I want to enjoy my first home-cooked meal in, what, almost two weeks I been gone?" With that, Tom directed his attention to a crispy chicken leg.

* * * * *

That same Monday, Billy called Roxie Lytell, once he was sure she'd be home from work.

Roxie had her feet up on the coffee table in her tiny apartment, watching TV and sipping a Coke when her phone rang. She got up, went to the kitchen, took the phone off the wall and said, "Hello."

"Roxie! It's Billy! How you been?"

"Well, I've been reading about the big 500 coming up and wondering if I can get a good seat."

"I guess I just assumed you'd want to go but didn't think that far ahead. Sorry."

"I've heard they sell out all the seats in the stands."

"Drivers get some complementary tickets for wives, family, friends, and so forth. So, I can get you a seat. Maybe you can sit with Andrea again. I could try to lean on that guy again for a room at the Speedway Motel. My deal depended on his wife being there that weekend and him wanting to make his girlfriend disappear."

"Let me know. I can just drive over the day of the race if that doesn't work out. I'll be there one way or another, Billy."

Chapter 7

Sunday, May 30—the race was always on the 30th, no matter what day of the week—promised to continue the streak of "Hulman Weather." The forecast was for almost no chance of rain, warm but not hot, a few clouds: conditions that assured a huge crowd. A military bomb signaled the opening of the gates at 4:00 a.m., unleashing a mad scramble of fans. Eager infield spectators in trucks, cars, and on motorcycles raced for choice locations on the turns and staked out their spot for the day. They backed up their trucks and cars, unloaded all their gear, and got their party started. Until recently, fans erected tall scaffolds in the infield—a practice that ended when one collapsed.

Fans cooked sausages, burgers, and hotdogs for breakfast and dinner on barbeque grills—even supper for those in no hurry to leave after the race. All that picnic food would be washed down with lots of beer. Many would not see the winner due to overindulgence. Many young men paid more attention to shorts-clad beauties than they did race cars. Fans would suffer from sunburns and hangovers on Monday. Little did they care. This is the Indianapolis 500 and the unofficial beginning of summer.

Billy was awake when a loud boom echoed over the Speedway, signaling that the gates were open. He hadn't slept well, waking several times to confirm he'd set the clock radio correctly. Roxie woke with a start, looked around and saw Billy peeking out of the drapes of their hotel room.

"What are you doing? It's…four o'clock? Come back to bed. Sleep!"

"Can't. I'm ready to go. I can't sleep no more."

"So, what are you going to do? You have to rest. This is a big…"

"I know! Don't you think I know that?" he snapped. "I just want to get over there and get started. But there's nothing for me to do really. That's all up to Caldwell and the crew!"

"Billy…"

"Go back to sleep, Rox. I don't want to go to breakfast till, I don't know, maybe around six thirty or so. I don't wanna talk now.

"Billy, come back to bed."

"Nah, I'm gonna go out and walk around a bit. You sleep more if you can. I'm sorry I woke you up. Go ahead, sleep some more."

Billy left to explore the grounds near the motel and was surprised by the crowds already partying on Sixteenth Street. He walked until he encountered a security guard.

"Hey, buddy! How'd you get in here?"

"I'm a driver, Billy Wallace!"

"Sure! And I'm the President! ID, come on, right now before I call the cops!"

Billy reached for his wallet and discovered his pocket empty. "Crap! I forgot to bring it with me."

"Sure, let's go!"

"Hey, get your hands off me! I'm a driver, Billy Wallace, middle of row three!"

"How can you prove that, kid?"

"The motel clerk knows me. Ask him!"

When they entered the motel lobby, the night clerk said, "Mr. Wallace, why are you up so early, and why is this guard with you?"

That settled the issue, and the guard apologized many times, ending with, "Good luck today, Billy! Can I have an autograph?"

Billy could think of several ways he'd like to respond, but in the end he wisely kept his mouth shut and signed the guard's 500 program, the one he'd whipped out from his back pocket. *Hope he keeps it so he can tell his kids and grandkids this story. Anyway, maybe I made a new fan. That will be a valuable souvenir someday—I'm gonna win this thing or crash tryin'!*

· · · · ·

Willy Caldwell had been awake for an hour when the 4:00 a.m. signal went off. He'd slept as well as he could on a fold-out cot in the garage alongside the Olsen Racing Special. He was no different than most chief mechanics, who'd been fussing and worrying over their cars since the last time the cars had been on the track, Thursday, for what was called Carburetion Day. When these cars *had* carburetors—that ended in the 1950's—the crews were given a last-chance practice day to set air/fuel mixtures. In time it became the last chance to check the race-day set up on the car. In the race, cars carried a full load of methanol fuel. That fuel load added nearly four hundred pounds to the rear end of the car. Speed was the goal for qualifications, so cars ran with just enough fuel for perhaps ten or twelve laps. Why add more weight than necessary when you want to go fast? Mechanics had to take that fuel load into consideration when adjusting the chassis for the race. They also had to consider the critical right front tire and how much stress it could bear without wearing too much, too soon.

Carburetion Day was another day to practice pit stops, to make sure that the wheel men quickly hammered loose the three-tab, knock-off wheel nuts; removed the worn tire; mounted a fresh wheel and tire; replaced the knock-off; banged it tight with a brass hammer—brass didn't create sparks or damage the wheel nut—and get ready to help push the car off. A fourth crewman plugged in compressed air for the in-car air jacks and was prepared to change the left front tire if necessary. The fuel man, most often the chief mechanic, had the most critical and dangerous job. He first slipped an asbestos sleeve over the hot exhaust pipe, then pumped sixty gallons or more of methanol—under pressure—into the tank. A man behind the wall offered the driver clean goggles and a paper cup of water, on a long stick. This was all to be done in twenty to twenty-five seconds, in order to remain competitive. That was the goal, but a goal not always met. Things could go wrong, so crews practiced their stops many times over.

But Caldwell was afflicted with fears of what he *knew* could happen and the uncertainty of unknowns that *might* happen. He must have checked fluid levels—engine oil, coolant, brake fluid—many times. He checked to see if all drain plugs—transmission, rear end, engine oil—were snug. He checked brake lines. He checked to see if bolts were tightened, and safety wired. How many times in the past had a car been denied a victory or a good finish by the failure of some ten-cent part? Sleep? Rest? He could do that on May 31. Now, he still had many hours to worry and work.

* * * * *

Eddie Spencer spent Saturday night at the home of his old friend, Charley Kirk, another old-time driver, though the two had never raced together. Charley raced in the late thirties and after the war, while Eddie had raced in the twenties, putting them about a decade apart. Eddie had continued his involvement in the sport in some capacity through the 30's, 40's, 50's, and now into the 60's. Charley and his wife lived in a five-room bungalow off Georgetown Road just west of the Speedway, where Charley worked year-round on the maintenance crew. Charley and Wilma often rented a room in their basement to young racers. Billy Wallace was one of those young men who enjoyed the Kirks' hospitality.

Now Eddie was taking advantage of that room. The old friends had a home-made spaghetti dinner Saturday evening in what Charley called "Wilma's Workshop." That kitchen appeared unchanged since the day the house was built thirty some years ago. It had white metal cabinets and a green Formica countertop, polished to a luster from years of cooking and cleaning. Over the sink, white curtains framed a window looking out on a small back yard. The kitchen table had chrome legs and a wide chrome band around the top edge. The tabletop matched the green of the countertop. A globe ceiling light was above the table. The chairs matched the style and color of the table. The refrigerator and stove were original to the house and had rounded edges popular then. The floor was made of linoleum with alternating cream and dark green squares. If one wanted to know what a working man's house looked like in 1935 or so, this was the place to see it. It was all neat. It was all clean. It was a picture of the past.

All through dinner, the old friends reminisced with "remember the time" stories, stories of great days and some bad days, of friends now gone, and how things had changed. They talked about how things were safer today—but not foolproof. They talked about Billy and Tom.

"Billy stayed here last summer, you know, Eddie," Wilma said. "Nice boy. Needs to settle down a bit, but that's the nature of the beast. You know how race car drivers are, sometimes."

Eddie's thoughts drifted. "If he learns, he could be a good… what word should I use…representative, or spokesman… maybe that's the word…for the sport. Got to be a gentleman in this world now. Television will be more involved someday soon, and these boys will need to learn to speak well. But the racing part—he will be good, I'm sure of that. Just needs a bit of polishing. He could learn some lessons from…well, Wilbur Shaw. He could teach Billy how to be a racer *and* a gentleman, but Wilbur's gone now, so Billy needs a teacher for that part."

"And Tom Lawton? What do you think, Eddie?" Charley asked as he lit his pipe. "You want a cigarette? Wilma, you still have them Chesterfields around here? She quit, you know."

"Threw them cancer sticks out, thank God!" Wilma said as she got up to clear the table.

Eddie shook his head, thought for a moment, and said, "Tom Lawton. I like that guy—a lot. But there's his age. The window is closing for Tom. He was so good a few years ago. But then his car owner sold the race car, extra engines, parts, trailer. Sold it all and got out. And Tom had been so damn good in that car! He struggled till last year when he subbed after Billy broke his arm. That helped him, driving Chuck Williams' car. Helped a lot."

"He's in that car full time now," Charley said.

"Yeah, and I think it was Billy who helped Tom this year," Eddie mused.

"How?" Charley asked.

"Well, Chuck fixed Olsen's car over the winter, after Smitty's wreck at Dayton. Then Billy left Chuck's new car to drive for Olsen. Tom took his rookie test in Olsen's dirt car. The way I figure is that Billy must have somehow persuaded Olsen to let Tom use that car."

Wilma offered, "Maybe Billy's payin' that back to Tom."

Eddie nodded and said, "However it came about, it was good for Tom. He's startin' way back, but things can happen. It's a five-hundred-mile race, no fifteen-mile sprint. Old Dutch is a clever man with a race car, and I'm sure he could show a lot of guys some tricks."

The conversation continued until each realized the others looked tired.

The Kirks and Eddie Spencer didn't have the same trouble sleeping that Billy and chief mechanic Caldwell did that night. Lack of pressure allowed them to sleep right through the 4:00 a.m. signal bomb.

* * * * *

Chuck Williams decided to stay home for the holiday weekend. He'd had a few calls from crew chiefs, trying to recruit him for help in the pits on race day, but he turned them all down, even from a former winner that he'd worked for years ago. He had school buses that needed attention and thought that Saturday would be a good day for that. Donny would probably be in back, working on his sprint car, and he could help if he needed an extra hand. Then Sunday he could work alone and uninterrupted on his new car, the number twenty-two that

Connors had driven at Eldora last week. What better way to spend Race Day—working on a race car, cold drink nearby, the radio tuned to WIBC and Sid Collins and "The Greatest Spectacle in Racing" with no distractions.

Then, around three-thirty in the afternoon the race would be over, and he could walk fifty feet to his own back yard. He could put some charcoal on his grill, wait until the briquets had a nice ashy look about them, then start the steaks that Ernie had gotten out of the freezer. No crowds, no drunks to walk around, no traffic to fight, no five or six hours in the pits with the heat radiating off the hot concrete. The advantages of staying home outweighed the reasons to go. *There'll be more Indianapolis 500-mile races for me, but not this year. Or…maybe you're getting' old, Chuck.*

* * * * *

Tom's car owner, Lou Turner, had reserved two rooms many months ago at the Holiday Inn on Sixteenth Street, across from the south end of the Speedway. He knew that if he didn't get his car in the race, he could easily cancel. The management would be able to get twice as much as the usual going rate. Demand was high and many fans were eager to get lodging just a few hundred feet from the track. So, he had a room for himself and his wife and a room for his driver, if he found one capable of getting his car in the race. He was happy to have found such a man in Tom Lawton. How lucky could an owner, and for that matter, a driver, be?

Tom and Janet took advantage of Lou's generosity and drove to Indianapolis on Saturday afternoon, leaving Tina in the custody of Missy Wilkins. Missy and Ray drove to the Speedway early Sunday morning with Tina and James riding along. They left Barton at "O dark thirty," in Ray's words for four a.m.

As they drove, Tom and Janet said little for the first thirty minutes, other than commenting about sights along the way: nice houses, sleepy country towns, farmers in their fields, a silly song on the radio, and similar chatter. Tom knew what Janet had to be going over in her mind and had no reason to bring it up. Why, at this point? And, anyway, there was no reason to replay such discussions of the past. He knew that his old line was pointless: "I drive as much with my head as my foot" didn't reassure Janet anymore. She knew too much, and she had seen too much.

Tom awoke Sunday morning at four a.m. when a loud bomb signaled the opening of the gates. He slipped out and walked across Sixteenth Street, excusing himself as he walked through the mingling crowd of fans. *Now this is odd. They'll be watching me in a few hours, and here I am saying' 'Excuse me, Pardon me, Ma'am.' They don't know me without a uniform on. I look like an…old man! Like their Uncle Morty, maybe!* Tom hoped he could get a look at turn two, stand quietly by himself and treasure the opportunity ahead of him. Reality and amazement filled his mind at the same time. *You're a gas station jockey, Tom Lawton—an unemployed one, to top it off—but today you're part of the biggest race on this earth. How lucky can such a man be?*

His chance to meditate was interrupted by the ridiculous sight of Billy Wallace walking with—or in the custody of—a security guard. *What did you do now, kid?* Tom watched as the pair went into the motel, wondering how Billy would get out of this situation. *How could so many things happen to him? That boy will have a lot stories to tell someday.*

· · · · ·

After breakfast at the motel, Billy and Roxie walked the short distance to the Speedway. Roxie took Billy's hand and chatted about the day ahead, asking questions that, even after a year of following Billy to racetracks, showed she had more to learn.

"I told you about the crowd, but you'll see in a few hours what I mean," Billy said.

"I get that. Qualifications Day was really something."

"Multiply that crowd by two or three. I kinda felt it last year, when I was just a helper. Those stands on the front stretch, the thousands of people there, all the bands, movie stars. It's really a big deal! You'll feel it, just wait."

"I remember the sound of those cars, but there were only two or three close together then. But thirty, uh, what thirty-five cars all at one time?"

"Thirty-three, Roxie. Eleven rows, three cars in a row. Quite a sight! Oh, who do you want to sit with? You could sit with Andrea and her people. Or Tom's wife will be here with some friends. I don't know how many seats she's got. I'll talk to Tom."

"I think I'd like to sit with Janet. I don't know her well, but she seems nice. More like me. Andrea's different, you know. Not as easy to be around."

Billy's pace increased as they entered the grounds, and his attention to Roxie seemed to fade as they got closer to Gasoline Alley, the pit area, and the main straightaway. They could hear the chatter of the PA announcer, a voice that rang up and down the main straightaway, echoed between the stands, then drifted out over the whole Speedway. Billy's focus increased, and he talked less and less. When they got to Gasoline Alley, Billy said, "You can't go in there—no women allowed in the garage area. Can you wait here by the gate? Stand here by this guard in the yellow shirt. I know him and he'll take care of you. I'll see if Tom is here yet. Then you can sit with Janet, okay? I'll be back, I promise." Billy kissed her and disappeared into the busy crowd of crewmen and officials.

· · · · ·

The schedule for Race Day was timed to the minute. The race was to start at 10:00 a.m., but there was a Central Indiana quirk. Indiana was in the Eastern Time Zone, except for Indianapolis, which was on Central Standard Time. Anybody coming from out of state had to know that peculiarity.

All cars were to be in their pits by 7:30. A low wall separated the stacks of tools, spare tires, fuel tanks, and equipment from the area where the cars would stop. On the wall in front of each assigned pit were painted the driver's name, car number, and car name. A chain link fence separated the spectators from the pit area, a fence that would be lined with eager fans all day.

Billy found Tom in his owner's garage. "Hey, Tom, ain't this something? A year ago we'd just met, and here we are today! The big show, huh? How you feelin'?"

"Okay, Billy, I'm okay. You?"

"Gotta admit, I'm a bit jittery, didn't sleep well last night. Up early and ain't been back to sleep since. I wanna get goin'."

"That's what I figure. Get in the car, you know—that's our world. We control that."

"Hey, Roxie needs a place to sit. Janet got some extra room?"

"She invited a friend from home and that friend's boyfriend. Then Tina and *her* friend came, too. Tina won't want to sit for five or six hours, so I think she and her boyfriend will walk around some. Janet can make room. So, yes."

"Great, she's out by the fence. I'll tell her."

Tom and Billy, in street clothes to be less recognizable, walked with Roxie through the gap between the stands and to the seating area behind the pits.

"Janet, got another race fan for you. Roxie'd like to sit with you, okay?" Tom explained. After "good luck" and "be careful" and a hug, Tom turned and walked down the stands.

Roxie nervously reached out for Billy's arm, pulled him close for a hug, and whispered in his ear, "Yes, Billy, good luck, but be careful. I…love you, Billy!"

"See you after the race, Roxie…in Victory Lane!" With that, Billy turned and followed Tom back to the garage area to change into his driving uniform.

* * * * *

Fifteen minutes later, Tom and Billy walked through the gap in the stands. The crowd applauded and shouted as they saw the drivers that they recognized. There were shouts of "Good luck!", and "Go get'em, Russ!", and "First place today, C.J.!", and encouraging words to the favorites and famous drivers. These fans had been reading about Billy Wallace, and his exploits on the track—and off, thanks to the Cam Turner incident—had earned him a degree of notoriety. There were shouts of "Let's go, Billy!" Tom understood that little of that acclaim was for him. He was not in the same category when it came to fan recognition. He didn't need it and knew that only fans who followed the sport for the whole season would recognize his name and appearance. This was a different crowd—a crowd that mixed once-a-year fans with true, weekend-to-weekend, all-season fans. The latter were the fans who knew him best.

The cars were lined up in their assigned pits, crews organizing for pit stops. Billy's pit was closer to the starting line than Tom's. Starting order shuffled the slower cars farther north, away from the control tower. Crew chiefs of the most competitive cars preferred that arrangement, knowing the time consumed by a pit stop was less. It was a faster way to get a car in and out of the pits

Billy found his pit. On the wall, painted in black, were words that he could not, a year ago, imagine seeing: Billy Wallace 17 Olsen Special

Tom looked at his young friend. "Good luck, today, Billy. Let's go one-two, okay?"

Billy shook Tom's hand and said, "As long as I'm that

number one. See you in a few hours, and take care of yourself out there, old man. Shoot! How many times will I have to take a leak before this race gets goin'? I better go back and take care of that…again! Damn, let's get racin', Tom! See ya!" With that, he headed back to the restroom to relieve his bladder.

"Ain't you a Nervous Nellie! That's not like cool and calm Billy Wallace."

"Gimme a break, pops!" Billy shot over his shoulder as he walked away.

Tom continued down the line of cars till he came to the red race car. *Red…again a red race car.* Color's been good to me, though. And it's number thirty-three! The number of cars in the race…*and three times eleven…eleven is the number of Chuck's sprint car. Kinda funny to think about that.*

Dutch was leaning over the open hood of the car, tinkering with something, worrying over every bolt and clamp and hose that he could worry about. "Tom! We got about an hour and a half till green flag. You ready? I'm ready, I hope."

"Yeah, it's another race. Longer, more people, more money at the end, but another race. I'm gonna tell myself that, at least. But I do want to go over your weight jacker in here and make sure I've got that all straight in my head." Tom looked at the handle, low on the driver's right side. The mechanism had been there all month, but the crafty mechanic had attached the handle to operate it just a week ago. Dutch knew Tom well enough to trust his judgment.

Dutch said, "You have to be reasonable with that, Tom. Don't go crankin' that thing a bunch. We'll give you a full fuel load on your first stop. Car's gonna feel heavy, so one crank might help make it handle better. It works on the left rear torsion bar, but it will also affect that right front a bit and give you more front-end bite, get some of that push out of it. Then after thirty, thirty-five laps or so, the car should be more balanced—you'll have burned off some of that fuel weight. So, reverse it and take some of that bite out of the right front, so you don't wear it out too quick. Remember, turn it right to add weight, left to take it out, but just a notch or two at a time. You give it one on the straight, when you got time, and see how that feels in the next corner." Dutch hoped Tom would keep that straight. "If you don't notice much change, give it another notch, but be cautious with it. Remember, right to add, left to remove. Or this, it's easier, till I think of something else: right is more; left is less. That might help. Left is less, okay? And keep this in mind—the car will eventually come back to you. It'll get better as it gets lighter. Be patient, Tom."

* * * * *

High school bands marched past, seemingly without end. Supposedly there was one to represent each state in the country. A shapely majorette in a gold suit led the Purdue Band. They had a drum so big it was in the back of a pick-up truck. That was to be the featured, and last, band to arrive on the front straight, where they would play "On the Banks of the Wabash." By then all cars were to be positioned correctly on the track in their starting positions—eleven rows of three.

Celebrities were introduced to the crowd a few minutes after nine o'clock. There were movie stars, politicians, the Governor of Indiana, astronauts, retired drivers, famous athletes, former winners, and beauty queens. During these festivities, some drivers milled about the assembled cars and crews; chatting with friends, sponsors, and those celebrities; joking with fellow drivers; talking with their mechanics and car-owners. Other drivers talked very little. Thirty-three cars, five or six crewmen for each car, an owner, a few hangers-on, reporters, photographers, officials. That all added up to a lot of people and a congested scene. Soon there would be a call for "Drivers, report to your cars," as if they had to be reminded, but there was usually one who arrived late enough to give his crew the jitters. By 9:30 the grid began to clear of non-essential personnel.

Then at 9:40 the Purdue band played the National Anthem. Five minutes later, the Armed Forces Color Guard played "Taps." Billy strapped on his helmet, looked in the stands where he thought Roxie was sitting, and waved, hoping she might be looking. Tom was already sitting in his car, tugging at his gloves, his goggles hanging loosely around his neck. Dutch leaned in and said, "This is a solid car, Tom. She's good for two hundred racing laps and a bit more. You ain't gonna lead the first lap, we know that. But you have the car, and you are the driver that can lead the last lap. Another thing—I'm fuelin' you up a bit light so you can run a little faster them first laps when it's easier to pass. The field ain't so strung out then so you can pick 'em off one at a time. I know how much fuel it's got and how far that will go. The man on the pit board will let you know when to stop, but it will be earlier than a lot of these guys. Goin' much past forty-eight or forty-nine laps is iffy though. If there's a caution in the forty to forty-eight lap range, ya gotta come in, okay? We got some good pit stop times in practice this week. I think we can get you goin' again with twenty-two or twenty-five second stops, if all goes right!" Then Dutch slapped Tom on the back and leaned on the car's roll bar.

"Sounds good to me, Dutch," Tom looked up to his right where the mechanic stood beside the car. "Now, you gonna get ready to plug that starter in?" Dutch smiled and went to the front of the car. Lou Turner gave Tom a thumbs-up. A helper used a hand pump to pressurize the fuel tank.

At 9:50, thousands of colored balloons were released from a tent, and an opera singer sang "Back Home Again in Indiana." Chuck called it the Hoosier national anthem.

Billy was ready. Tom was ready. Thirty-one other drivers were ready. The grid was clear now, except for crews, cars, and drivers.

At 9:53, Tony Hulman took to the microphone and said, "Gentlemen, start your engines!"

Thirty-three electric starters whined, and thirty-two engines coughed to life. One car, directly in front of Tom, did not start. A crewman opened the hood and squirted fuel into the injector horns as the chief again engaged the starter. A crewman placed his hand on the exhaust pipe. The noise was so great now that one more engine couldn't be heard, but a hot tail pipe meant the engine had started. Thirty-three crewmen had a hand in the air to indicate "engine running."

Each car crept slowly forward, crewmen pushing to boost the cars on their way. Tom Looked to his left as he passed the area where Janet was sitting and waved.

The cars crept down the front straightaway in ragged order, some cars sputtering, their cold engines firing unevenly. Tom had to dodge to his right toward the retaining wall as a car directly in front of him, a silver car with red trim, slowed to a near stall. The driver put the clutch in, and revved the engine, hoping to clear it. The car suddenly shot forward and nearly rammed the car in front of it. Tom wound through groups of crewmen still on the track, pulling starters and battery carts to their pits, clearing the track.

There were to be two preliminary laps. The first, the Parade Lap, was a "get lined up" lap, when all cars were to take assigned positions. As they came down to start the second lap, the Pace Lap, drivers were expected to wave to the fans. The fans stood, and many would remain standing until at least ten laps were complete.

Far ahead but out of Tom's sight, the pace car—a new white convertible—was leading the first row into turn one. C.J.

and his rear engine car were in the middle of the second row, fifth position. Directly behind him was Billy in Olsen's yellow number seventeen. There were four rows between Billy and Tom, who was on the outside of row eight. The field of thirty-three cars straggled through turns one and two. Fans stood and waved. Tom could clearly see some with cameras, some with binoculars, young men already bare-chested, women in sunhats, a child waving a souvenir checkered flag.

When the field reached the back straightaway, it took on a greater semblance of order, although some drivers were accelerating, edging out of line, then falling back. The driver in front of Tom disengaged his clutch and tried to clear a sputtering engine. In each row of three, the middle car had roughly six feet between it and the car on its left and right. Between each row there was approximately one car length, about sixteen feet. As the cars rounded turns three and four, drivers steered into correct order. *Now, time to wave and make nice to the people paying you, Tom. You wouldn't be here without them,* he told himself.

Front straight—thousands of people on their feet, waving and shouting, though crowd sounds were drowned out by engine noise and muffled by a crash helmet. Turn one—excited fans in the most coveted location, seats often passed down through generations of families. Turn two—fans standing in the sunlit bleachers. And then the long, wide open back straightaway, the "cheap seats" on the infield bleachers, nothing on the outside of the oddly low retaining wall, except a few trees. Then turn three—the same, no seats outside the track but bleachers inside the turn. Turn four—huge, uncovered stands outside the track, thousands and thousands of fans. And then the front straightway, cars increasing speed, drivers striving to maintain spacing, but also eager to edge ahead, speed up, and get a jump on the cars beside them. Chief

Steward Porter had told the pace car driver he wanted a ninety mile-an-hour start. The only driver who knew miles-per-hour was the man in the pace car; no speedometers in race cars.

Midway down the front straight, the pace car pulled into the pit lane entrance, and the field accelerated as one. The starter waved the green flag. At Christmastime, eight or nine years after they had gotten married, Janet had given Tom "Gentlemen, Start Your Engines," the autobiography of three-time 500 winner Wilbur Shaw. Tom found that what Shaw had said of his first 500 start was so true. It seemed as if a vacuum was pulling his car along and even if he wanted to use his brakes, they would hardly slow him down, the energy created by those cars was so great. Tom's first goal was to find a clear spot to settle his car, and get in line, as did many drivers, save for an enthusiastic rookie who seemed eager to get to the front as soon as possible, driving high through turn one. *Better not try that after sixty laps or so, Buddy. There'll be lots of crap up there that'll put you into the wall!* Tom entered turn one ahead of the car starting in twenty-third place, to his left. The car that started on the inside of row eight drove with his left side wheels below the white line in turn one. Tom steered his car in an arc that would take him to within a few feet of the wall in the short chute, followed the car ahead—twenty-second place—and lifted slightly as he entered turn two. Midway through the turn, Tom accelerated hard to approach the long back stretch with as much momentum as possible. This wouldn't be his fastest lap due to the ninety-mile-an-hour start but knew he could drive the next three-fourths of a lap as fast as possible, traffic permitting.

Focus! Got to be alert, you know. Remember your shut-off points. Focus. This ain't no movie and you ain't no star! Remember your job here today, don't get carried away. He thought about what he once told Tina. *Driving for me is thinkin' all the* time—about what other drivers might do, where to try to pass a guy, how the engine sounds. Like you and that horse. You're constantly aware of how she's reacting.

The field sped into turn three, visually so unlike turn one which seemed enclosed by the huge stands. The car in front of him was slow to accelerate into the short straightaway leading to turn four. Tom knew that crew chiefs started with a fuel load near sixty-five or seventy gallons, adding several hundred pounds to the weight of the car. And that weight was not evenly distributed. A full tank, being at the rear, tended to lighten the front end and reduce steering effectiveness. The driver approached turn four very low on the track. Tom was able to pass and move into twenty-second place. He arced close to the outside wall and accelerated onto the front stretch. Tom approached turn one this time at racing speed, watched for his shut-off point, and steered low through the turn, allowed the car to arc out to the wall in the short chute before dipping low in turn two. He followed the same principle that he did at any racetrack—try to make his path as straight as possible. Especially here and at these speeds, he tried to be smooth and deliberate, avoiding sudden, drastic movements unless circumstances demanded them. The most he moved the large steering wheel in a turn was perhaps twenty-five to thirty degrees—much different than racing on a half-mile dirt track, where wheel thrashing was the order of the day.

Tom maintained his place, aware of only the two or three cars immediately in front of him. As he passed the pits to end his second lap, he saw that a car was stopped, and the driver was out. That left thirty-two cars in the race. *At least I won't be last!*

At the end of ten laps, Tom was in twenty-first when another car in line ahead of him retired with mechanical problems. Far ahead in the field, C.J. was in fourth place, and Billy was right behind him in fifth. Tom relaxed his grip on the steering wheel on the straights, giving his hands a few seconds of rest from the engine vibrations.

Tom moved up on the car holding twentieth place. He could see that the driver was struggling with a poorly handling car. The car had an obvious understeer condition, or "push," that at the very least compromised performance. Tom could see—as he maneuvered to the left of the car in turn one—that the driver had the front wheels angling inward, or "snowplowing," to control the situation. The car was probably heavy with fuel, a situation that would improve as it burned off. Tom backed off slightly and followed him through turn two. He followed the car closely down the back straight, stayed in his slipstream, and made his move to pass just before the pair entered turn three. Tom passed and advanced another place. His pit board read **"POS-20"** as Tom completed lap twelve.

· · · · ·

Back in the stands, Missy yelled over the constant roar, "I can hardly tell what's going on here, Jan!"

Janet turned and spoke into Missy's ear, "Look at that tower, Miss. At the top, they show who's in first place, second place, and so forth. See number 20? That's Tom."

Roxie offered, "Yeah, it says Billy's in fifth place. He moved up three places. Billy says that C.J. guy is the one to watch, the guy in that little car. He says the engine's in back and thinks he'll be fast."

Janet said, "It's going to be a long day. They still have over a hundred and eighty laps to go. It'll get a bit more interesting when they start pit stops. Those guys can change tires and put in gas so fast. You'll see. Tom says that usually starts around lap fifty-five or sixty…around then, at least."

Just then, the track announcer said, "Caution lights are on, fans."

Drivers responded by slowing. According to race rules, positions were to be maintained. Passing was not allowed, and drivers were not supposed to advance their position on the track. If a driver was entering turn one as the car in front of him was exiting that turn, the following car was supposed to keep that distance. Some drivers did as expected, and some did not. It was such an easy way to make up ground, and a few drivers used it to their advantage.

"There was debris on turn three, fans. This should be a short caution period," the announcer said. He'd hardy finished his explanation when the flagman waved the green flag and the race resumed. James had a transistor radio up to his ear. "On the radio they said there was something right in the middle of the track on turn two. It may have fallen off a car."

· · · · ·

Laps twenty through forty were mostly uneventful, and Tom made modest progress. On lap thirty-seven, Carl Connors, who had led or run second, was passed by both C.J. and Billy as they exited turn four. Tom improved one position—aided by a retirement—to nineteenth. He was able to advance another three spots, with another retirement and more aggressive driving. *This is goin' okay, I think. Not sure exactly where I am, but I passed a few and ain't been passed. Dutch said, 'Do your passin' early' so I'm tryin'.* Dutch had a chalkboard that he used to inform his track-side man holding Tom's pit board. The track-side man then gave the same messages, on his chalkboard, to Tom: his position, how far he was behind the car in front of him, threats from behind, how many laps until his first scheduled stop. Dutch had figured that laps forty-five to forty-eight was their best window. On lap forty-two, Tom flashed by his pit and read, **"Pit 3 Lps."** He ran that lap thinking the car had never felt better and that it would be a shame to load it with all that fuel, at roughly seven pounds a gallon. *This thing will feel like a cow with all that!* Tom thought. Then, just as he exited turn four, to complete his forty-fifth lap, the track lights all flashed yellow.

How lucky can we get? Yellow right about when we wanted to stop! Tom made a split-second decision to enter the pits, threw up his left hand to warn cars behind, and braked hard. Pitting under yellow was preferable to stopping under race conditions. Cars were going slower during a caution period, so a car in the pits wouldn't lose as much ground during the twenty to thirty seconds that the stop would require. *They gotta be ready for this! They were tellin' me to pit in a few laps, so probably Dutch has them all set to go, least I hope so. Might be surprised, but they can handle it, probably.*

He didn't know the reason for the caution was right behind him. A car had slid while exiting turn four. The car behind it, attempting to avoid a crash, had spun into the grass. Once stopped, its engine still running, it continued on its way, but that first car had stalled and stopped, blocking the pit entrance. Drivers who wanted to take advantage of the caution period to make a stop, were prevented from doing so by the stalled car. That obstacle was *behind* Tom.

Dutch and his crew looked surprised to see the red number thirty-three racing toward them, but they were ready. Tom brought the car to a stop, put the transmission in neutral, put his foot on the brakes, and kept the engine racing. Five men jumped over the low wall. Dutch fueled the car, dumping sixty-five gallons of pressurized methanol into the tank in seventeen seconds. As Dutch refueled the car, the man assigned to change the left front wheel—rarely changed—inserted a high-pressure air hose into a fitting on the left side of the car to activate the on-board air jacks. He then cleaned the windscreen. Three other men attacked the right front, right rear, and left rear wheels, banging the three-tab wheel nuts loose with their brass hammers. The sixth man, not allowed over the wall, offered Tom clean goggles and a drink in a paper cup by means of a long pole. Tom looked back to his left, watching Dutch for his signal to go. When all three wheelmen stood up to indicate they were done, the fourth wheelman pulled the air hose out. The car settled back on the concrete apron, Dutch yelled, "Go!" and slapped Tom's helmet. The two rear wheelmen pushed the car, helping Tom get back on the track. The man with the long pole shouted, "Twenty seconds, Dutch!"

The car that had blocked the pit entrance prevented several cars from taking advantage of the caution period, while most stayed on the trck with no intention of pitting. Apparently, many found that the timing did not suit their pitstop schedule. Many of the front runners stayed on the track.

When Tom returned to the track, he had dropped from sixteenth to twentieth place; he knew that many others would pit within ten to fifteen laps, and he would in turn pass many of those cars as they made their stops. Stopping in a caution period had great advantages, and this time luck was on Tom's side.

* * * * *

Sixty miles away, Chuck Williams sat in a lawn chair positioned between his two sprint cars. His red car was the one that Billy had driven to his first Midwest sprint car win at the high-banked Dayton Speedway. His new car, built over the winter months, was painted a gleaming pearl white with red and blue striping. It was numbered twenty-two and lettered as the "Precision Tool and Machine Special."

Chuck smoked a cigarette, nursed whiskey on ice, stretched out his legs, and leaned back in a lawn chair. He tinkered with his new car while he listened to the radio broadcast of the 500. Ernie—Ernestine—had made one of her big breakfasts, and he was enjoying the contentment of a full stomach, and slowly realizing that real work would not likely take place today. Anyway, he didn't really want to work. He was satisfied to just "fuss with the cars" and "putter around the shop." That was the way to spend this day. Getting into some serious work could just distract him from the pleasure he took in listening to the race on the radio. He'd been there many times, and he could see it all in his mind's eye. Here he was surrounded by his two creations. Well, number twenty-two was his creation, built from the ground up. He'd cut and bent the tubes of the frame, welded them together, and attached every part. On occasion, he liked to sit in a car, not often, just often enough to remind himself that sitting in such a car was his limit. He loved his cars too much to do to them what had to be done to win a race. Under their gleaming paint, they were brutes that had to be handled as such to be competitive.

Ernie walked in with a cup of coffee. "How many laps in? Hear anything about Billy or Tom?"

"After thirty laps, they said Billy was in fourth. Top ten was all I heard," he said and motioned for Ernie to sit and listen with him.

Ernie sighed and took a seat. "Well, I sure hope Billy keeps his cool today."

Chuck mused, "Yeah, you know, you take our two guys—Billy and Tom—those are two sides of a coin. I been thinkin' about them. Billy is an all go wide open, jump without lookin' kinda guy, and Tom—he could use some of that fire. Each could gain some from the other. Maybe their friendship has done that to them, I don't know."

"But you know, that coin, heads or tails, it spends both ways. Ain't no better side for buying something. Maybe that's our two guys—different ways to win."

"Well, that is some philosophy! You might be right about that. Anyway, I'm okay stayin' here today, Ernie. I been over there enough for that race. I like it, all the excitement and stuff. But I'm older and today I'm happy to just listen."

"Don't you miss— "

"Shh! They said there's been a wreck." Chuck turned his attention to his radio. "Oh, it's just a spin…listen."

"They say who? "

The announcer excitedly told about the tangle in turn four and how Tom quickly darted into the pits.

"That could be a lucky break for Tom. He got in the pits the instant that caution period started. Might help him in the long run."

Ernie said, "So, a hundred and sixty laps or so to go?" She changed the subject. "Donny coming over here today to work on the race car? I could fix more supper for him, you know."

"I doubt it. He worked on it some yesterday, fixed that broken shock mount, but fact is, it don't need much now, early in the season. And it ran just fine at Salem. Anyway, he talked about drivin' over for the race today."

"How come *you're* out here today? Gonna fix buses?"

"Not on my day off! New car needs tinkerin' around the

edges, you know. At least, that's what I tell myself…and you, too. But you know me pretty well by now. I just like to mess around with my cars, Ernie."

"And all this time I thought you had *so much* work to do! Of course, I've known that for a long time, old man. Two cars though…that one too many?"

"This may come as a shock, but I've given some thought to sellin' that car to Donny. He does practically everything on it now, as it is."

"Don't that boy have a girl to occupy some of his time? You'd think that would be of interest to him."

"He says he can't figure out how to deal with girls. He says, he's awkward when it comes to 'that side of the fence.' That's the way he puts it."

"That could be part of the problem right there. A guy that thinks about girls on, what did you say, the *other side of the fence*? That boy needs *help,* Chuck."

"Right, but that help ain't gonna be me."

"Lord, I know that!"

"Tell you what I think, though. He needs a girl that sort of gets to know him, and he gets to know her, a little at a time, over a *long* time, a few years…maybe longer, so he didn't even have to think of how to approach a girl. So, he just gets to know her through friendship, and bein' around her, without all the dates and stuff. Then that romance and attraction may just, later, kinda *sneak* up on him…them." Chuck stopped, surprised at what he'd said.

"Well, you call me a philosopher, Chuck. Who are you now, Mr. Lonely Hearts? Never heard you mulling over relationship advice. I'm going back up to the house before you start advisin' me 'bout *my relationships!* I got to get some things ready for supper. You going to have enough appetite for those steaks?"

"I ain't too old for sirloin!"

Chuck took a sip of his drink, stood, and dusted his two clean and shiny race cars with a clean shop rag.

· · · · ·

Late Saturday night, May 29, Donny Housman decided that listening to the race on the radio was not enough this year. "His" driver—that is what Tom had become in his mind now—was one of the thirty-three starters in the big race, and he *had* to be there to watch him. Donny waited until nearly ten thirty until he told his mother.

"Mom, you think Dad's settled in for the night? Things will be okay now?"

"Sure, I know how this will all play out now. It'll be okay now. He'll sleep like a baby until maybe nine or ten. Till the booze wears off. Why?"

"I'm goin' over to the Speedway tomorrow. Wanna see Tom."

"You should, Hon. I'll be okay. You don't need to worry about me—us. Go on."

"If you're sure."

"Yes. Go." Sally Housman—Chuck Williams' sister—smiled and hugged her son.

"I'll leave around three or three thirty then, Mom."

"I ain't gettin' up to make breakfast at that hour, but I'll make some sandwiches and things you can take along. A few bologna sandwiches can be breakfast, dinner, or supper. It don't matter what time you eat it. I'll leave some things on the kitchen table for you. You better get to bed and sleep a while. Sunday will be a long day."

"Thanks, Mom. Listen on the radio, you know, since Tom is in the race, okay?"

Donny had called a friend earlier in the evening, a friend who lived on Thirtieth Street, just northeast of the Speedway grounds. He'd asked his friend to save one parking spot in his front yard for him. "One spot for you, Donny! I'll rope it off and put a 'Reserved' sign on it." Parking there might make his walk to the Speedway a bit longer, but he'd have less traffic to deal with, both coming and going.

After parking his truck, and walking past jammed traffic, Donny bought a general admission ticket that gave him access to the grounds. Walking and standing rights. Not great, but he had to be there today. He could only get *glimpses* of the cars, but that would be enough. After the race—he had no reason to rush home—he was sure he could see Tom and Billy in the garage area.

* * * * *

During his stop, several cars passed Tom, but not as many as under green flag conditions. One of the cars in the mishap had quickly been removed and towed to the garage area. The driver of the other car had been able to re-join the race, though he would need to stop at his pit.

With the track clear, the officials switched the lights to green, and racing resumed. Tom immediately found that his car had a much different character now—as did all cars after refueling— with nearly four hundred pounds of fuel in the tank. *Should I use Dutch's weight jacker? Guess I'll go with this as is for a while, burn some fuel off, see if it comes back in ten laps or so. Ten laps are twenty-five miles, and at three miles a gallon, that'll burn about eight gallons or so. Hmm. Well, fifteen laps or so will use about twelve or thirteen gallons. Dutch said we started the race with about forty, so those fifteen or twenty laps at racing speed should…uh…well that would bring the tank down to around fifty gallons or a bit more. I guess I'll wait and see how it goes.*

At this point in the race, seven cars had retired, mostly due to mechanical difficulties. Neither of the cars in the turn four mishap returned to the race. Tom held his position, though he knew that would change as cars made their first scheduled stops. Last year's winner, Russ Stevens, led. CJ still ran second with Billy close behind. Connors had closed back up on Billy. Those four cars, though not exactly nose-to-tail, passed by within six or seven seconds. Tom ran near the back of the pack, position twenty—only six cars were behind him. He remembered what Dutch had said: *Be patient, Tom—the car will come back to you.*

Drivers began to make their first pit stops, including the leaders. Billy Wallace entered pit lane just before he completed lap fifty. He took on three tires and a full fuel load, in a so-so time of thirty-one seconds. Olsen wasn't pleased to see his driver lose places, even though he knew that his position would move forward as others stopped. CJ stayed in the race, although he faded to seventh place.

Tom Lawton saw his place in the sequence improve, as pit stops shuffled the order. He still found himself trying to adjust to a much different car. The near full load of fuel created a few challenges. The car was slower to accelerate and sluggish in the turns. It was like adding a much bigger kid on a seesaw: the back end of the car dominated the front, making the steering lighter and "pushy." Tom found that now he turned the steering wheel to the left a few degrees more; the right front tire had less traction. He didn't feel confident, a feeling that was confirmed when he was passed on the backstretch. Tom decided to try the weight jacker. He turned the handle to the right two clicks, hoping to give the right front a bit more bite. *We'll see what that does.*

The car that had passed him two laps before peeled off to the left exiting turn four and into the pits on lap forty-eight, giving Tom one place back. At this point, he had not burned much fuel, so that would not be a factor in his car's handling. Tom reached for the weight jacker, hesitated, then pulled his hand back. *Just ride it out, remember what Dutch said.* The race was near the quarter mark and Tom was past the excitement he felt at the start. *Settle in, move up when you can, stay out of trouble, and endure the long haul, but keep moving up.* As he passed his pit to end his fiftieth lap, his pit board said, **"POS 20"**.

· · · · ·

With twenty-six cars still in the race, there was nearly constant engine noise, not conducive to easy conversation. Missy leaned close to Janet, shouted, then realized that there was a momentary lull. In her normal voice she said, "Sorry, guess I don't have to scream at you. I'm lost! Where's Tom now—first, last, second? I thought I could follow him, but those cars came in and I lost track. I'm confused!"

Janet began to answer, then paused as two cars went by, side-by-side, followed by another a few seconds later. "Look at the tower. It shows car number thirty-three—Tom—in twentieth place."

"Okay, I get it. But he was in sixteenth and there was that wreck and the yellow lights—to slow down, I guess. Then he went to his pit. Now it says twentieth."

"Well, a few cars passed him when he was in the pits! When all the cars have made their first pit stops, the order will settle into their real positions. You'll see. Aren't you enjoying this?"

"Guess so, at least it's fun knowing our guy is out there. Is he doing okay, you think?"

"Like I said, we'll know more after this first round of pit stops is done. That sorta resets it all, and then they're more equal. Some pit crews are really good, but others don't change the tires and put the gas in so fast. Tom got about a twenty second stop. That's good. Like, well, if some other driver takes forty seconds in the pits and Tom has a twenty second stop—that twenty-seconds difference is like makin' up a part of the straightaway and more. The pit crew gained it for him."

"I guess I see."

Janet waited for some cars to pass. "Here, Miss, think of it like this. Let's say we both left the farm store to go to, uh, Lima, each in our own car. After two miles you stop for a fill up, and I go right on by. I get a lead on you, but then I stop for a fill up and the guy is really slow or something makes my stop longer than yours. So, you pass me, and I don't get back on the road for five minutes. You get a really good lead on me and get to Lima long before I do."

"But some get fast stops, right?"

"Yep, but the ones who don't, well they lose that much time, and they go back in the order."

Tina, James, and Ray were directly behind Roxie, Janet, and Missy. Tina leaned forward and shouted over the engine noise, "I'm hot and thirsty, Mom. James and I want to walk around some and get a soda. Maybe a hot dog, too. That okay?"

"Sure. Bring back some Cokes for us, too. Here's some money."

. . . . .

"This is getting boring. The bands and famous people…all that was neat, and the start was *really* neat, but nothing's happening now," Tina said as she and James walked behind the front straightaway stands. The roar of the engines was diminished there, and conversation was easier. "Let's get some sodas and look this place over. A friend told me to look at the crowd inside turn one. She said it's a real riot, like you won't believe how some of them—lots of college kids and hoods, especially—get wild and carry on."

James got two Cokes and popcorn at a concession stand, backed away, and was bumped by a bare-chested young man being chased by another, apparently inebriated. "Come back here, you jackass! You owe me a beer! Hey, watch where you're goin' kid!" he said, looking back at James, who was getting in line to replace the two sodas and popcorn in the dirt.

"So, is that what your friend was talkin' about, Tina?"

"I guess, but from what she said, it's a whole lot more than that." They walked on past the end of the stands. Safety trucks, wreckers, and ambulances were parked on the grassy apron inside turn one. Tina understood what her friend meant when she saw the crowd near the first turn. Young men were passed out, lying in the grass at this hour, eleven o'clock. Shirtless and sunburned, some tossed footballs. A young couple lay entwined on a blanket in the grass behind a parked car. Another group crowded around a car trunk filled with coolers and picnic food. Several young men, oblivious to the race, used a blanket to toss a girl in the air.

As they took in the spectacle, a few attentive fans stood and pointed towards the track. "Whooee, check that out!" one shouted. A red car slid high out of the groove—a path darkened by tires that the cars mostly followed—bounced off the outer wall and ricocheted back to the grassy area inside the turn. The driver sat motionless for perhaps fifteen seconds, then waved to show he was alright. Many in the crowd applauded. One man shouted, "That's just a little taste of Indiana concrete, buddy!"

"That's a red car, Tina! That's not your dad, is it?" James asked.

"No, that car was red and black. Dad's car is all red."

"What are those guys clapping for? Cause there was a wreck? That what they want to see?"

"Dad says they're glad the driver's okay. But I wonder sometimes, I really do, when I see some of them. Let's go back, James. I've seen enough now so I can compare notes with that girl back home."

As they headed back to the stands, James said, "How can you watch this, you know, with your dad out there and all? It must be a hard thing to do."

"You mean like that back there, that wreck?"

"Yeah, I guess you…you think about what might…"

"We don't say *anything* about that. It almost never comes up, and if it does, Dad has his standard answer…"

James said, "I know this, he told me a couple times: 'I drive as much with my head as my foot.' Is that it?"

"Yeah, that's Dad's line. But we don't talk about it. So, *we*—you and me—aren't going to talk about it, okay?" There was a long pause as they walked through the infield crowd. Finally, Tina said, "So, Mr. Senior Boy, what will you do next year after graduation?"

"Not sure. I've done well in mechanical drawing class, and I like that pretty much. So, college, some tech school? I'm not sure. When I was helping your dad clean out some old stuff at the station for the sale, he talked about me doing something like that."

"Really, my dad? What's he now, guidance counselor, too? Next career, after auto racer?"

"He told me that he once thought about college or something, like studying engineering, after high school, before he got married. Even gave me a drawing set, the kind that draftsmen use. Said some guy gave it to him, but he never used it and thought maybe I could."

"Really, Tom Lawton, that's who you're talkin' about? He may talk to you more than he does me! Hey, we gotta get Cokes for Mom and the others."

· · · · ·

After he'd parked his car in his friend's front yard, beside several others who'd paid the three-dollar fee, Donny walked past long lines of cars and trucks inching toward infield parking. He entered the northern part of the Speedway grounds, between turns three and four. The stands outside turn four were about half full. The infield was already alive with parties and picnics. Young men were throwing frisbees and footballs in the grassy areas, trying to avoid the fans on blankets crowded up to the fence but at the same time trying to make dramatic catches near the most attractive girls.

He bought a program and walked by a souvenir stand selling cheap toy cars, checkered flags, and crash helmets for children. He folded the program and stuffed it in his back pocket. He had two sandwiches left, jammed into the pockets of his jacket.

The infield bleachers inside of turns three and four were filling. They required a ticket for admission, which Donny didn't have. He found a gap between two couples who had their blankets up to the fence—their plot for the afternoon.

One couple was dozing, lying on their stomachs. The young man had his arm draped across the girl's back. Her skin glistened with suntan oil. She had the back of her blouse rolled up and her bra unhooked, trying to get a good start on her summer tan. On his other side, a young lady lay on her back with her young friend beside her, propped on his elbows. He ran his fingers through her blond hair, whispered in her ear, and began kissing her. She whispered something, put one finger on his lips to stop him, made another comment, and then enthusiastically kissed him.

How can people DO this, right out here? Donny began to reconsider his viewing choice. *No way I can stay here! And it don't bother them at all, me standin' here! Jeez! I'll stay and watch the parade and then drift away, I guess. I thought everybody came here for the race! What's wrong with ME?*

· · · · ·

On lap fifty-six, the track announcer said, "Caution on the track, fans. Caution." There was a noticeable decrease in engine volume as drivers slowed.

Janet's immediate thought was *Where's Tom?* She stood and craned her neck to the right, looking far up the front straightaway to the fourth turn. Even on her tip toes she couldn't see the familiar red car.

Roxie and Missy rose from their seats. Roxie said, "Billy hasn't come by for a while. Well, maybe I missed him a lap or two ago, but I haven't seen him or Tom yet."

"They come by about every minute, plus a few seconds… at least when they're racin', but they'll slow down now. Be a little longer until they come around again," Janet explained, talking as much to herself as her companions.

The track announcer said, "All right, folks, we have a report from turn one. That was Jimmy Dawson who spun and tapped the wall, but he got out of his car on his own and waved to the crowd!" Janet sat, relieved, a feeling that was confirmed when Tom drove by seconds later. Experience had taught her that the first story might not be the whole story.

"Oh, there's Billy!" The yellow car drove by, noticeably slower. The scoring tower showed car number seventeen, Billy, in twenty-first place and car number thirty-three, Tom, in nineteenth place. Three cars and about half the length of the straightaway separated them. The three women sat down just as Tina and James returned with sodas for all.

Janet said, "You got here just in time, kids. Break time in the race and we could all use a cold drink."

"Mom! We were standin' over by the turn when that guy slid. You know, Billy was just in front of him. Dad wasn't anywhere nearby. But *some of those people, Mom! Ugh!*"

"I know, I know. You can see it all here. I guess I should have warned you."

Missy and Roxie turned to Janet in unison, and it was Missy who asked the question both women were thinking. "What? What's she talkin' about, Janet?"

Janet ho-hummed an answer. "Well, it's spring in the Midwest. Schools and colleges are on vacation. Young people have been cooped up for a long, cold winter, and this is the unofficial start of summer. They're ready to loosen up and that's what you see there. Kids loosening up. What more can I say?"

"As I said before, ugh!" Tina took a sip of her drink. James grinned and said nothing as did Missy and Roxie.

"Girls, look at the gap between Tom and Billy," Ray said as the field drove by. "There's one car between them. Janet, you said drivers are supposed to maintain their place and spacing, right?"

"Supposed to, Ray, but Tom says some guys cheat. They try to close the gap between them and the others."

"The blue car behind Tom keeps gettin' closer each lap. At least it looks that way."

Janet said, "And what will happen is, the cars behind will move up too, just to keep that distance. Don't want the blue car to get too far ahead. Tom don't know they're creepin' up. No mirrors, you know."

"That hardly seems fair," Missy said. "Don't the officials do anything about it?"

"Tom says not that he knows. They just get the big lecture talk before the race and hope that'll take care of it. But truth is, they almost all edge up a little, some more than most. Like that blue car," Janet said. "Oh, and Missy, things are gonna get sorted out a bit now. Most crews will use this caution period for a pit stop. They all should have made a stop around lap sixty or so. Here come a few now."

At the end of sixty laps the track lights went green, and the race resumed. Tom moved into eighteenth place, and Billy moved up to nineteenth. C.J. did not pit and ran in second position. Tom improved another position when a car slowly and silently coasted into the pits. C.J. headed for the pits on lap sixty-two, moving Tom and Billy up to sixteenth and seventeenth. C.J. rejoined the race in twenty-second place after a poor pitstop.

Roxie bounced in her seat and clapped when Billy passed Tom, almost directly in front of the Wallace-Lawton fans. "Oops, I guess I shouldn't act like that, Billy passin' Tom, you know."

"Oh, shoot, I'd do the same thing. We're cheering for our guys. They're friends, we're friends, you know."

"Yeah, you're right, but they're doing well, right? You know much more about this than I do, Jan."

Laps seventy through ninety were run with no cautions. All cars had now made one stop. With the re-shuffling, Billy advanced to sixth while Tom moved into tenth. Observant fans took note as C.J. made up for his bad pit stop and advanced toward the leaders.

Janet said, "Now, Missy, here's what I wanted to explain before. They've all made one stop, so the order is close to… oh, what would I say? Natural? Real? Accurate? Something like that 'cause now they're more equal, on account of the pit stops. So, the fast guys are up front, not way in back like when they made a stop. That's how those slower guys get way up front, until they have to stop. Then they get passed and go back in the order."

"Ah, I see what you mean, I think," Missy said. "Like I said, Jan, this is all Greek to me." She turned around and said, "Hey, Ray, the big tower says ninety laps, about halfway. Want to escort me to the facilities? I'd like to walk a bit."

The approach of the halfway mark at one hundred laps seemed uneventful to the crowd, but not to the drivers. Billy moved into fifth place on lap ninety-five as C.J. continued his pursuit of the leaders. He passed Tom on lap ninety-seven.

Soon after, Tom noticed a fan very close to the crash wall near the exit of turn one. He stood out from all the others because he wore a big cowboy hat, painted Day-Glo red. Lap after lap, the fan stood and raised his middle finger when C.J. and Tom raced by. *I never noticed that guy before. What the hell is that about? Why would anybody do that to me?* Tom began to watch for the fan each lap, and on each pass he was there. Tom tried to ignore it but found it uncommonly odd and unforgettable. *Some weird stuff here.* Tom finished the first half of the race right behind C.J. His car handled better now that he had burned off fuel. His pit board read **"POS 11"** as he passed to complete one hundred laps—halfway home. *Should I tinker with Dutch's weight jacker? Probably not, at least for now. Remember what Dutch said.*

· · · · ·

Eddie Spencer had been assigned to the same observation post that he'd occupied during practice. There was near constant chatter between observers and officials in the control tower. Some observations were routine, but occasionally he or his partner would report possible liquid dripping from a car, smoke, or another issue.

"We're in to the 'droning' stage now. Less than two hours and this thing will be all over."

His partner said, "Got any predictions, Eddie? You seen a bunch of these, I bet. How many times you been here?"

"Drove twice. Then I worked every race, right up to the war. After that, I only missed one. That was in fifty-nine when my wife was sick."

"So, maybe around twenty or more. Seen anybody that looks really good to you today? "

"Them first three or four cars, obviously. And that yellow car, Billy Wallace. Then that rear engine car—he makes passin' look easy here."

"Seems he can pass low or high. That car looks like it's on rails."

"But that's a stock block engine. Bit 'iffier' here. Those NASCAR guys can run them things near wide open for four, five hundred miles, but here? You think that Kelco Customs guy can make a Chevy run that fast, that long? Keller knows a quarter mile at a time—drag strips, for God's sake. Quarter mile at a time, and how many trips up the strip on a typical day. Seven, eight, ten?

"Well, he's got about two hundred and fifty miles in and he's lookin' good so far."

Eddie said, "I know, I'm just sayin' that you gotta consider his amount of—and kind of—experience. That's all I'm saying. Right now, if I was a bettin' man I'd have to think about these last twenty laps or so. Spectators find this middle part of the race to be boring, but the frontrunners are setting the stage for the finish. They want to stay close to the leading car, within striking distance for the finish. You got those two guys up front, and Wallace has been comin' on real strong since his first stop. He came from eighteenth to fifth. I've been watchin' C.J. in the Kelco car, the one they call the 'toy car', rear-engine thing? After his stop, he's come from twenty-something to eighth in thirty-five laps or so. The winner is up front there as long as he doesn't have a problem—mechanical or something."

"Guess I need to pay more attention. So, your money's on C.J.?"

"I never bet on auto races, just sayin' what I'm seein', that's all."

"Hey, Eddie! We got a hot one comin' in!"

Eddie looked toward his right and saw a car trailing the tell-tale sign of engine trouble—clouds of smoke. The driver quickly got out of the racing groove and headed for the grassy apron inside the back stretch.

Eddie said, "That leaves twenty-four cars still in the race. Really pretty good, reliable performances so far. And except for that tangle in turn four, no big wrecks. Back to C.J.'s car. That's Keller's car. They call him Snooky, runs that Kelco shop out in L.A. You know what they call that place, don't you? Well, at least some guys call it Killco. They say the cars he builds aren't safe. Anyway, I was over at Mates' tavern the other day, drinkin' a beer with Charlie Kirk. Willy Caldwell, he's Olsen's wrench man, was sittin' with Dutch. Dutch was talking about his car—that Epperly laydown that Lawton's drivin'—and how a full load of fuel ain't gonna upset the handling as much as it will in Olsen's car."

"What's he mean?"

"Dutch says the center of gravity in his car is better. That fuel weight is gonna be lower in his car and won't have as much effect on the car in the turns. Caldwell says something—so loud anybody on the sidewalk could hear—says something to the effect of wait till race day. Then Snooky Keller, C.J.'s mechanic—the builder of that car—sittin' at the next table, put in his two cents and talked about his fuel tank. Keller says, 'Think about them dinosaurs of yours. Every drop of fuel is in the rear. You add four hundred pounds or so when you put in a full fuel load. All in the ass end. Your driver forgets about that when he hauls down into turn three for the first time, and he's lookin' at where's he's been when that thing swaps ends. Or if he figures it out and keeps goin' the right way, that car is gonna handle like a cow till he burns off twenty or twenty-five gallons.'"

Eddie continued, "Caldwell—you know how short his fuse is—says, 'Junior, you got it all figured out here don't you? Your first year, and you know it all!' Keller says, 'My car puts the weight of that fuel on the left side between the front and rear axles. All that weight spread out more evenly over the whole car, and it's in the *middle,* not in the *rear.* So, wait till race day. We'll see.'"

"Mates' White Front is the center of great wisdom here, isn't it Eddie?"

"That tavern is the second center. Gasoline Alley is the first center, and the White Front is the other." Eddie chuckled and said, "They're the MIT and Harvard of auto racing!"

* * * * *

Lap one hundred one marked the start of the second half of the race, and the next round of pit stops would soon begin. Stops depended on team strategy. Billy had stopped on lap one hundred five and re-entered the race in seventeenth position. Dutch's plan had been to start Tom light on fuel, and it was their good fortune that the yellow light and caution period came just before their first planned stop. The window for stop two began to close around lap one hundred twenty, so Dutch began to send signals to the man with the pit board. On lap one hundred five, Tom read **"STOP SOON"**. On lap one hundred seven it read **"STOP IN 2"**. As he was to complete lap one hundred nine, Tom came out of turn four, angled left to the inside of the track, and entered the pit lane.

All the wheel men were waiting, new tires beside them, brass hammers in hand. Dutch stood near the wall, holding the fuel hose. Firemen, extinguishers in hand, stood by the car. As soon as Tom stopped the car, the fourth man inserted the high-pressure air hose into its fitting on the left side of the car, and the car rose on its on-board jacks. Dutch flipped open the aviation-style fuel cap and slammed the nozzle into place as another man replaced the left rear. A man behind the pit wall, handed Tom a drink of water in a paper cup on a long stick. This time the man who inserted the air jack hose put on a new left front tire. Tom kept the engine racing, transmission in neutral, brakes on. When the right front wheel man was finished, he laid the worn tire down and stood near the front of the car, watching for Dutch's signal that fueling was complete and that the other wheel men were done. He signaled to let the car down from its jacks. Tom turned back to his left. Dutch pulled the hose out, slammed the cover closed, lifted the fuel nozzle high, and slapped Tom's helmet. The two rear wheel men then pushed to help boost the car back out to the track. Tom glanced back to his right to make sure he wasn't pulling out in front of an incoming car. The engine skipped a few beats, then caught, and Tom accelerated down the pit lane, shifting quickly into race gear. Dutch's fifth man looked at his stopwatch and said, "Twenty-two seconds, Boss! Two good stops!"

Dutch said, "Got one to go. Hope we can do that once more."

When Tom completed lap one hundred ten, the tall scoring tower showed he had dropped to fifteenth. There were twenty-four cars still in the race. C.J. stopped on lap one hundred eleven, but his stop dropped him to sixteenth, right behind Tom.

· · · · ·

Chuck Williams climbed the steps leading to his house's back stoop, opened the screen door, and walked into Ernie's kitchen.

Ernie kidded, "How, or maybe why, is it you come in here every day like clockwork at noon? You don't punch a time clock, but you live like you're on the clock. Explain that, Charles."

"Now, I punched a time clock plenty after the war until I got my fill of that kind of life. Habits, you know, Ernie. When I was a kid workin' on Dad's farm, no matter what he was doin', noon or a few minutes either side of it, Pop would head back to the farmhouse, wash up at the pump handle outside, and go in for lunch. He could be in the back of the big field, quarter of a mile out from the house, he'd pull up the plow and head in. He never wore a watch…kept his eye on the sun or listened to his stomach. Guess I get it natural."

"Old men, old habits. Anyway, what's goin' on in the race? Got the radio on yet?"

"They're just a little past halfway. Tom and Billy had good stops, but C.J. got held up by a problem in his pit. By the time he got back on the track, he was behind Tom. Billy is running twelfth, but he'll move up after all the second stops and all that shuffling are done. Those were green flag stops. They probably couldn't gamble on waiting for a caution. There's two cars been up front most all day so far. Last year's winner, Russ Stevens, and Connors have been leading or in the top ten all day."

"*Carl* Connors? The guy who's been driving your new car?"

"Yep. He's got a lot of experience, and this year he finally got a car to match his talent. He ain't flashy, like Billy. But he can drive a car and tell you what it's doin'. He's been good for me, you know, gettin' that car sorted out. I hope this goes well for him."

"That 'goes well' could mean you'll be lookin' for a new driver, Chuck."

"That's okay. My cars are just steppingstones. I'll never make a fortune racin' cars on half-mile tracks anyway. And for that matter, no driver will either, unless he gets up to the big time."

"Really? I thought we were just one win away from a new house and a trip around the world!"

"I consider myself a successful car owner at the end of the year if my ledger book ends with a black bottom line, even by a few dollars."

"Maybe I should start keeping your books for you."

"That extra work might be too much…"

"I hear you! Those cars are your toys. But those toys are much better than some men's entertainment."

"Anyway, Ernie, got my lunch ready?"

"Yes, siree! Open the fridge. Whatever you find is your lunch!"

* * * * *

Donny wanted to get to the walkway behind the pits, hoping he could watch one of Tom's pit stops, but the guards asked for his reserved seat ticket. He had no way to get a close look, so he continued to wander, listening to what he so wanted to see. He wandered north to an area of the infield that still had a grove of trees, close to the fourth turn. *This is amazing. Trees inside a racetrack! And they're old trees, too. Huge—perhaps fifty, sixty feet! Old oaks, maples, big old poplars. Why in the world would they keep these trees here? Must not be too concerned about fans having a clear view.*

Donny settled in the shady grove, resting with his back against the grill of an old, rusty pick-up truck, its doors labeled "South Side Wrecking Yard." Directly in his view—perhaps fifty yards away—there was a gap between the sets of bleachers. Through that gap, Donny caught sight of the cars flashing by at nearly a hundred and fifty miles per hour. From Donny's vantage point, the retaining wall obscured most of the cars, leaving him with only a split-second image of the drivers' heads. *Jeezow, look at that! Nothing but a little hoop roll bar! And a head going…how damn fast? Someday I got to give Tom a hard time about that! I'll say, 'Tom, I saw your head go by at a hundred and fifty!' He'll probably say, 'And it wasn't fast enough, Donny-Boy!'*

Donny searched the pockets of the jacket tied around his waist for his remaining bologna sandwich. It must have fallen out somewhere while he wandered around the infield. He went to a concession stand, got a hot dog and Coke, and headed back to the grove. The junk yard truck now had two men sitting in the bed, drinking beer, so he sat down at the base of one of the trees to have his lunch. Halfway through his hot dog, he heard a girl's voice. "I CAME TO WATCH THE RACE!" Nearby, a car door slammed, and a young girl stormed off toward the bleachers.

What the heck am I missing here? Guess some didn't come here for what I did!

· · · · ·

A spirited contest for the lead began after the second round of pitstops was complete. It lacked the intensity of a final ten lap sprint, but it seemed as if the top three or four drivers were seriously testing each other, trying to get a feel for any weakness their opponents might have. Stevens and Connors dueled with each other as they raced back to the front of the pack. By lap one hundred thirty-two, they were running in first and second, trading the lead. Billy advanced to seventh place after the fifth-place car retired.

Tom moved into the top ten followed by C.J., who was rapidly working his way up to the leaders. *What's with the red hat man in turn one?* It was impossible not to see him. In a sea of people, he stood out—even at a hundred and forty miles an hour—lap after lap. Now, however, there was no middle finger extended, but the guy was still there. *Don't try to solve the mystery now, Tom. You have better things to do.*

Tom's goal was to hold off C.J., who was right behind him in eleventh place. But there was no denying the superior handling of the rear-engine car. Their cars were closely matched in straightaway speed, though Tom had a slight advantage over the production-based engine in C.J.'s car. C.J. passed Tom in turn three on lap one hundred thirty-eight and soon moved up to fourth place, behind Billy who had picked up another spot. Tom moved into sixth place on lap one hundred thirty-nine when the car in front of him bobbled in turn three, had to back off, and lost momentum. That allowed Tom to easily slip by in the north short straight. A car running near the back of the pack retired, leaving twenty-two cars still on the track, and the fifth-place car made an unscheduled stop. Tom's pit board read **"POS 5"**.

By the end of one hundred and fifty laps, Stevens had regained the lead. Billy was now in third place, closing the gap on first and second. A three-car train—Stevens, Connors, Billy—was positioned for a dramatic finish. Each had one more stop to make, putting pressure on the pit crews. The race could be won or lost during those last stops.

C.J. and Tom were within a few seconds of each other, but there was a half-straightaway gap between them and the leaders. On lap one hundred and fifty-one, the three leaders exited turn two in close order and accelerated onto the back stretch. A blue car, occasionally emitting puffs of smoke, had been lapped several times and was just entering turn three. It could present an obstacle or an opportunity for those three drivers. The car might serve as a blocker and allow one or perhaps two cars to advance. That situation would not present itself on this lap but could soon.

The blue car was well off the pace of the leaders, perhaps six miles per hour less than the leading trio; when they entered turn three, the blue car was exiting turn four and smoking more. At their current speeds they would likely overtake the ailing car on the next lap. Stevens, Connors, and Billy headed down the front stretch nearly nose to tail. Stevens saw that the blue car was in the fast groove, high on the track, close to the outer wall. He saw the flagman edge out onto the track surface to display his black flag. The driver was being ordered to enter the pits for consultation on his next circuit. Officials would likely remove his car from the race to prevent more oil being spilled on the track.

The driver did not immediately move out of the groove, so Stevens darted left, preparing to pass at the end of the straight, and so be positioned to enter turn one in, not the best line, but one that would protect his inside from Connors. Just as he committed to that move, the driver of the ailing blue car darted left, into Stevens, and the two cars locked together, sliding and grinding toward the outer wall. Connors tried to veer to the left to avoid the two cars, but his right rear wheel hit the tail end of Stevens' careening car. Connors ricocheted left, twirling and heading for the inner wall. Billy saw the mishap developing but had neither time nor an avenue for escape. He steered to the right, aiming for a gap between the two locked cars and the wall. The gap shut as the cars ground along the wall. Billy's escape route was closed, and his car was jammed between the wall and the two cars. C.J., following far enough behind the leaders in fourth place, was able to find open space to his left and skirted the mass of crashing cars. Billy's car began a series of end-for-end flips high in the air. Tom Lawton drove by to the left of Billy's car as it leaped high over the track. Tom could see his young friend, belted in the car, holding the steering wheel. *Oh, my God, Billy! Oh my God!* Tom couldn't believe his eyes. *He's going to be killed!* And then just as quickly as that awful sight had materialized in front of Tom, it was gone as he passed the accident and assumed second place in the race, with C.J. now the leader.

Roxie, Janet, and Missy were stunned by the suddenness and violence of the accident. They had been following Tom and Billy closely during the long, green flag period. Fans had been standing for many laps, enthralled by the two-car contest between Stevens and Connors. When Billy moved up to challenge those two, Roxie and Janet paid closer attention. They had more invested with Billy involved. Missy comprehended less of the race than her two companions, but now even she had a reason to watch. The women saw the cars coming towards them but didn't understand the complication presented by the blue car.

Missy had seen the flagman step out on the track. "That guy with the flags ought to find a better location. Can't he stand somewhere else? What's that black flag he's waving for?"

Janet answered, "That blue car is smoking a lot, so he's supposed to come in on his next—" but she never got to finish her explanation, instead throwing a hand over her gaping mouth, watching in horror as the disaster unfolded.

Roxie shot to her feet and froze, incredulous. Her vision was filled with Billy's yellow car tumbling over and over just yards away from her. The awful sight shocked her senseless. Her body shook, her mouth was open, but speechless. The crowd, which had been cheering and urging on their favorites just seconds before, groaned a collective "Ohhh," and then fell silent.

Janet looked to her left, saw the terror, shock, and fear in Roxie's face. She grasped Roxie's arm and said, "Let's go. Right now! We got to get out of here!" Janet knew that this was no place for screaming or a breakdown. *I've got to get Roxie out of here to…where? Someplace quickly! That café…is it open, is it quiet? Where can I take her? Restroom? No!* Janet and Roxie left their seats, pushing, stumbling on feet, sidestepping past standing and murmuring fans. They went down the steps and through the gap between the stands to the area underneath the stands. "Here, Roxie, let's go in this office. No, that's the press room. No way we're going in there. USAC office—that's good, for now. Come on!" She led Roxie into the office of the sanctioning body. *Now, if there must be screaming and crying, okay, we're out of sight of those thousands of people.* Ernie Williams had taught Janet that there was a way for a racer's wife to behave in such a situation, a lesson that Roxie hadn't heard about.

All the lights around the track flashed yellow and the cars slowed, weaving through the debris and wreckage of the four cars. The yellow car lay battered, but right-side up, Billy slumped forward, still in his belts, motionless. Emergency crews rushed to the cars. Stevens' car and the blue car were jammed together, against the wall. Connor's car had come to a halt against the inner wall, near the pit exit. Billy's car ended up in the middle of the track, sitting diagonally. Fire crews stood with extinguishers ready, although there was no sign of fire.

* * * * *

Donny, relaxing in the shade of the trees, was drowsy from the constant drone of the racing engines. Suddenly an audible "Oh!" rose from the thousands of fans on the front stretch jerking him wide awake. The announcer said, "We have two, no, three cars tangled on the front straightaway, fans! There is caution on the track! There's a yellow car and!" Donny only heard "yellow car" and knew that could be Billy. He ran behind the bleachers, behind the tower terrace stands, past Gasoline Alley and the garages, dodging fans, bumping into some and excusing himself, trying to get as close to the scene as he could.

* * * * *

As Tom drove through the south turn, he couldn't shake the image of Billy. *That car could turn over once, twice, who knows how many times? And how would it come to rest? Upside down? Still a lot of fuel in the tank. Would the roll bar protect Billy?* Tom knew the history of this place and how such incidents could have fatal results. Many fans in turn one had seen the accident and were standing, some pointing toward the scene. As Tom reduced speed for the caution period, he took advantage of the break to relax. On the long backstretch, he took his right hand off the wheel and flexed his fingers. He shook, then opened and closed it several times. He switched hands and did the same with his left. The long green flag period, nearly an hour, was interrupted for Tom by one pit stop. His single-minded concentration did not register anything close to an hour. This was his first opportunity to rest. Tom knew that positions were frozen in a caution period and advancement was impossible. But he was nearly on C.J.'s tail when the accident happened, so he knew he could follow closely without bending track rules.

When he drove by on his next lap to complete lap one hundred fifty-three, Tom's view of Billy's car was blocked by the emergency workers, safety trucks and ambulances. Billy was probably still in the car. An empty gurney sat alongside the battered yellow racer.

Tom stayed close to C.J., not letting him pull away. As Tom passed his pit and completed lap one hundred fifty-five, his crew signaled **"P2, STOP SOON."** There would be no comment on the accident from the crew. All were focused on the final phase of the race, as Tom should be. He saw that several ambulances were parked near the inside of the track, rear hatches open to receive gurneys.

As Tom completed his next lap under caution, only one ambulance remained. *Injured drivers taken away?* It wasn't until he and C.J. completed lap one hundred fifty-nine that Tom could see that Billy's car was empty and the ambulances were all gone. The fans near the scene still stood, but those farther away had returned to their seats.

The track was cleared of the wreckage, and clean-up crews were sweeping the last pieces of debris. This caution period changed Dutch's calculation. Driving more slowly in the caution period, Tom had not been burning the usual gallon of fuel every two or three miles. That meant they could put in less fuel on the last stop. The other positives were that putting in less fuel meant the car would be lighter—and faster—and the stop could be faster.

Tom entered the pits on lap one hundred sixty-two. He was surprised when C.J., directly in front of him, darted into the pits, also. The two pit crews would go head-to-head. This last stop might determine the winner. C.J.'s pit was farther toward turn one and would require a longer approach. Tom arrived at his pit first, and his men were already working on his car as C.J. approached his own pit. The other side of that coin was that when C.J. was ready to go, he was already closer to turn one.

Dutch and his crew had performed flawlessly all day and this stop was no exception. Dutch knew how many gallons he could pump in per second, and he planned for thirty-seven gallons, enough to get to lap two hundred plus a few extra. His wheel men replaced the usual three tires. When fueling was complete and Tom was ready to go, Dutch yelled and pointed to the in-car weight jacker. "Two cranks, to the RIGHT!" He held up two fingers. Tom nodded. Dutch and the two rear wheelmen pushed on the car as Tom accelerated away.

One crewman said, "What's the deal with that tire marked 'Last Stop LR?'"

"I let some pressure off that tire—little softer so the car might handle a little better—and had Tom crank a little more weight into that left rear. We went a little light on fuel so the tail end is lighter. I wanted to plant that back end as much as possible. I want Tom to run hard, harder than he ran all day. And that'll give that right front more bite, too. We're racin' to win, ya know."

"Damn, Dutch! Nineteen seconds!"

Dutch said, "Well, we pumped in less fuel. Takes less time, right?"

At the same time, there was near panic in C.J.'s pit. The right rear wheelman had lost the spinner nut. The car was fueled, and the other wheel men had completed their tasks and were ready to push the car away, but the frantic crew man was shouting and waving for C.J. to stay. By the time the nut was found under the car and hammered on tight, forty-two seconds had elapsed. Not catastrophic yet but not what the crew had hoped for. As C.J. waited in his pit, Tom passed him, essentially for the lead. On the track, still under caution, the two cars were fourth and seventh in order, but the three cars ahead of them still had to make their last stops, which they would do soon since the track was nearly cleaned up. Track crews were sweeping up the last of the Oil-Dry. Racing would soon resume.

Drivers knew that the remaining laps would be more like a sprint. Cars would have fresh tires and enough fuel to reach the finish, so there would be no long-range planning. All the pieces were in place for the last dash to the finish. The three cars in front of Tom and C.J. made their last stops, and Tom took his rightful place at the head of the pack. *You are leading the Indianapolis 500, gas jockey!*

The flagman indicated that the green flag would wave on the next lap, one hundred sixty-nine. As Tom drove this last lap under caution, the red hat man in turn one was standing and waving his hat. *That guy hasn't stopped this whole race! Is he drunk or crazy or both? But he ain't givin' me the finger! That's for C.J.! I get it now! Red hat man is my cheerleader! Damn, Tom! You're slow to catch on sometimes!*

· · · · ·

Roxie and Janet stood at Billy's bedside in the medical building. Billy looked dazed, and his uniform was bloodied in front. The nurses dabbed at his face, cleaning him up. For once, he had little to say. His world, for two hours, had been one of speed, noise, heat, concentration, and tension. That all ended in seconds on the front straightaway. Lying there, he was able to hear the cars circulating, though obviously slower. This room was quiet and calm as were the doctors and nurses attending him.

A doctor nodded to a nurse, turned and then said, "We'll send him downtown, ladies, just for a check-up. He was knocked out there for a while, so we need to be sure. That blood? Don't let that fool you. He got a bloody nose! Must have bumped his face into something. Steering wheel? Oh, and he'll have two black-eyes. That's part of it, too. He got some bad scrapes on his arms—track burns, probably. But all things considered, he's good!" Roxie sobbed, and the doctor paused to reassure her before leaving. "Really, Miss, he's fine. Very *lucky*, but fine."

"Billy, I don't know what to say! I was so scared! I still am. I don't know how I got here, don't remember leaving my seat, where I've been for the last…can't say—hour?" Roxie looked at Janet.

Billy smiled and looked at Roxie. "I was in the race car—running so good—and then…I don't remember much…except trying to get around that mess…and…it just happened so fast!"

Janet moved to the foot of the bed. "Roxie, just sit here beside Billy. We left the stands together, remember? Went to that office for a while, and then the men brought us over here. It'll all come back to you. You'll be okay, Billy's fine." Janet took the young woman's hand and considered asking the doctor to give Roxie a mild sedative. "Are you okay going along with Billy by yourself? I can go along if you want company."

"No, I'll be fine, but I should stay with him tonight. They might keep him, you know, just to be sure. Run some x-rays and stuff."

Even inside the medical building, Janet heard the track announcer. "Fans, we have a new race. Tom Lawton and C.J. Jones are our leaders now. Both have made their last stop so they are ready to race these last laps!"

"You sure you're okay, Roxie?"

"Billy needs company, Janet. Now, you better get back to the stands. Tom is doing well. I'll be okay."

"I'll call the hospital when the race is over so we can plan what we're going to do. It's all so…well, I'll call." Janet hugged Roxie, squeezed Billy's arm, and rushed out, back to the front stretch bleachers.

. . . . .

Miles away, near Muncie, Chuck Williams continued to linger in Ernie's kitchen long after finishing his lunch. He was drinking coffee and smoking his second cigarette. *Just two so far today. I'd like to quit them, but coffee and a smoke are so damn good together!* Ernie was at the sink, washing lunch dishes and all the baking paraphernalia from the rhubarb pie she'd made for supper. They had their radio tuned to WIBC in Indianapolis, listening to Sid Collins and his team of reporters describe the race.

Sid said, "We have action on the front straight! Three, no, four cars! One car flipped several times! Let's go to our reporter in the south pit!"

The reporter said, "Sid, I'll wait until we have positive identification of the cars involved. I can see that one is a yellow car!"

"Let's be sure, so we don't alarm any family and fans unnecessarily," Collins cautioned.

Ernie turned around, looked at Chuck, and said, "Yellow car? That could be Billy!"

"Right, and just like Billy to be in the middle of things, too. He was running third. Had a good race going." Chuck walked out the kitchen door and headed back to his shop. "Rather hear bad news by myself, Ernie."

· · · · ·

Janet worked her way back up the Tower Terrace stands, excusing herself as she sidestepped past spectators, many standing for the re-start. There was a subdued atmosphere in the stands, perhaps a recognition of the occasional, deadly violence that was a part of this sport. There were concerned glances and whispers. A few wives stopped Janet, asking what she knew. Her answers gave them visible relief. There were hugs and "Thank God" expressions, and Janet nodded, smiled, and returned to her seat. Some said, "Tom's looking good", others "That number thirty-three is leading now," or "He's right in there now!"

Tina leaned forward to her mother. "Shouldn't you stay with Roxie? I mean, she can't be alone, not now." There had been no official announcement yet about Billy, though the other three drivers were reported to be uninjured.

Missy laid a hand on Janet's arm. She didn't know what to say or how to even bring the subject up. Janet turned back to her right so Missy and Tina could hear. The cars, circling during the caution period, had passed by so there were a few minutes of relative quiet. "Billy was awake and talking."

"My God!" Missy started, paused, remembering where she was, and then continued in a near whisper, "after that? How can that be? No injuries, broken bones?"

Ray and James, sitting behind Janet and Missy, listened to the radio broadcast on transistor radios. "Nobody's sayin' anything on the radio about Billy, though. You sure about that, Jan?" Ray asked.

"Well, Billy's gonna have two big black eyes. His face is all bloody—well, was bloody. He must have hit his face hard on something, maybe the steering wheel. He was out for a while so they're taking him downtown to the hospital, just to check him out. They always worry about head injuries, you know, with unconsciousness. Just a precaution, the doctor said. Roxie's riding along. She may spend the night there. We'll have to go down there when the race is over."

Tina said, "Mom, that could have been—"

"It wasn't."

"Yeah, but—"

"It wasn't!"

· · · · ·

When the starter waved the green flag, C.J. accelerated past Tom, leading the field into turn one. C.J. was able to build a lead using the advantages of his rear engine car—superior cornering and a multi-speed gearbox. He quickly pulled out a six or seven car lead on Tom, who was slower to reach race speed. At the end of the long back stretch, Tom regained one car length, but as they raced through turns three and four, C.J. made up that distance and added more. As the pair started lap one hundred seventy, Tom's greater straightaway speed allowed him to shorten C.J.'s lead. But C.J. again negotiated the south turn faster, adding to his lead. The fans began to realize the inevitable: Tom was faster, but C.J.'s car handled the turns so well that Tom was steadily falling behind. An exciting and promising finish was steadily turning into a run-a-way, and fans sat down, though some were already picking up coolers and picnic baskets. Except the for red hat man, who gave the finger to C.J. every lap; and as soon as Tom appeared, he began jumping and waving his hat, urging Tom on.

* * * * *

Dutch stood on the pit wall as C.J. raced by on lap one hundred eighty-six. He watched and listened as the car went by. The crew chief in the adjoining pit looked quizzically at Dutch. Dutch shrugged his shoulders as if to say "I don't know."

As C.J. passed by to complete lap one hundred eighty-seven, Dutch was sure of what he'd heard. There was an obvious difference in the sound of C.J.'s engine. Dutch wrote a message for his pit board man to relay to Tom. As Tom sped by on his next lap his pit board read **"CJ TROUBLE! GO!"** Dutch's sixth man, the master of details, said, "C.J.'s lead is slipping, boss! I got him down to about ten seconds!"

Tom could see that C.J. was closer. About halfway down the back stretch, he thought he saw a puff of smoke from C.J.'s car. As he completed that lap, Tom's pit board read **"CJ 8 SECS."** CJ's car seemed okay on laps one hundred ninety through ninety-two, though Dutch's stopwatch man timed the gap at seven seconds. On lap one hundred ninety-three, Tom was exiting turn three as C.J. was entering four, and there was more smoke from C.J.'s car. Tom's pit board read **"CJ 6 SECS."** The situation on the track now had the full attention of the announcer, who said "Fans, we have a situation! Lawton is gaining and it looks like C.J. Jones may have trouble!" Red hat man was no drunken fool. He could see what was happening, and his enthusiasm matched the excitement of the moment. Those who had been preparing for an early departure stopped to watch the final laps.

By lap one hundred ninety-seven, a thin stream of blue smoke trailed C.J.'s car, and Tom had closed the gap to two seconds—roughly five hundred feet. Dutch's message to Tom on the pit board was simple: **"GO GO GO!"**

The flag man waved the white flag as C.J. and Tom completed lap one hundred ninety-nine. They had one lap to go, and Tom was nearly within one second of the leader. The fans were standing, shouting, waving. Tom thought just for a moment he could hear them, but was that possible? He knew he had one good shot at the lead. C.J.'s car may have been crippled, but it wasn't dead. The handling advantage he had in the turns was still there, but his speed wasn't. Tom figured his opportunity to pass was better now because C.J.'s straightaway speed was compromised even more. That one second lead was about one football field. Tom's car was still strong, as strong as it had been all day, but as they entered turn three for the last time, he still wasn't close enough to pass. But Tom could see the inevitable: he *could* eventually pass C.J., in three or four laps, at this rate of closing. He had the speed, C.J. didn't, and C.J.'s engine would not last much longer. *Too bad we don't have two more laps, even one more after this one. I'd win this!* But they only had one more turn and one more long straightaway.

As the two cars raced out of turn four, they had about a half mile to the finish line. Tom steered left to pass. C.J. could have swerved to block him, but he held to his own path, racing Tom fairly. Dutch and his crew stood on the pit wall. The fans were standing, waving, cameras clicking. The flag man had the checkered flag raised. The announcer was saying, "Here they are folks! Who…will…win?" Janet, Missy, Tina, James, and Ray were standing, looking north at the two cars, Tom to C.J.'s left and just feet behind. The cars were nearly side-by side, just dozens of feet from the starting line when C.J.'s engine erupted in a cloud of blue smoke. His car immediately slowed and Tom gained—but how much? Enough to get to the finish line first?

Tina was jumping. "Mom! Mom! Did Dad win?"

"What just happened, Janet? Did that car explode or what? Is that man alright?" Missy asked.

James looked at Ray. "H-O-L-Y crap! Who won? I dropped my darn radio!"

The public address announcer was stunned and silent for the first time today, perhaps for the first time ever.

Ray said, "Radio guy isn't sure, but his unofficial call is C.J. won by just a nose. The officials will make the call or look at the finish photo. No one's saying anything right now."

Tom knew. He could see it as the two cars crossed the one-yard-wide strip of bricks. C.J.'s front wheels were on the finish line when Tom's were about one foot back. *One more lap! That's all I needed! One damn lap! You don't get many chances like this. Everything was just clicking along. If I had…well, if I had…then another thing may have happened.*

· · · · ·

Tom Lawton sat grimy, exhausted, and emotionless in his car, his crew surrounding him. He'd slipped his goggles down but still had his helmet on. He had "reverse raccoon eyes"—his face was black except where his goggles had protected him. His open-face helmet had allowed a black coat of oil, rubber dust, and track grime to accumulate over the five hundred miles and three and a half hours. Dutch was the first person to Tom's side. He crouched at the open right side of the car and looked at Tom without saying a word. The fans in the stands to the left were cheering and shouting. The crowd behind the pit wall swelled as fans tried to get closer. Those across the track to the right were standing, many not sure of the outcome but cheering, nonetheless. They'd witnessed one of the most dramatic days ever at the old racetrack.

Tom couldn't hear well. Five hundred miles of his own unmuffled engine exhaust, just feet from his ears, deadened much that was said. He ached all over. The sudden cessation of noise, tension, intense concentration, and emotions left him unable to verbalize, so he just sat, hands on the wheel, staring straight ahead. Dutch finally took both of Tom's hands in his own, put them down on Tom's legs, and unbuckled his belts. Lou Turner stepped over the pit wall and stood on the left side of the car. "In my book, Tom, you are our 500 winner! I know what the announcer guy said. You're some kind of race car driver!"

"How's Billy?" Tom asked. He knew that Lou Turner had said something, but it didn't register, and it wasn't his primary concern. Tom tried to get out of the car but sat back and waved to anyone and everyone. The cheering resumed. He leaned his head back on the car's headrest and took a sip of the water someone handed him. One by one the crewmen shook his hand, clapped him on the back, or patted the top of his helmet, one brushing tears away with his sleeve. Crewmen in adjoining pits offered their congratulations. He simply smiled back in silence.

"But...how's Billy?" he repeated.

Dutch said, "About the time you made your last stop, they announced that Billy was awake and talking, and that they were taking him downtown for a check-up. He's one lucky boy, Tom."

"No kidding. Luck is usually in the car with that boy, thank God."

Then Dutch said, "What more could I have done, Tom? I don't think we could have given you better pitstops. If I could have given you three more feet somehow, you'd be up there in Victory Lane."

At last Tom rallied from his daze. "I'll stop you right there, Dutch. That has to be the most spectacular second place finish in history. So many things could have been just a little different. I could have passed one more car sometime, could have run a few laps a little faster, had a better first lap, qualified better and started closer to the front…but…this was a *damn* good day. Who can say they wouldn't be proud of what we did here today? You and Lou took on an old rookie. Maybe some other guy—a younger driver—would have given you that extra foot or so there at the finish line." Tom paused and raised his hands up as if to say 'Stop!' "I'll say it again, this was a damn good day! Now, how about you guys push me back to the garage? I don't have the strength to get outta this thing yet."

Dutch, the crewmen, and Lou Turner either pushed or walked beside the red car to the cheers of the crowd. Tom stayed in the car, smiling and waving, as he steered the car down pit lane, through the gap between the stands, and into Gasoline Alley.

· · · · ·

Sitting on the workbench in the garage and cleaning his face with a shop rag, Tom talked quietly with Lou Turner. Some crewmen wiped the car clean of race grime, while others spoke with fans in the crowd gathering in the lane between the two long garage buildings. Dutch stood in the middle of the two open doors where he'd strung a rope to mark the limits of his territory. After the race, Gasoline Alley was open to fans, and many walked from garage to garage, hoping to see drivers, and, if lucky, get an autograph. The garages of Carl Connors, Russ Stevens, and Billy Wallace were closed to discourage any morbid interest in rumpled race cars. The garage doors of C.J.'s winning car were closed. That car, its crew, owner, and C.J. himself were still at the south end of the front straightaway in Victory Lane. That disabled, oily car would soon be pushed in for fans to see. C.J. would be busy with his new duties: victory lap in the pace car (his now), interviews with reporters, and all the miscellaneous responsibilities that went with his transition from mere driver to 500 hero. His life was forever changed. Minutes ago, just a few inches made him the winner and Tom an "also ran", although one that will be forever remembered by true fans. If it had gone the other way, Tom would be that hero.

Tom slid off the bench and slowly shuffled toward the crowd of fans gathered at the open doors. Spontaneous applause rose from the knot of people waiting to get an autograph on their programs, shake hands with Tom, or just say "Nice job." His ears still rang, and he felt as if his body was vibrating and buzzing, an odd sensation he'd never had. But he had never raced five hundred miles in one sitting. This was no ten-minute sprint race. As he stood talking to a fan, he heard Dutch say, "You're Tom's wife? Guess we never met, Mrs. Lawton. Just call me Dutch, ma'am."

Tom looked to the back of the garage and there stood Janet, Tina, Missy, James, and Ray. Lou Turner had his back to Tom and was talking to the group. Tom struggled to attend to fans while catching snippets of the conversation in the back of the garage.

"Mrs. Lawton, this was the…"

"I left Billy's girlfriend to get back…"

"I talked to Olsen and he said…"

Then he heard Tina say, "Hey, Daddy, guess you're not a 'joppy' driver anymore!" Tom turned to see Tina waving and smiling. When she was very young, Janet had explained to the child that her father was busy many Sunday afternoons at the local dirt track driving jalopies. The young girl had turned that into 'joppy.'

"That's about the best thing I've heard today." Tom smiled, and turned back to the fans, and saw Donny Housman standing behind the rope.

"Tom, will you sign my program? I'll tell people from now on that Tom Lawton used to drive my car till he dang near won at Indianapolis!"

"Get in here, doofus! Why would I quit one of the best ever sprint cars?" Tom lifted the rope for his friend to enter the garage.

"I thought you were goin' to do it, Tom! So close, so close!"

"Yeah, I know. An hour from now, a day, a week, a month—it might all look different sometime. But, you know, we did what we could. If I look back at the day—we were one hundred percent in everything. If we had bad stops, I could say, 'We lost it in the pits" but it all went well. We have nothing to feel bad about, Donny. Nothing."

"I don't know how you can be so…so…I can't think of the right words, Tom."

"Like I said, an hour, a day, a week—I may think another way then. Hell of a day, Donny. Hell of a day."

· · · · ·

Eddie Spencer walked through Gasoline Alley, stopping at garages to speak with drivers and their teams. He knew that finishing this race was no mean achievement. He'd run one full "500" mile race here in 1926 and scored a ninth-place finish. These modern cars didn't have the most comfortable cockpits, but at least the track was smoother than the brick surface that Eddie had raced on. Ninth place today finished the race in about three hours and forty minutes compared to the nearly five and a half hours it had taken him to finish in ninth. He knew that any driver deserved recognition for what he'd done, even though fans tended to gather at the garages of the top few finishers. He stopped at any garage that was open, congratulating drivers or offering consolation for a less than satisfying result. They all deserved respect and recognition.

Eddie especially wanted to see Tom Lawton. He had a connection to Tom and to Billy Wallace. He'd known Tom for many years, some good and some not so good. He was happy for Tom's success this day and hopeful that it would continue the rest of the season and beyond. Eddie had played a role in Billy's advancement. Tom had introduced Eddie and Billy last year at a race at Winchester, Indiana, when Billy was sidelined with a broken arm. Eddie then showed Billy around the Speedway in May, introducing him to some owners and crew chiefs. It was Eddie who had told Cal Olsen about this young, talented newcomer. That led to a ride in one of Olsen's cars at Milwaukee, where Billy's performance had produced this more permanent ride as Olsen's number one driver. He figured that if anyone knew about Billy's condition, it would be Tom. They had been teammates on the sprint car circuit.

He worked his way through the crowd gathered at Lou Turner's garage. Tom was still behind the rope that held the fans back, chatting with admirers and signing autographs. His face was still grimy, and his uniform was oil and sweat-stained, but Tom was gracious and smiling, savoring the moment in spite of his fatigue.

"Thanks, Ma'am." "Here you go, son." "I appreciate that." "How should I sign this?" "Next week? Milwaukee? Not sure." "Sure, stand here. I ain't too presentable for a picture, but let's do it!" "I know, but them's the breaks." Eddie watched Tom and smiled. *He would be a hell of a man in Victory Lane! So damn close! How often does a guy get a chance like that? At his age how many more chances can there be?*

Tom noticed Eddie. "Speed Spencer! Come on in! You got the time so we can catch up?"

"I'm a retired old man. All I got is time!" Eddie ducked under the rope and walked to Tom's family and friends standing near the back of the garage. "Mrs. Lawton, I'm—"

"Call me Janet, Eddie. I remember you, and Tom talks about you a lot, anyway. Billy too."

"Sometimes I wonder who knows me anymore, with my age and all. Glad you remember, Ma'am, er, Janet. You know anything about Billy? Tom know?"

"I went with his girlfriend to the track hospital, so we got to see him. He was talking fine and was kind of bloodied up a little. Must have smacked his face on something. They took him downtown 'cause he was out for a while. Want to watch him for concussion. But…seems mostly okay."

"A lucky boy. I didn't see it, but I heard about it over my earphones. Sounded bad."

"Lucky is hardly the word for what we saw. You'll see what it looked like, if anybody got film."

"And I just heard a description of the finish. Couldn't see it from my position. I saw Tom come by but not C.J. From what they said though his engine blew, and he couldn't take his victory lap."

"Yeah, he crossed the finish line, engine up in smoke. Then Tom passed him and went on around, and C.J. just steered to the inside. It took a few minutes, but they declared him the winner, and his crew pushed him down to Victory Lane."

"You talked to him about any of this—Billy, that finish and all? What's he got to say?" Eddie asked.

"No, he's been busy with the fans for, I don't know, darn near forty minutes. They're so excited, and it looks like he's loving it. How can you drive like that, at that speed, for three and a half hours, and not be exhausted?"

"It must have been so close, Janet. Another ten inches or a foot and you'd all be over there in the winner's circle."

"I know, Eddie, I know."

"His life, and yours, too, would have changed forever, you know. And there's the money, too."

"Geez, I never thought about that!"

"Winner gets around a hundred thousand, and the usual split is forty percent to the driver. Second place…forty or forty-five thousand or so, I think…well, you do the math. Not as good as winning, but nothing to sneeze at."

"Money was the farthest thing from my mind, Eddie. Until just now, I swear," Janet got quiet and looked toward the open garage doors. Tom turned around, smiled and held up one finger as if to say, "Just a little more time here."

"Excuse me, Janet. I'd like to talk to Lou and Dutch for a minute." Eddie maneuvered the tight quarters of the garage, working his way to the car owner and crew chief and offering his hand to both. "Gentlemen, I've seen a lot of races here. I've seen some teams get a win snatched away from them in the last few laps, and I've seen others win a race they never expected to win. You guys have every right to be disappointed, but I don't see disappointment here. You guys, all of you, handled this like winners." Eddie, Dutch, and Lou then reviewed the day and all the "couldas" that may have changed the results.

A man with press credentials asked, "Tom, how about a picture? Could we get your wife in the photo, too?"

"Sure, if it's okay with her. Janet, you okay with a picture? Man wants both of us."

Janet stood beside Tom as they locked arms and smiled for the press photographer. It became a ready-made pose for fans who took advantage of the opportunity to add a photo to their souvenirs of a very dramatic day. There were many "Thanks, Tom," "One more," "Tom, Mrs. Lawton," and similar requests.

"Jan, hon, maybe the fans will start to thin out pretty soon and—"

"You just stay as long as you want to…or can. You must be exhausted, though."

"I ain't never seen fans like this. Makes that second place feel quite a bit better. But I think today maybe I should have driven a bit more with my foot rather than my head."

"Tom Lawton, you just keep driving the way you always told me." Janet smiled and squeezed her husband's arm. And then, more seriously, "Sure, you could have gone a bit faster on this lap or that lap, you could have passed one more car somewhere along the way, your pit crew could have given you a little faster pit stop. All or some of those things could have happened. And you know what? That may have put you right up there in Billy's wreck. Think about that! Now, stop second-guessing yourself and go back to these fans. Sign some autographs, buddy, while you can. Next year you might finish last! Who's gonna want your autograph then?"

"I can always count on you for a dose of reality, Jan!"

• • • • •

Ernie Williams paused in the doorway of Chuck's garage. Chuck leaned on the rollbar of his red car, his back to the doorway. The radio was still tuned to Sid Collins' race coverage. For the longest time, there was no radio chatter, just the sound of race cars as they passed the silent, open microphone, seemingly abandoned. The dead airtime seemed like hours. The lone sound of racing engines magnified the lack of commentary, which had been nearly non-stop for four hours.

"What happened? Does anybody there know what happened, Chuck?"

Chuck turned around. "I ain't never in my life ever heard of anything like that! What happened? I don't know, radio guys don't know, but they got to say something soon. Our guys, Ernie! First Billy and his event and then this with Tom!"

"I was listenin' in the kitchen, and then it all seemed to go crazy that last lap. Really, just that last straightaway. I guess Sid couldn't call it…it was too close."

"Shh! Sid's comin' back on the radio now. Listen."

At last, Sid Collins broke the radio silence. "Fans, we just now heard the track announcer declare C.J. Jones the winner of this year's 500 by mere inches over Tom Lawton in a finish that…that I have never seen and, speaking for the observers here in the master control tower, no one has seen."

"I shoulda been there, Ernie. I shoulda been there. Wouldn't change anything, but those are our guys. Could have shared in it all with them. I couldn't do a thing to help, but just bein' there, you know. Could have talked to them, just stood beside them before the race. Just another guy around helps sometimes, good or bad times. Especially a guy that has a connection with them."

Chapter 8

In recent years, the Milwaukee 100 had been scheduled to take place one week after the 500, and so was the first track to feature the "stars of the 500", which was how the promoters advertised the race, drawing on the publicity generated at Indianapolis. Many of the same drivers and cars would be entered for the one-hundred-mile race. The track was well-suited for those same cars because it was a paved mile track, though flat. Still, the advantages of a "roadster" style Indianapolis car made them first choice for owners and drivers. Indianapolis, Milwaukee, and Trenton were the only paved tracks that the United States Auto Club used for its Championship division. The remaining tracks on the circuit were all one-mile fairgrounds dirt tracks, where an Indianapolis "roadster" did not perform as well. On those one-mile tracks, a "dirt" car was much more suitable. Nevertheless, Cal Olsen entered his yellow number twenty-seven, dirt track car for the Milwaukee race. The car Billy Wallace had crashed at Indianapolis was what Cal preferred, but there was no way repairs could be completed in such short time. Billy had been released from the hospital on Tuesday following the 500 and though he was in no condition to race, thought otherwise. Cal Olsen had phoned him on Wednesday. "Billy you're not drivin' any of my cars for...a while, till you're okay. We'll see how long, but it won't be at Milwaukee. Ride along up there, okay. You can help out, but you're not gonna be in the car. Matter of fact, you can be an advisor for my driver. I think you know him—Tom Lawton."

"Tom Lawton! Can't be the Watson car. You're puttin' him in the Kuzma, the dirt car?"

"Sure. It worked good for you there last year. Lawton's good. He'll be subbing for you."

Billy thought about the situation. *Lawton subbing for me again after an injury. Again! This is gettin' a bit strange. Well, Lawton's been good to me, maybe this will help him. Maybe Roxie would like to go along.*

* * * * *

Billy called Roxie Lytell on Wednesday. "Roxie! It's Billy. How you doin'? Get rested up from the big weekend? Guess it was quite a weekend, huh?"

"I haven't been home long. I worked late, just tryin' to catch up. Staying at the hospital Sunday and Monday was…well, if you weren't the new hot shot at Indianapolis and famous…I'll just say that you being Billy Wallace excuses some things for me. Coming back to work Tuesday got me back on the good side of my boss, even if I was late. He wanted to know all about the race and how you are."

"So, can we expect you to get out of the office on Friday? Or could that be a problem?"

"A problem I don't want to cause, Billy. Why?"

"The Milwaukee race—you remember that from last year, don't you? That's the next race. We could go Friday. Take the afternoon off."

"I can't do that, Billy. I've been missing too much work lately, and I stayed with you in Indianapolis. And…I need the money."

"That's okay. I got plenty of money now. They scored me

in eighteenth place. My share of the winnings was twenty-two hundred bucks! You believe that? We can drive up Saturday, early. I'll come up to Muncie Saturday morning. Or, better still, I'll drive up Friday afternoon and stay at your place."

"I just can't go. We got a family thing this weekend. I better go to that. I'm sorry."

"Damn, that's too bad. And we had so much fun, too. You sure you can't work out something? Maybe we can…can try another time, okay?"

Roxie's response was not enthusiastic. "Yeah, I…hope so."

* * * * *

Tom and Billy rode with Cal Olsen's mechanic, Willy Caldwell, to Milwaukee on Saturday. One day, one long drive, and three men who had only one thing in common—racing. After two hours discussing the current state of the sport, the conversation stalled. Caldwell was an overworked crew chief, not one that could be called optimistic, and an easily frustrated man. So far in this season, he had come back from New Jersey with three damaged cars, and the wreck at Indianapolis had undone the repairs that he'd performed on Olsen's Watson. Getting that car back in competitive condition would not be as easy this time. The frame was bent, the front axle needed replacement, and there was a lot of bent and broken body work. At least now the nose and tail sections were molded fiberglass. Those could be bought new and wouldn't have to be hammered and smoothed out as in the past, when sheet aluminum was the favored material, a job requiring the services of talented craftsmen.

The wrecked Watson chassis was back in Olsen's shop in Indianapolis. On Sunday, Tom would drive Olsen's dirt track car, number twenty-seven, the one Billy had driven to tenth place in last year's two- hundred-mile race. It was a car most suited to dirt tracks but was still competitive on Milwaukee's pavement. As recently as four years ago, a similar car had won at Milwaukee. But the handwriting was on the wall. Such a car's days were numbered on a paved track—the Indy-style roadster was superior, and owners were buying those. Thus far, the season had been costly for Cal Olsen. His dirt-track car was ready to go, so he decided to enter that car. At least he might recover a few of his expenses.

When conversation in the car lagged and died into awkward silence, Tom tried to offer up a few topics. Fishing was a non-starter. Caldwell said, "That sport has the wrong name. Why not call it waitin'? It ain't fishin' for me 'cause all I ever do is the waitin' part with no catchin'!" Billy didn't say anything. Then Tom tried music. Billy said, "I like them Beach Boy guys. I can't dance, but I like to watch girls dance to those songs." Caldwell snickered and said, "For me, if it don't come from south of the Ohio River, it ain't music!" Tom gave up, leaned his head back, and pretended to sleep.

In the front seat, Caldwell and Billy eventually found a mutual interest as they drove through Fort Wayne. Billy saw a cute girl in short shorts on a street corner and said, "Oh my lord, Caldwell, would you look at that!" Billy whistled loudly and hung out of the car waving.

Caldwell did as directed and outdid Billy. He blew the horn, stuck his head out of the window, looked up, and howled like a wolf baying at the moon. That was just the start. Front seat discussion in the car went downhill from there, as the libidinous young man and the leering, middle-aged man vied for the most outrageous comments on any woman or teenage girl that had the misfortune to fall into their sights. Tom slinked down in the back seat, trying to avoid public association with his companions. They were funny, but he could only think to himself, *You've got a young daughter at home, about the same age as those girls!*

· · · · ·

On Sunday, Tom qualified with a time of 34.801, putting him in seventh place in the field of twenty-two cars. That was better than Billy's performance last year. There was only one other dirt car in the race, and it started in twentieth place in the field of twenty-two cars. That car was a rarity. Its owner/mechanic had installed a Chevy V8, a common engine to use in a sprint car, but the Offenhauser—Meyer-Drake—still dominated the longer, mile tracks and Indianapolis. The engine was proving successful in the short, brief sprint races, often lasting just ten or twelve minutes. In a few rare hundred lap races on half-mile tracks the stock-based engine performed well. But one hundred-mile races on a mile track lasted right at one hour. Many thought the Offy had proved its rugged durability, though C.J.'s win at Indianapolis had many thinking.

Tom's starting spot put him on the inside of the first turn as the race started. The driver beside him steered to the outside and out of the groove as they drove into that turn. The field was still bunched up, jockeying and bumping through much of the first lap.

He moved into sixth place on lap three, a position he held until lap thirty. Tom advanced to fifth place, slipping by a car that had bumped another and was forced to slow down momentarily. The third-place car spun and hit the turn one wall on lap forty-two, causing a nine-lap caution period. That misfortune put Tom in fourth, his highest place of the day. Carl Connors, forced to start near the end of the starting order, passed Tom as he made a desperate drive to the front of the pack. Then on lap ninety, Tom made his own push to the front. That effort was too aggressive and too late. It was enough to expose the wear marks on his right front tire, forcing Tom to slow down to save it, allowing a competitor to pass.

Cal Olsen was the first to greet Tom when he pulled into his pit. "Good job today, Tom!"

"Thanks. This is a good car. I think Billy will do well with it."

"You're right. It's Billy's car and he'll be in it on the miles. But remember, we took two cars for the Trenton race this spring. There's another race there. If we take two cars, you want to drive this one? And don't forget, there's a two-hundred-mile race here later this summer."

"Unless Lou Turner wants to run his car, sure. I'm not sure how committed Lou is to run all the pavement races. He picks and chooses, somehow. I don't know why he does that. He wasn't at Trenton in April. And for some reason he didn't want to run here. That's a *fine* car. He doesn't have a dirt car, so I'm lookin' for a ride for the miles."

"I don't see a problem there. Lots of guys would like to have you drive their cars. I'd be one of those, but Billy's my guy. Unless he gets banged up again! Ha! You know Billy! Oh, Tom, here's your pay." Cal handed Tom a wad of cash.

* * * * *

"Do you mean Daddy will be gone *every weekend*, all summer? I thought he'd come along to watch some of my shows!" Tina stood in the kitchen of the Lawton home, her hands on her hips. Her mother was dressed for work and about to leave. It was the Monday after the Milwaukee "100" Championship race.

"Dad's second place finish in the 500 earned him money *and* points that, with a good season, could give him the championship and the bonus money that comes with it. He has a good start to build on. His reputation has gone up considerably in the minds of car owners. He's at an important place in his career now, Sweetie. I'm sorry, but yes, he'll be gone almost every weekend now through September. And probably some week nights, too."

"Where is he now?"

"He got home really late last night, or this morning. Still sleeping."

"How did he do?"

"He ran as well as he could, finished in sixth place. He said the points will keep him in the running. Better than not racing at all, he said." And he said the money was good. Sixth place paid about fifteen hundred and his share was over five hundred."

"What about that lucky C.J. guy?"

"His winning car didn't get repaired…well it did, but not good enough. Dad said C.J. parked it in morning warm-ups. Then he talked his way into another car and finished fourth. So, he stretched out his points lead on Dad."

"I'm going out to the barn and wait for Mr. Carlson. He's supposed to take me and two other kids for our driver training hours today. Oh, Gloria Anderson called Saturday and said the Putnam County Fair is weekend after next. She thinks I should enter that one, okay?"

"Sounds good. I'll go along." Janet knew there was a conflict with Tom's schedule. That was the weekend of the rain date for the New Bremen race in May. *I can't be in two places at the same time. But this time I'll go with Tina. I'd like to say I'll enjoy it…and I will…but my thoughts will be miles away. It's always better to be with Tom, at the race. Distance always preys on my imagination. Images of what could happen are hard to erase. My mind has a mind of its own.*

* * * * *

Mid-week, Wednesday, after the Milwaukee 100, Roger Hicks called the Lawton home asking for Tom. Janet took the call. "Janet, so good to hear your voice. This is Roger. Is Tom home?"

"No, I'm sorry, but Tom drove over to Muncie this morning. He wanted to talk to Chuck Williams and Donny Housman, race-car guys, you know. Is there anything I can help with?"

"I wonder if Tom could stop in the office tomorrow sometime. I'm in all day. Let's just leave it like this: if he can come in, that would be great, but if that doesn't work, ask him to call when he gets back. He can call me at home, but I'd really like to talk to him here."

"Is there a problem, Roger?"

"No, Jan, nothing like that. I just have a few ideas, okay?"

"I'll let him know."

* * * * *

On Thursday, Tom entered the new office building of the Maxcell Corporation just outside the city limits of Barton, Ohio. The receptionist called Roger's office, "Tom Lawton is here, Mr. Hicks…Okay. Mr. Hicks will see you now, Mr. Lawton." The secretary rose from her chair and led Tom to Roger's office. She smiled and said apologetically, "Uh…uh, my son is a big fan and the race this year…well, I wondered if I might…"

"He'd like an autograph, I'll bet. This is a new thing for me, miss. I'd be happy to do that! When I leave, okay?" Tom was still surprised at his new notoriety, and still pleased. "Thank you."

From behind his desk, Roger Hicks said, "Tom! Have a seat! I, well, *everyone* in town, is so proud of you. Little old Barton, Ohio, has a big-time race driver now!"

"Oh, thanks, Roger. But that was just one race, you know."

"Still, just a few inches the other way, and we'd be proud to call our Tom Lawton an Indianapolis winner! Just a few inches!"

"You know I was very lucky. Lucky that one owner loaned me his car for my rookie test. Lucky that another owner took a chance on me. Lucky to get in the race as a rookie. Lucky to have a great mechanic and crew. Lucky…well I could go on. You get the idea."

"Yeah, but it takes more than luck. And you got that. Skill, Tom! How many men can do what you do? Huh?"

"It's all kind of routine after a while, like a lot of jobs."

"Routine? At what, a hundred and seventy miles an hour? That doesn't seem routine to me, Tom. That finish sure wasn't routine! I never heard of anything like that! What was that like, driving down to that checkered flag, seeing that you could win and then almost…almost. You came up short by two feet? That was so damn close!"

"It was even closer than that, Roger. I'd say it was more like a few inches, but I knew as soon as we crossed the line. C.J. was there, like I said, a few inches before me. Yeah, I knew. But I was thinking almost as much about Billy Wallace."

"The big wreck there on the front stretch?"

"I saw it all, Roger! I drove right by him when he was flipping. Must have been fifteen feet up in the air."

"But he was okay. They told you that on one of your stops. So, you knew he was okay."

"No, there's no time for chat during a stop. Anyway, there's the noise of your engine, other cars going by, and the helmet makes communication difficult. I drove another forty laps or so thinking he could be dead. So, Billy was on my mind. That boy and I…we've had…several career connections over the past year or so, Roger. I've been told not to make friends with other drivers, but that kid, I can't help but think of him as a friend."

"I never heard of Billy Wallace much. He going to be good, you think?"

"If he catches some breaks. Well, he's gotten a lot of lucky breaks, but I sure hope he doesn't get…doesn't get his career seriously sidetracked by *misfortune—that* may be the polite way to say what I mean."

Roger leaned back in his chair and folded his hands. "Well,

Tom, the reason I called is sort of related. Janet answered the phone the other day and said you'd gone over to Muncie. It was so nice to hear her. It's a shame we don't get together more often. Suzy would like that. We should all go out—dinner or movie, something. Just like old school friends again!"

"That'd be fun, Roger."

"Back to what I was saying before about careers and luck. For you, or any driver, a career lasts how many years? What comes after you retire? You'll have a number of years to work. Would you like to come back here to Maxcell? I don't mean after you retire, I mean now."

"That'd be a problem. Racing is why you had to let me go back in May. The schedule makes a job very questionable May through October, and even after, in November."

"We could work something out, I'm sure."

"I think it may even get a little worse. Some promoters pay me just to show up at a race now with the Indianapolis thing and all."

Roger narrowed his eyes. "We can be flexible. Some weeks you could work four, maybe five days. Other weeks just two or three days. How about that? It would be good for you—a steadier income. *And*, good for us here at Maxcell, too."

"I got good money for that second-place finish. Money that makes up for losing my gas station. And that Milwaukee race paid well, too."

"You sure, Tom? We can be, as I said, *flexible*."

"Thanks, Roger, but I have to say, 'No'. I think I can make racing my job now. I've got a good car and probably even more offers. No, but this means a lot to me."

Roger stood, extended his right hand, and said, "Think it over, Tom. Keep an open mind, okay?" The men shook hands and smiled. Tom turned when Roger repeated, "Just think it over, Tom."

Tom waved back to Roger as he left the office, then stopped at the secretary's desk. "Now, ma'am, about that autograph."

* * * * *

In the early evening hours of that same Thursday, Chuck Williams and Donny Housman worked preparing their cars for the race on Sunday at New Bremen, the make-up day for the May rainout. Donny hoped that they could duplicate their experience in hot laps that day when the track, car, and driver had been "right on the money." Part of him worried it had been a rare combination of those three elements, something not easily reproduced.

"Donny, what gear you gonna run at New Bremen? You looked at the book yet? You ain't lost that book, have you?" Chuck Williams leaned over the engine in his number twenty-two sprint car and groaned. "This isn't the best position to work in, gets to an old man's back!"

"I looked at it back in May when we got rained out there. Tom ran like a scalded cat in hot laps, you know. Anyway, this is what you wrote in your book: 'gear set number 9, 4.97 gear.' We talked about it, I remember."

"Yeah, go ahead and tell me what we talked about. What do you remember about last year?" Chuck watched Donny change spark plugs on Tom's car.

"Well, I remember that we were changing the car after the Eldora race. Billy finished that race in eighth, after he started way back. That was his first race back, after his broken arm. He was sorta spooked till you and Tom tinkered with his head, got some of the old Billy back." Donny chuckled and smiled.

"Yeah, that tire thing was an old trick. I've used that kind of thing before. Sometimes a driver thinks *he* knows it all, and I know damn well what works better at a certain track. One time—I forget who my driver was that day—he came in after hot laps and told me that the left rear torsion bar was all wrong, needed a stiffer one on that corner. So, I said, 'Okay, I'll get right on it.' Went back to the trailer and got another bar. But I told my helper—this was before you, Donny—to somehow take that driver away. Take him to check out a new car with you, or kids that wanted autographs…tell him a pretty girl wanted talk to him—anything, just get him away for a few minutes. So, while they're gone, I make like I'm changing that torsion bar, but I ain't changing anything. He came back and I told him, 'She's ready to go!' He went out and ran second in the feature and said it handled like a dream. Said whatever I changed was just the right thing." Chuck closed the hood on his car and smiled.

"But Donny, when Tom talks, I listen. I never did that kinda thing with Tom. Never! And I'd advise you to do the same. Well, back to the gears. That set was good last year, that 4.97 works well at a lot of tracks, except for ones with tighter corners. I think that Bremen race came right after…Eldora? Is that what you said? Anyway, New Bremen and Eldora are pretty much alike, you know, except Eldora's got them high banks. Driver can carry a lot of speed there, so I usually run that 4.97 gear or 5.04 sometimes, depending on conditions. Both seem to work there."

"I'll take both boxes of gear sets. One for your car, one for mine. Tonight, though, I'll put in the same gear you ran last year, which, you'll be interested to know, is what I ran there in May, that 4.97. But I'd like to know what your thinking is about how Eldora and Bremen are different, Chuck."

"Like I said, Eldora's got them higher banks. That's the main thing. It's a faster track, so engine speed is up and can be kept up. The 4.97 gear is a higher gear, getting' a *little* closer to something like a top gear in a car. But New Bremen is a bit flatter, and a driver has to back off more for the turns. Otherwise, those two tracks are alike. If you ever had an airplane ride and overhead view of them, you'd see. They'd look much the same: long sweeping turns and short straightaways that are even bent a little. That's why some guys say Bremen is a 'Little Langhorne,' closer to a big circle."

Donny said, "Well, changing gears doesn't take too much time. If the track is a little different, we can do that in a few minutes. Your book also said the track was dry and slick after twenty laps in the feature."

"Billy ran well, if I remember right."

"Book said, 'Fourth in feature.'"

"You gotta keep in mind, if it's hard and slick again, you sure as hell don't want a gear that's too low. Driver'll get on the power and sometimes the back wheels will just spin, tires can't get a grip. He'll have to watch so it doesn't get away from him. That higher gear won't respond as quick. Sometimes you can run faster with a bit slower engine speed. That's odd, ain't it? But true!"

"So…what are your thoughts about a dry slick track at New Bremen?"

"Make sure you take some higher gears, like 4.93, 4.85. Anyway, what else you gonna do?

"It's still set up for our last race at Winchester. I stiffened up the front end with a half wrap spring on the right front and ran that right front wheel reversed, like I ran at Salem last month. I have to change those two things. What you got to do yet? I can help, Chuck"

"I'm going to unhook the shocks on each corner and put the car on my scales so I can get an accurate weight on each corner of the car. That'll take away some of the guess work. Lifting on each corner is okay, but this way I'll know more exactly how many pounds I got on each wheel."

Chuck jacked up the front of his car, wheeled a farm scale under each tire, and let the car settle on the scales. He went to the rear of the car and did the same, settling the rear wheels on two more scales. Then he took out his notebook that had a large X on the page labelled "New Bremen" and the date for the race. At the top left point of the X, he wrote LF; then at the top right point, he wrote RF. At the bottom of the right point of the X, he wrote RR, and to the left at the last corner, he wrote LR.

"Okay, Donny, what do the scales read?"

"Left front: three hundred fifty-five. Right front: three hundred seventy-five." Donny walked to the back of the car. "Right rear: four hundred eighty-eight. Left rear: five hundred fifty. Damn, Chuck! That's slick! Takes out the guess work."

"Yes, in-deedy, boy. Of course, there's just a few gallons of fuel in and no driver, so that'll add weight to the rear end. But my plan is to do this here, with the same amount of fuel, before each race. Maybe put some weights of some kind in the seat, like a driver was sittin' in it. Set that as the place to start, and always measure from that."

"Anybody else doing this?"

"Some guys at Indianapolis do, of course, that's a bigger ball game. But sprint car guys? I don't really know."

Donny said, "This will add a few things to your new testament. Your set-up book for the new car. I wonder what your scales would tell us about number eleven here."

"Wanna try it?" Chuck asked.

"Dowty's mechanic told me to put a jack under the center of the rear axle—on the pumpkin—and raise it up. The left rear wheel shouldn't go up as high as the right. How far that left droops gives you an idea about how much weight you got on it."

"I used to do that, Donny, and it worked okay. But after a while I just knew what to do. This new car…well, I'm gonna use my scales till I get to know the car better."

"Maybe someday, but I'll stick with your book, Chuck, for now, at least. Let me learn my way around this car the old way. Then maybe I'll try your scales next year. Car's workin' good now, so…" Donny shrugged his shoulders. "What did Connors say about your car on Sunday? He must have felt comfortable, finishing second. That's good for a new car, one that you're still trying to sort out."

"Connors is…good, but he says a lot about what he thinks the car needs. He'll come in after a few laps and tell me maybe it has the wrong tires, or he'll want to change gears, or something else. I could use less of that laundry list now. I like to solve one problem at a time instead of changing two or three things. We're still learning, Donny. I worked with number eleven there so long. I had that thing all figured out. But a new car and a new suspension, for me at least, will take some refining. Second place is good, you're right, and I don't want to be complaining. How about you and Tom? You got them problems worked out?"

"Tom was fine with the car, said it was good till it wasn't. He qualified fastest and would have won his heat race, but then, you know, engine started missing. Magneto went bad. At Indy, that's a common thing, or at least that's where they like to lay the blame. But in these short races? On a good race day, that engine runs maybe seventeen, eighteen minutes or so, if everything goes just right, or thirty minutes if it doesn't. The magneto isn't our most common problem. I thought I had a fix on it, but Tom ran one lap in the consolation race and dropped out. That was the end of *our* day. I'm puttin' in a new Vertex mag tonight. But you—good day for both of you, running second, and of course, Billy has to be happy the way Olsen's car ran."

"Billy did have the field covered though, didn't he? That was a good comeback for the kid, and Caldwell musta been happy, considering he's been fixing Olsen's busted-up cars since early May."

Donny smiled and said, "Here's my way of thinking about it: If Tom can't win in my car, then Connors in your car should win, Chuck. If neither of our guys win, then Billy should. I still think of him as one of our guys, you know. And crap, you put that car back together for Olsen after Smitty's wreck at Dayton! So, is that your car, too?"

"Kind of a complicated family, isn't it?"

* * * * *

Soon after lunch on Thursday Tom had gotten a call. An owner asked him to drive his midget race car at Anderson, Indiana. Tom had agreed, somewhat reluctantly. He knew he'd make some money, though not a great deal, and there was no assurance of "appearance money" with the promoter. Some of the luster of his near win at Indianapolis was dimming. The farther he got away from that event…well…it was just second place. "It's a chance to keep my name out there," he'd told Janet. "It's fairly close, so I'll get home at a decent hour."

"I can't go along, Tom. I've got to work Friday, and I know we wouldn't get home till…midnight, or later."

"Sure, I know, that's okay."

"I'd always rather come along, but I'll sit this one out, hon."

"I know, I know. Take Tina out to drive. She still needs practice. We'll catch up then in the morning."

* * * * *

Janet woke with a start and looked at the clock radio beside the bed. It read 1:30 A.M. and Tom's side of the bed was neat and unslept in. *This hour and he's not home? What's going on?*

She passed Tina's room, looked in and saw that she was asleep. From the top of the stairs, she could see that the kitchen light was on. The house was silent: no radio, no TV. She found Tom sitting at the kitchen table, still in his driving uniform, smoking a cigarette, an empty beer bottle on the table and a bottle of whiskey beside it. His uniform was oil-spattered and sweat-stained.

"Tom? You coming to bed? It's late. You been home long?"

"Got home about, oh, it must have been a little after midnight."

"You okay? Not hurt or anything are you?" She knew that was an unnecessary question. There were no signs of injury. "But you…you…got something on your mind, don't you?"

"Jan, a guy who does this stuff knows. He knows what can happen. But I have a hard time with it. We can't say 'That's racing' and go on every time. It's getting harder to make that excuse."

"What happened, Tom? Billy?"

"Shoot, no. Billy smoked everybody tonight. Some new kid, though." Tom refreshed his ice and poured another drink.

"Who? What happened?"

"I never saw this kid before. They told me he was just driving stock cars a little last year and thought he was ready to try open wheel cars. He found some owner who was willing to give him a chance."

"Who was it?"

"That makes it even worse. I can't remember his name… except for his first name—Jackie. It'll be in the newspaper, sure, but…Jackie…something. I was lined up to start, third in the feature, right behind Billy. He started on the pole. I was standing beside my car, Billy was already belted in, and I was getting ready to climb in. Then this kid—I tell you he looked like James, that young and skinny—ran up and said, 'Tom Lawton! Let me shake your hand! My name's Jackie.' Then the announcer said some stuff and I didn't get his last name. 'I just wanted to say that I wanted you to win the "500" so much. I was listening to the race on the radio, and I was jumpin' and yellin' so hard for you to catch that guy those last few laps!' And then one of his guys—mechanic or owner—came up and told him to hurry back to his car. He said, 'Good luck tonight, Tom! Gotta go!' Then he shook my hand again. I hardly had time to say anything. I think I said 'Thanks' but he was gone. I didn't even say 'Good luck.'"

"Yeah?" Janet sat down at the table, knowing the story wasn't over. "And what happened?"

"Well, this Jackie started way in the back, last row or somewhere. I followed Billy at the start and got into turn one right behind him, passed the guy who started second, and held that spot for the first lap. Billy took off like a rocket, and I knew damn well nobody would touch him, unless he blistered a tire or wrecked—it's Billy, you know."

"Yeah…Billy."

"Anyway. We came around to finish the second lap, and all the track lights went yellow, and almost immediately went red. Billy slows to a crawl, way down on the inside of the track, and I follow him, and the whole field creeps along, too. We came out of turn two and there were two cars tangled up against the outside wall. One car was upright and the other is sorta tipped on its side, left-side wheels up in the air, and the cockpit is right up against the crash wall. I saw the cars, but, you know, I don't know those guys as much."

Janet got up, went to the refrigerator, and poured some milk to make hot chocolate. "You want some hot cocoa? It'll help you sleep, Tom." She stood behind him and put her arms around him.

"Not on top of this." Tom motioned toward his drink.

"I guess there's more to tell, though, right?" She cradled his head against her chest.

"Yeah. So, the whole field stopped on the front stretch, and the ambulance crew went out there to the wreck, red lights flashin' and all. Some drivers never got out of their cars, sat there with crews standing around. I got out and talked to Billy a little. He said, 'That new kid—Mitchell kid, huh?' That's it, Janet, Jackie Mitchell. I talked to Billy a while and then went back and got in my car. Once in a while, you get a feeling, just by the look of things when that happens, and how the emergency crew works, and how long it takes for them to… well, do their job. The other driver was okay, and he walked back to the pits with his owner while they loaded his car on the trailer. After, I can't say for sure…twenty-five, thirty-five minutes or so…the ambulance drove away. There was no siren, although the red light was flashing. It was all real quiet. Odd, sad or…not sure what more to say."

"And…"

"And we finished the race. Billy ran away from everybody. I lost sight of him, even though I ran second for most of the race. I expected he'd come around and lap me. I blistered a tire and had to back off, so I wound up third. When I settled up with the car owner, I asked about the kid. All he said was, 'It ain't good, Tom. As far from good as you can get' is the way he put it. He's a friend of the kid's car owner."

"No wonder…you…why you're awake." She didn't know where to go with the conversation. She knew her husband's thinking well enough, knew the conflict he lived with but seldom spoke about. She also realized she couldn't push him away from doing what he loved, as she couldn't walk away from him.

* * * * *

On a Sunday, Janet sat in the bleachers of the equestrian arena at the Putnam County Fair. Just minutes ago, she'd left Tina and her horse in the ready ring. She'd hugged her daughter and said, "You know this routine today and so does your horse. How lucky can you be? It's one you spent so much time on."

Tina smiled tensely and nodded, "Thanks, Mom."

Janet sat waiting, hands clasped tightly in her lap, as the first horse and "rider" were called. Rider was a misnomer in this event because the handler, probably a more accurate description than rider since there was no riding, led his or her horse through prescribed maneuvers.

She knew there was nothing she could do; it was all up to her daughter. The little that Janet knew about this event, and horses in general, was what she'd learned by helping Tina and listening to Gloria Anderson, the trainer that had taught Tina so much. Janet's help was more that of an educated fan. Now she understood more of what her mother had experienced when Janet's older brother had played high school sports. When young herself, there were a few times that she'd sat with her parents instead of sitting in the student section with friends. Her mother usually seemed tense and uneasy. She calculated the minutes of playing time in her mind. She kept track of less than perfect passes, missed shots, fouls. All those negatives loomed so large in her mind. Why? Back then, Janet had no way of knowing how challenging it had been for her mother.

Now, Janet understood that, like her own mother, there was nothing she could do. Her child was out there alone, in the arena, on her own, and there was absolutely *nothing* she could do to help. It was all up to her daughter to perform. Sure, the judges and audience understood these were young people and judged them accordingly, but her daughter would judge herself more harshly than anyone, and Janet would have to deal with those emotions. Her daughter, now sixteen, had somehow endured and survived challenges in the past. Janet remembered her learning to walk, though later than most children. Conquering that milestone had been complicated by her cerebral palsy, but she'd done it and probably hadn't found it as traumatic as her mother had. Then, when she tried to run with other children, she would always fall far behind. "Mommy, how can they run so fast?" Tina would ask. Answering without tears was a skill that Janet had learned to master.

The announcer said, "Next, we have Tina Lawton and Candy."

Tina led her horse from the gate to the first cone. She walked with the normal, slight "hitch in her get-a-long", as Gloria had said last year. Tom's share of the payoffs in recent races had helped to equip Tina in a new western style outfit. The rules were specific and occasionally odd. Long-sleeve shirt? Perhaps suitable in March, but in the summer? The shirt must have a collar. The "rider" must wear a bolo tie or a kerchief about the neck. Boots and hat—yes, that's understandable. And then there were expectations for the horse: manners, cleanliness, behavior. The horses tack—lead and halter—had to fit, be clean, and presentable. And the horse had to obey the handler's commands.

Tina and Candy paused for a few seconds at the first cone. Janet thought *That's too long*. They trotted to the second cone and made a right-hand turn. *That seemed okay. Did Tina look like she was pulling Candy? Oh, jeez!* Then Tina "clicked" with her tongue, and her horse smoothly accelerated to an extended canter and advanced to a third cone and another right-hand turn, where they slowed to a walk again. *Doing okay now,* Janet thought, gripping the hard, wooden bleacher seat. Tina and Candy advanced at a walk to the last cone where the judge stood waiting with her clipboard.

Horse and "rider" stopped at the judge where the horse was to "square up" with legs placed neatly in pairs, not staggered. Tina stood to the left of Candy's head. The judge, on the right, made notations. Candy was an attractive and well-proportioned animal, but those were not today's criteria. Tina was to demonstrate to the judge that she and her horse knew what to do, and that Tina had control of her horse.

The judge moved to the right rear flank of the horse, and Tina, still holding the lead, moved to the right side of Candy's head; she was not to allow the horse to be between her and the judge. After making a few notes, the judge walked by the left side of the horse, and Tina moved back to the left side of Candy's head. The judge then flipped the horse's mane to the right side. Candy didn't move a muscle. *Good!* Tina then "fixed the mane", moving it to its original position.

The judge spoke to Tina, and Tina applied slight pressure to the animal's halter; Candy backed up two paces. Janet said to herself *So far so good.* When Candy stopped, though, her feet were no longer perfectly "squared up" as necessary. *Oh shoot, horse!* Tina directed Candy to square up, a command the horse did not always respond to. But the horse obeyed. *She did it! She did it!*

Next, Tina nodded to the judge and turned Candy clockwise in a circle, pivoting on her right rear hoof. *But that was good, maybe the transition from backing to turning was so brief that...that...the judge won't notice? Fat chance!*

Candy came back to her original position and stood motionless, as did Tina, waiting to be dismissed. The final part seemed to last for hours, as horse and rider stood in the hot sun. *Tina, you had to have that black and turquoise outfit. Wish you had something cooler now? I tried to tell you!*

At last, the judged dismissed Tina and Candy to the area in front of the bleachers where they were to wait patiently for the other contestants to finish. *Going second is good, but that means waiting until the next six horses are finished. How will they handle that, in this heat?*

Her daughter's pattern work over, Janet relaxed for nearly half an hour, as she watched the other competitors in the sixteen and over category. Janet had a direct, across-the-arena view of Tina and her horse. Once, she thought she made eye contact with Tina, but if so, there could be no acknowledgement. Rider and horse were to stay in position, waiting patiently and silently, not communicating with fellow contestants or crowd. One horse was fidgety and tried its rider's patience and control, stamping its fore feet and snorting. Janet was thankful the horse wasn't beside Candy. In spite of liberal application of fly repellant, some of the pests were not deterred. Every horse had to contend with flies, stamping, shaking its head, and swishing its tail. *Just how long will this take?* Janet wondered. After what seemed like hours, but in truth was perhaps thirty minutes, the results were ready.

"All right, folks, we have the results now for the sixteen and up Western Showmanship competition. Handlers, when your name and place are called, move to the center of the arena, pause for the photographer, then exit by the far-left gate. All right. In eighth place we have Mandy Wilson and Tiger." The audience applauded as rider and horse advanced, then stopped for photos. *At least we're not eighth of eight!*

"Next, in seventh place, we have Ann Carter and Jewel." *Ok, one better. A little better.* The announcer advanced through fourth place, and Tina had not been called. "Third place is Amy Jackson and Nelly." *Oh my God! Second, or first! And Tom's not here!*

The two remaining riders and horses stood motionless. Demonstrations of emotion were discouraged. Competitors were to be restrained in their reactions, all part of the protocol, though riders and family found it difficult to exercise that restraint. Janet's hands were clasped so tightly they were drained of color.

"Second place today is Carla McCoy and Solo." *Oh, oh, oh. Tina!* Janet shook and sobbed in joy and relief. *Can't I run to her and hug her now?*

"And today's champions are Tina Lawton and Candy! Thank you all, contestants and fans. We'd like for the first, second, and third places to return to the center of the arena for one last photo." Janet beamed, wishing that her husband could have seen this.

An hour later, Janet and Tina were halfway home, chatting and reviewing the events of the day: competitors and their horses, funny things that happened, and their own personal observations. It was an unusually hot day—low nineties—for late June, and the open windows of the truck provided plenty of ventilation, though the air was hot.

"I'll bet you're worn out, Tina."

"I feel fine, Mom, I really do. In spite of this being my first show, I'm okay. Relieved, but I feel okay. *You* look tired, though."

"I just sat and watched, so why would I be tired? I'm not saying you had it easier. Never would I suggest that. But watching is hard. All you can do…is well, *watch*."

"Seems easy to me, Mom."

"You know, Grandma Richardson watched a lot of your Uncle Jack's high school basketball games, and she said it wasn't easy and fun all the time. She worried about him so much. Parents do that, you know. Can't stop themselves 'cause they want the best for their kids. You'll probably find out some day," Janet said, turned and smiled.

"Don't know about that, but it went okay for me. I wasn't really very nervous. I had things to do, but I guess you just sat."

"Right, and then in the back of my mind...."

"Was Dad, I suppose, huh?" Tina said with slight irritation.

"I can't help myself when it comes to that. Sorry, hon."

The truck remained silent for several minutes as they drove through Van Wert and turned south on the road that would take them home to Barton.

"Mom, there's one little thing in the back of my mind, and...well...forget it."

"What?"

"No, forget it, Mom," Tina turned to look out the side window.

"What? Tell me, okay?"

"I shouldn't say this, but it won't go away. And I know, I'm sure it's not so, but it won't go away. Do you...do you wonder that the judges thought 'Oh the poor little crippled girl' and they..."

"Absolutely not, Tina! Get that out of your head. It's all judged on horse and rider communicating and doing all those moves right. Appearance is not the big thing, other than how the horse *appears* to cooperate and perform. Judges stick to those things. You, of course, your outfit, is part of it. But it's how *you* and your horse perform, how well you've trained and can control her. You were just another rider to them."

"Well, when you put it that way, I don't feel..."

"That's what you want to be—just another rider. No special

breaks, I guess is the way I'd put it. Isn't that what you want? Be just like any other kid?"

"I sure hope so, Mom."

"Well, let's try to get those thoughts pushed down and out. You did such a great job today! Just think about what you can tell Dad when he gets home." Janet smiled and turned her attention back to the road.

"I've been thinking of entering in the Horsemanship class next year, anyway. I'll actually ride instead of walking beside her. That would eliminate that whole issue, wouldn't it? But…understand me now, Mom, that's not easier. So, I'm not running away from anything."

"You never have, Christina, you never have."

⋅ ⋅ ⋅ ⋅ ⋅

Tom sat in Chuck Williams' red number eleven. The cars were lined up in their starting order on the front straightaway at the New Bremen half-mile speedway with Tom on the pole position, by virtue of his qualifying time of 18.92, a new track record. He had then proceeded to win his heat race in a convincing manner, nearly lapping the last place car but failing to break the old eight-lap record.

Billy Wallace was starting in second place, just to Tom's right, in Cal Olsen's car. Willy Caldwell fussed with something on the engine as Billy stood between his car and Tom's. Billy cinched his helmet tighter, stretched his fingers out in his leather gloves, and flipped his face shield back. His goggles still hung loosely around his neck.

Tom looked to his right and considered his young friend and how far he'd come in a little over a year. Perhaps he hadn't won a great many races, but he was always a factor in any race he entered and insiders knew his future was bright. Just like the Heisman Trophy winner was an odds-on favorite to be an NFL star, or the MLB Rookie of the Year might enjoy a long career and end up in the Baseball Hall of Fame, Tom knew that Billy could be an Indianapolis 500 winner someday. "Those are some fancy boots you got there, boy!"

Billy turned and smiled. "These are the latest, old man! Like a boxer's shoes. Light, so my feet can dance on the pedals! Just follow me and find out, Tom!"

"Those are nice, but I like my old leather boots. I've had enough hot oil and water blown back to teach me a few lessons. Good luck, Twinkle Toes!"

Billy said, "Hope you finish second, Tom!"

"Follow me, Billy! I'll show *you* how to finish second!"

Carl Connors, in Chuck Williams number twenty-two, lined up to start in fifth position, inside row three. Chuck leaned on the roll bar of his car. The push truck nudged up close to the push bar at the rear of the race car. Chuck absently stared ahead, looking at the outer crash barrier in turn one, the one that many drivers said was still not suitable—still too low. Connors sat in the car, twisting the steering wheel left to right through a few degrees of movement. The old recording of "The Star-Spangled Banner" scratched through the last few bombastic bars. Fans replaced hats and opened another beer. Kids scattered away from the high, but uncomfortably flimsy-looking fence that separated the crowd from the track, as they gave up any last chance for an autograph or good photo. A young boy shouted, "Let's go, Billy!" Stepping into his yellow racer, Billy looked to his right as he leaned on the seat back, half-standing, and waved in the general direction of the voice. As he did, several fans waved and whistled at the crowd's young favorite.

"I made a few changes, Tom, while you were standing with Billy watching that last race," Donny Housman began, tentatively. "I talked to Chuck about it, too." Donny sounded sheepish, reluctant to admit what he'd done.

"Well, what can I do about it now, Donny?" Tom said and smiled. "If I can't trust your judgment, I can't trust anyone's. Just give me a good car, and I'll work with that."

"I did two things. I put in a smaller injector pill to give you a little richer mixture. Maybe we won't burn a piston."

"Okay, sounds reasonable."

"And I changed the rear end gear set so we got a 4.85. The track is really drying out and this place don't get much of a cushion. I'm afraid with that other gear, you might be more likely to do a lot of tire spinning. No big changes, just tinkering around the edges, you might say."

"I can handle tinkering, Donny. You learned your lessons well from ol' Chuck!"

The track announcer said, "Okay, Fans, this is what you came for—thirty laps of racing by the finest drivers anywhere! Let's give them a big send-off. Remember, on the lap before the start, let's give them a wave and show them your enthusiasm."

Both Billy and Tom signaled their push truck drivers with a hand motion indicating "forward." The push truck drivers accelerated hard in low gear, and Tom felt the rear of his car rise. He waited a few seconds as the engine chuffed, flipped the magneto on, and the engine burst to life. Billy did the same. Tom pulled ahead of Billy through turn one and two, idling along, allowing the oil to warm. Billy did the same but punched the gas on the back stretch and easily passed Tom.

The first four rows, eight cars, began to fall in line. They slowed and drove close to the outside wall on the front stretch as the next group of cars were being pushed off. There weren't enough push trucks for the field of eighteen cars to all be started at the same time, so some had to wait their turn.

Most fans were standing, as they would for the first five or six laps. Many owners and crew men had staked out vantage spots: some on top of tow vehicles, some on top of trailers, some inside the first or fourth turns, a few on top of mounds of dirt that surrounded light poles for night races. (Tom once had looked at those mounds and wondered how any driver could complain about a guardrail that was too low and not be concerned about hitting one of those "ramps.") Of the six or seven thousand individuals gathered, there were few sitting, except the eighteen drivers.

In less than four minutes, the field of cars had nearly assembled into correct order. One official with a clipboard in hand stood at the start/finish line, looking carefully at the nine rows of two as they idled by. Seeing something he didn't like, he signaled to the starter in his perch atop the outside wall. He exaggeratedly shook his head, indicating for the starter to wait. As the field came by, the official with the clipboard pointed to a car outside row six to move up in the order. The driver did as he was told.

As the cars made another pass by the flagman, the official looked them over carefully. Impatient fans shouted, "Let 'em go!", "Let's go!", "Turn 'em loose!"

The official nodded to the starter. All was ready for thirty laps of racing. The field made one more pass by the starter, drivers and fans waved. The starter had his green flag furled in his hand, held up so the drivers understood that this was, likely, the last preliminary lap. Tom, as pole position starter, had the responsibility of setting the speed of this last pace lap. He had no desire to trick anybody, including Billy, by lagging and purposely bunching up the field. Nothing more dangerous than eighteen race cars all packed together closely. Add to that the open wheels of the cars. One may run up on another's tires and the resulting clash might launch one or more up and into another car. Better to accelerate steadily, allow all to find their spot safely, and then race.

Tom led the field at an even pace through turns one, two, the back stretch, and turn three. Exiting turn four, he mashed the accelerator down. Billy stayed right with him, as if they were tied together. Billy's position gave him a better approach to turn one, closer to the racing line, high and near the wall in the straight, allowing him to enter turn one three quarters of the way up the track. Tom found his line into the first turn perhaps not ideal, but good enough to get a half car length lead that he held through turn two. Tom's momentum took him toward the outside wall on the back stretch, forcing Billy to back off and follow Tom. In turn three, Billy tried to dive under Tom and pass him on the left, but he drove too low and got into the part of the track that had less banking. As Long as there was some moisture where Tom was, closer to the wall, that was the fast way around. Billy stayed low through turn four, raising clouds of dust. Two more cars tried that route, but like Billy, found it to be a poor approach. That could change in another twenty laps, but Billy and most other drivers soon moved into the higher groove.

Tom never looked back, never heard another engine coming from behind, never saw the nose of another car threatening to pass. For the next twenty-five laps he was alone in this dusty world, seeming to circle faster and faster, until his perception of location on the half-mile oval dimmed: straight, turn, north, south, front, back—they all nearly disappeared for him. His vision narrowed until all he saw was a band of brown earth rising before the nose and two front wheels on his car, wiggling left and right with his steering corrections.

Race cars were noisy beasts, even discounting the unmuffled exhaust. They generated a cacophony of sounds: greatest, of course, was the unmuffled engine exhaust, the rattling and shaking of body panels; the sucking of the injector throats only feet away; the thudding of the car as it jolted through ruts and growing holes in the track; the rasping of tires as they churned over the bumpy, hardening clay; the rush of wind at nearly a hundred miles an hour. Race cars also created unique physical sensations for the driver: G forces that flung the driver to the right side, forcing him onto the seat tab or his belts; the wind tore at his clothing; sweat soaked his thin uniform and the bandanna covering his nose and mouth; his helmet was not ventilated and sweat trickled down his neck; arms ached from constant steering to control the sliding car.

Tom saw no faces in the crowd, just a blur of color on his right every twenty seconds or so as he passed the front stands. There was the flagman with his green flag fluttering in the swirling gusts of wind stirred up by clots of cars as they passed under him. Every five seconds a green light swept by his right side—the four track lights never changing color for those twenty-six—or twenty, or twenty-eight, or twenty-one, or nineteen—he had no idea where in the thirty laps they were; figures flashed by: Donny, Chuck—he wasn't sure—some men inside the front straightaway—just figures, but

Tom had no recognition of individual faces. A brownish haze rose and surrounded the entire half mile circle, swirling and getting sucked into momentary, billowing clouds as cars drove through it; the front stretch wall swept close to his right side with each lap as did the back stretch barrier; he aimed his car for the approximate middle of the track on each turn and allowed the car to drift up close to the crash barrier on each straight, turning the oval into as much of a circle as he could, trying to make it into the "little Langhorne." He had lost awareness of almost everything outside of this circle. He ran in the clear, by himself with no threats from behind for ten laps but then began lapping tailenders. They were easily dispatched, except for the car holding eighth place. He was running the same groove as Tom and ignored or did not see the "lay-over" blue flag with the horizontal orange stripe. That car was a momentary obstacle, that Tom avoided by leaving his accustomed groove as he exited the south turn, passing on the left. He had no perception of time, of the eight minutes that had elapsed since the start.

Donny knew Tom was on his twenty-sixth circuit. He kept a metal counter in his left hand and clicked it each time Tom crossed the finish line. He made his twenty-sixth click as Tom passed by, then looked to his right, searching for Carl Connors and Billy. Then Donny heard an "Oh" from crewmen nearby and saw them point to the left. Tom was lapping a car in his accustomed, proven groove. The driver apparently tried to make room for Tom, moved left, but caught a rut that lurched him to the right just as Tom was passing. His right-side wheels bashed into the left-side wheels of Tom's car. A more perfect match couldn't have been planned and practiced; eight or ten inches either way and one car could have easily ridden over the others' tires, possibly launching it out of control.

The shock of the collision sent a jolt through Tom; he lost focus for seconds and his foot lifted off the pedal. The other driver recovered momentarily, made one complete loop and drove on. Tom rebounded to the right, slipping up into the loose dirt thrown up near the crash barrier between turns one and two. The collision had thrown him to the right side of the open cockpit, and he leaned partially out as he struggled to regain control of his car.

Damn! Get with it! Must be about half the race over, huh? He felt as if he had been shaken from a long sleep. This was a new sensation one he had verged on a few times but never so completely, like being lost in a…he had no word for it…a dream or fog? The experience was neither pleasant nor unpleasant. It was as if he'd vanished for minutes or hours—but where he'd gone, he had no idea.

With effort, he regained his composure and attention. He shook off the "fog" and forced himself to concentrate on his location: the backstretch, the New Bremen Speedway. He told himself to push his foot to the floor, he told himself to drive closer to the backstretch wall, he told himself to twitch the wheels left then quickly right to throw the car into turn three and steer to the right to hold the sliding car through turns three and four, he told himself to steer to the front stretch wall, he told himself to look for Donny as he completed lap—*I have no idea what lap I'm on, but Donny had up two or three fingers, I think.*

A yellow car with a seven painted on the tail appeared ten or twelve lengths ahead. *Billy, I ain't seen him since the start!* He had been at the top of his form in a car that was giving him all it had. *I could pass him. I could pass him if I had five more laps, but there's only two to go.* But whatever he'd had for the first twenty-five or twenty-six laps was much diminished now. It had all been so automatic, but now—that collision had been like a slap in the face. He had to think his way around the last few laps.

Billy's car drew closer to him on lap twenty-eight, and as the two completed lap twenty-nine, they passed under the flagman, his white flag waving. Tom had no idea of Billy's place in the race, only that he had not seen him since the start. *How many cars did I lap? That…trance. Is that what it was? But I never saw that yellow car.*

On the last lap, Tom moved to within one car length of him in turn one. Billy's rear tires spun on the now slick and dry track. On the back stretch, Tom moved up even closer to Billy, and as they entered turn three he shook the wheel quickly left and right, to shake the back end loose. He drove higher on the track than he had so far, trying to pass this one last car. Doing so meant he'd have lapped the whole field. Billy ran low, Tom high as they exited turn four and headed for the checkered flag. He had the speed to pass Billy…but enough room between him and the wall? He would have lapped the whole field. But he backed off and didn't do it! A thought momentarily flashed through his mind: *Tom, you use your head too damn much!*

* * * * *

Tom sat slightly apart from Donny, Chuck, Billy, and Carl Connors in the shady grove behind the front straight stands. His sparse, graying hair was still wet with sweat. His uniform was dusty and sweat-stained. His hands were steady. They no longer shook as they had during the trophy presentation thirty minutes before—not from fear, but from the pure excitement of driving fifteen miles in ten minutes and fourteen seconds, a new track record. A race that was never interrupted by caution flags or accidents. Fans still approached him with comments, picture and autograph requests. There were many "Great job," "Congratulations," "Can I shake your hand?" "What a race,

Tom," comments. His three companions ate their chicken dinners, and Tom, staring down at the boxed chicken dinner in his lap, was about to eat a drumstick when a pair of dusty, wing-tip shoes entered his line of sight.

"Excuse me, Mr. Lawton, I hate to bother you now. Looks like you're just getting started."

Tom looked up from his boxed lunch at a man holding a large, Day-Glo red cowboy hat.

"Mr. Lawton, sir, I was at Indianapolis this year and—"

"Holy crap! You were in one of the rows closest to the wall at the exit of turn one!"

"Yeah! How could you know that?" The man, dressed in an old oil company logo t-shirt and what had once been dress pants, held out his race program. "I don't understand."

"I noticed you around…not sure…after my second pitstop? Or after that big wreck. I couldn't figure out why you were giving me the finger because…"

"That wasn't for you, Mr. Lawton! It was for that little, funny-lookin' car! The guy who won!"

"It took me a while to figure that out. But I saw you! You waving that hat! I figured out you were cheering for me, at least that's what I thought!"

"Absolutely, Mr. Lawton. But you saw me? At a hundred and…forty, fifty miles an hour? Nah, I can't believe it!"

"How could I miss that big red hat and a guy flipping me off? But, yeah, I could see a few people in the stands, especially the one I began to call Red Hat Man!"

"You saw me and you…remember? I'm, I'm—"

"Let me sign your program. That okay?"

"Okay? Sure, but what you've said means so much to me, even more than an autograph, Mr. Lawton."

"Can I look at your program, uh…Red Hat Man?" Tom looked at the program. He was amazed at the detail. All the drivers' names were printed neatly in ink, along with car names and numbers, their first and second qualifying lap times, preliminary race lineups and finishing orders, and race times, feature race lineup and finishing order, and elapsed time of race. He'd written the weather conditions, the route he'd taken to get to New Bremen, and the track conditions. He even had the size of the crowd. "Where should I sign this? I don't want to mess this up."

"Front cover okay, Mr. Lawton?"

"You can call me Tom, okay?"

Tom turned to the front cover of the program and wrote, "Many thanks to my turn one, row one fan—Red Hat Man. You just made a new friend, Tom Lawton, car # 11 and car # 33." He handed it back. The man read what Tom had written, smiled, shook Tom's hand and backed away, holding the program like a holy relic.

Donny said, "Red Hat Man? You've got to explain that to me on the way home today, Tom."

Chapter 9

Roger Hicks wandered through the aisles of the Barton farm store, looking at anything that caught his eye—bird seed, motor oil, garden hoses. He'd stopped on his way home from Maxcell to get a part for his lawn mower but had lost focus. He was in no great hurry, and his lack of direction may have been a convenient ruse. He knew that Janet Lawton was working. He had seen her when he'd entered, ringing up a sale for a customer, but had no desire to distract her.

Missy Wilkins called over her shoulder as she went out the front door, "See you tomorrow, Jan."

"Okay, hon, have a good evening…goin' out with Ray, right?"

"Yes, ma'am."

Roger put a bag of bird seed back on the shelf, looked around the store and saw that he was the only customer. A stock boy was straightening up items in the tool aisle. The only people in the store were that boy, Roger Hicks, and Janet Lawton. Roger picked up a lawnmower wheel and went to the check-out counter, where Janet stood with her back toward him, reading a newspaper. Roger put the wheel on the counter. Janet turned around.

"Roger! Good to see you! Still dressed for work I see. Well, that makes sense, doesn't it? It's just a little after five."

"Jan, I haven't talked to you in…I don't know how long. Kinda funny, isn't it? Such a small town and going to school together for twelve years. We started first grade together and were in the same class all the way. Well, it changed in high school a bit, taking different classes and all."

"Yeah, you took all that math and science. That wasn't for me—just took what I had to. I wasn't a great student, you know that."

"But you were such a pretty girl—are a pretty girl, well, woman, I mean…still are pretty. I blew that, didn't I?" Roger looked away.

"Let's face it, we aren't teenagers anymore."

"Yeah but go ahead and say something to pay me back for that. Say, 'Your forehead is a lot longer now.' That would be fair," Roger grinned and ran his hand over his thinning hair. "But twelve years of school, and we've been out another… sixteen years, right?"

"That's a lifetime!"

"Say, I read about Tom all the time in the newspaper. He's having one heck of a year!"

"He's been very fortunate, so far. Ever since the 500, things have really been going his way. Knock on wood." Janet rapped on the counter and smiled. "Superstitious, ain't I?"

"Well, July's almost over and, by my count, Tom's won four races, right?"

"Yeah, four wins, two seconds, two third places, and…oh, I lose track of it all. But he's leading in the points count. And he didn't even enter the first race, out east. Oh, I forgot, there was one race when his car broke down. Now, next month, his schedule gets even busier. This month there were just two sprint car races and one Champ car race—in New Jersey. So, he's filled in some idle time with midget races. That's where he is tonight—over in Columbus."

"He races those, too?"

"Makes a little money. It helps. But next month, as I was saying, he has three champ races—two of them in two days, back to back! Then another one a week later. Then throw in three sprint car dates. Lot of racing, *and* a lot of traveling to get there. He'll be gone a lot, but the season is half over already."

"You know, I talked to him about some part-time work, but he said it probably wouldn't work too well."

"He told me about that. That was really…nice…well…*helpful* isn't the right word, but it *could* have been helpful, if the scheduling thing worked out better."

"Maybe sometime. I was serious about that. Still am. Maybe when he slows down, retires from driving."

"Thanks. That means a lot," Janet said, smiling.

"Of course. Say, Christina must be about what, fifteen or sixteen now?"

"Sixteen. Learning how to drive. Matter of fact, she'll be ready for her driving test soon."

"She looks so nice on that horse. I drive by on my way home from work a lot, and she's out there in that field."

"That's out of your way, going by our place like that."

"Uh, well, I like to…to…enjoy a little longer ride home sometimes. Driving with the windows open, just ambling along and looking at the farms and fields. It helps me unwind from a day in the office."

"Stop in some time."

"Really? I might do that." There was a pause and Roger reached for his wallet. "Christina looks so *nice* on that horse. Just…like a young lady. You must be proud."

"I…we…are proud of Tina."

Roger put a ten-dollar bill on the counter. "Does she have any thoughts about what she'll do after high school? College or business school…or something?"

"She's starting to think about that, but you know how it is. When you're sixteen how can you pick out a job for *life*? That's the way it is for most kids."

"I'll take your word for it. Suzy and I are outsiders when it comes to parent stuff. As much as I work—and Suzy is *so* busy all the time—it's probably just as good we don't have children. She loves teaching, says those second graders are *her* kids. But if I had a daughter, I'd want her to be just like your Chr…Tina. I'll get her name right."

"That's quite a compliment. Sometime, somehow, I'll tell her, and Tom, what you said."

"Okay. Give Tom my wishes for him, to keep this good season going. If there's anything I can do for you, Tom, and Tina, too, for that matter, let me know." Roger walked away, but stopped when he heard Janet call to him.

"Hey! Did you forget something, Roger?" Smiling, Janet held out the wheel and his change.

He returned for his change and purchase. "Oh, jeez! What was I thinking? Guess I wasn't thinking, huh? See you later, Jan."

"Thanks, Roger." Janet watched him walk out the door. Her old, old doubt momentarily rose until she pushed it down.

* * * * *

Roxanne Lytell sat at her kitchen table, eating a cold-cut sandwich, chips, and enjoying a cold bottle of Stroh's beer. Her feet were on the other kitchen chair—there were just two—and her high heel shoes and hose were on the floor, under the table. The kitchen blended into the living room that had a hide-a-bed couch, one occasional chair, an end table beside the chair, and another by the couch. There was a small, portable black and white television set on a metal stand. There was a small bathroom. That was Roxie's apartment. More like a motel room. A place to sleep but it met her needs and, just as important, perhaps more, gave her the independence she desired. It was close to the local university and was often rented by students. She was about to finish her meal when the phone rang.

"Hello, may I ask who's calling?"

"Roxie! It's Billy! So good to hear your voice!"

"Hi, Billy. You're not racing tonight? Oh, shoot, what was I thinking? It's a Wednesday. Nobody races in the middle of the week."

"Well, they do, and I have—quite a lot lately. But not tonight."

"So, what's going on with you?"

"There's a track up north of you, well, north of Muncie somewhere. They run a lot of stock cars and modified stocks. They started running midgets a while back—some Indiana group. Now they're wanting to step up their game some, get USAC to run a midget show there. They hope they'll get some Indianapolis drivers then."

"So, you're racing up there tonight?"

"No, I'm just goin' up there to watch, look around, and then go back to the office in Indy and tell the officials if I think the place looks okay, how well they're organized, if the place looks safe. Stuff like that. I thought maybe you'd like to go along. How about it? Want to go?"

Roxie scratched the paper label on the beer bottle. She gazed out the open window. "Billy, that's a night race. I'd get home at…eleven or midnight?"

"We're young, Roxie. It won't be *that* late!"

"But you don't have to get up and…a girl's got a lot of stuff to do in the morning. Hair, make-up. And you can sleep as long as you want to. You don't punch a time clock."

"Aw, come on, Rox. One night ain't gonna take that much out of you. Take a nap the next day. Sleep late on Saturday. It'll be a good time."

"Billy, I just can't go with you."

"Don't turn me down again, Roxie. You were so good to me, stayin' at the hospital and all after the 500."

"I'm sorry, Billy."

There was an awkward pause. Finally, Billy said, "Maybe I'll stop on my way home. I can leave a little early, and maybe you'll still be up. What about that?"

"Oh, I usually go to bed around…well, if I'm still awake, maybe. Don't be knocking a whole bunch. If I don't answer after two knocks, you'll know I'm sleeping."

"Okay, see you later, maybe."

. . . . .

Roxie got up at six o'clock and started her morning routine. Billy was still sleeping when she sat down on the bed beside him. "Billy, honey, wake up…Billy." She ran her hand over his cheek.

He roused slowly and blinked his eyes open. "Roxie, you are beautiful. I've never seen you dressed for the office. What a sight to wake up to!"

"Billy, I've got to say some things to you. I want you to listen, and I don't want you to interrupt me. I don't want to stop once I start saying what I have to say, okay?"

"I don't think I can do that."

"I meant what I said. If you can't, I'll walk out now and you'll never understand. You'll just get mad and…and…you just won't understand. And I want you to *understand* me and not think awful about me."

"Okay."

"Billy, I like you a lot. I *love* you, Billy. I have *never, ever,* in my life said that to a boy, or a man. And right now, I don't know if I'll ever tell a guy that. I love *you.*"

"That's—"

"Billy, I want you to listen to me without saying anything!"

"Okay."

"When I saw you in that car, flying and flipping upside down! I *saw* you in there! The car was way up in the air! The guy I love! And when I got to the hospital…there you were all bloody and…If you had landed one way, maybe a few feet this way or that way. If the car landed upside down time after time…or if another car ran into you while you lay there…or if the car caught on fire! How many things could have happened differently? I *can't* live with the guy I love…risking that, living like that week after week, year after year. I want you to know that I love you, and that's why I can't see you anymore, Billy. I cannot see myself losing the person I love. And, if we continued the way it had been, it seemed to me that this wasn't just a casual fun thing. It seemed to me we were…going…*toward* something."

"Yes, I think so."

"And how could I go on without you then. And there might be children, too, sometime. I can't risk that, Billy. I can't see myself losing you, losing the father of our children."

Roxie was sobbing, and her neatly applied make-up was ruined, running down her cheeks. She was gently running her fingers over Billy's face. She leaned down and laid her head on his. She spoke quietly and directly through her tears. "Billy, I'm going to leave now. I want you to remember what I said, but don't hate me. I love you, and that's why I have to do this. I love you so much that I can't lose you that way." She kissed him on the cheek through her tears. "Goodbye now, Billy." Then she walked out the door, leaving a silent Billy Wallace behind.

· · · · ·

Eddie Spencer and Walt Morrow—the sponsor of Chuck's new car—walked out of the Linden Tavern late on a Thursday night in October. They had left the monthly meeting of an auto race fan club in Dayton, after the film of the recent Indianapolis 500 but before another about the Daytona race in February. The Indy film brought back bad feelings for them— their disappointment for Tom Lawton— which they didn't want to dwell on. Nor were they interested in all the amateur advice they were likely to hear about how, "Tom messed up when…" and "His pit crew should have…" and "Them damn officials…."

Eddie stopped at Walt's car. "So, Walt, how do you feel about being a sponsor?"

"Eddie, I know that if I put a few thousand dollars in a car, I'm not going to see a lot of money coming back to me in new business at the shop. Not at this level. Sure, there will be some. But it's another way to get our name out to the public. I love this kind of racing and want to support it. My advertising budget pays for the sponsorship, so to me it seems kind of free. Kind of."

"You still okay with Chuck's work though? That car does look good, and I hear the track announcers all the time calling it the 'Precision Tool and Machine Special.' You're getting good publicity."

"Sure, I know all that, but I just like getting back into it all again. I'm making enough money now that I can have some fun. And that's what the race car is…fun for me. I don't have to work on it, I don't own it, and I don't have to worry about all that. I'm happy with it all this way, Eddie."

"Chuck told me that he's having a hard time getting used to that new car. It's different in some ways than his old one, the one that Lawton drives. And his driver wants to change things on the car all the time. Billy Wallace drove it a few times before he got in Olsen's cars. Chuck said Billy could make any car into a winner. He could overcome any problem with just the talent and determination he has."

"So, one guys wants to change everything, and another guy just takes the car as is and won't say much of anything!"

"Right, so Chuck listens to Connors, nods his head, and then does what *he* thinks is right. In the past, Chuck would look at his set-up book to see how he ran it last year. Then after Tom hot-lapped it, the two of them would get Cokes or coffee and just go off by themselves, away from all the other drivers and mechanics, and just talk about the car, the track. I don't think he has that kind of communication with Connors. Your car is brand new. Chuck told me he looks at his old book and uses that to get started, but he does a lot of experimenting."

"My feet are killing me. Let's sit down. Get in the car." Walt motioned for Eddie to get in the passenger seat of his car. "I just bought this thing last month. Really like it."

"Pontiac, right?" asked Eddie. "Geez, this is nice!" Eddie ran his hand over the center console and floor shifter.

"Grand Prix, brand new Pontiac. But let's get back to Chuck and that new car. What do you think of Connors taking over for Billy. I thought that Billy in the new car and Lawton in the other car was going to be a hell of a one-two punch. But Wallace took off for what he thought were greener pastures."

"Billy has the whole deal now: Indy roadster, dirt car, sprint car, even a midget. He doesn't have to go from team to team. It's all there, and a pretty good crew chief in Caldwell. And a salary! I can't blame him a bit."

"You're right, yeah." Walt paused, leaned back in the driver's seat, was silent for a time, then mused. "It's all kind of…odd…or I don't know how to say it, but now you have two good friends, former team-mates—Lawton and Wallace—running one-two in the points standings for the championship this season."

"*Former* team-mates, like you said. I wonder how Chuck would handle it if they were *both* still driving for him."

"You know Chuck a lot better than I do, Eddie. What do you think?"

"I talked to Chuck a little after the Salem race, the hundred lapper. Billy drove a heck of a race and lapped everyone except for second and third. He lapped Tom in fifth place. Chuck was okay with it, he's not bitter about Billy leaving to drive for Olsen. That's the way it is—drivers go for what's best for them. Anyway, you could almost say that Olsen's number seven has a lot of Chuck in it—he rebuilt it. And he likes Billy, respects his talent."

"That'll be some showdown out there at Ascot next month. Lawton is up by…how many points?"

"I'm not sure, but I know Billy has a mathematical chance to beat Tom. Tom's ahead in points, but if he has a bad night: mechanical trouble, wrecks. Anything can happen, you know that. And if Billy wins, well, then he's the champion. Winning that big race at Salem is what got him in the hunt. I'd love to go, but that's a long trip to watch a ten-minute race. You going, Walt?"

"Nah, things are too busy at the shop. But I'm like you on that…like to go…*but*. Hey, Eddie, good talking to you. I better go."

"Yep, same, Walt. This'll all be decided before the next meeting. Take care." Eddie Spencer got out of Walt's Pontiac and realized he couldn't remember where he had parked. He wandered around among the cars. *Damn there it is! Right where I parked it, beside the blue pick-up truck!* He leaned on the side of his car to catch his breath. *They used to call me Speed! That ain't the right name anymore!* Eddie opened the car door, got in, and drove home.

Chapter 10

On a Monday in early November, Tom lingered in the kitchen of his farmhouse, his arms around Janet, saying his last goodbyes. He would ride with Donny Housman in the tow truck, ready to start the trip to Gardena, California. Chuck Williams would pull the new car. They hoped to make the two thousand plus miles in three or four long days, or one non-stop trip, if they felt up to it. Tom had packed two bags. His helmet bag had his uniform, boots, goggles, gloves, and assorted "track stuff," Tom's description for some back-up items. Another suitcase—from their honeymoon and rare vacations—was packed with street clothing. He kissed Janet then pulled her close, holding her for a long time.

"Well, Jan, with luck I should be home a week from Wednesday or Thursday, maybe really late. I'll call after the race Saturday night. No, that's a bad idea. Three hours difference means the race will be over around…uh…one in the morning out here, if everything goes okay, you know, no delays. I'll call you Sunday morning. Eight o'clock out there means eleven here, so that should work. Then we'll go on to the Sacramento race."

"I wish you weren't going, Tom."

"I know, and in a lot of ways I feel the same way, but this is different this year. The promoter wants some "500" drivers, and he'll pay just to get me there. And if I don't go, well, Billy will most likely be the champion. I can't just give it away like that."

"*If* the points race wasn't so close, *if* you had a bigger lead on him, *if* Billy hadn't won that Salem race," Janet mused.

"All true, all true. But I don't have to drive like I'm not the points leader. I've got enough of a lead on Billy that even if he wins, all I have to do is finish seventh or better. I can drive 'with my head and not my foot.' You know what I mean?"

"Sure, I do, but I don't really think you're going to do that. You race to win."

"We all do, but I'm going to race to win the *championship*. I can afford to back off, save the car, make sure it lasts for thirty laps."

"Okay, okay. I hear you. Be careful, and just take care of yourself."

"He kissed her one more time, hugged her, then walked to his truck. Janet brushed away tears and waved. Tina was in the field on her horse. Tom stopped, got out, and motioned for Tina to ride over to him.

"I'm leaving, kid. Time to drive over to Chuck's and head out west."

"Call us, Daddy, when you can. Think you can do that?"

"Why not? Sure, I'll do that. Now, lean down here and give me a kiss."

Tina bent over to her right, low as she could to reach her father. As she did, a silver chain fell out of her shirt with a high school ring on it. Tom stretched up, put his hand around the back of her neck, and kissed her right cheek. "I love you, Tiny Tina."

"How long has it been since I've been Tiny Tina? Ten, twelve years?"

"To me, you'll always be my Tiny Tina, even when you're

forty years, fifty years old! When I'm an old man sitting in a rocker on the porch, in my mind you'll still be Tiny Tina, even if you're six feet tall. Even if you make me a grandpa!"

"You're looking *way too far* ahead for me. Dad, you're something special." The horse snorted, impatiently.

"That old nag will never like me, will she? She's jealous!" Tom joked. "Hey, I'll see you in about a week. Take care, and help Mom, okay?"

"Sure, Dad. Love ya." Horse and rider returned to the center of the field. Tom watched his girl, no longer Tiny Tina he realized, but that girl was somewhere on her inevitable path, away from him. A sad but true thing, but inevitable, and ultimately good.

· · · · ·

Tom took a turn driving Chuck's car. Chuck, weary but not sleepy, talked about his many years of involvement in auto racing. Tom steered and listened, adding an occasional comment, just to let him know that he was listening.

"I've got two more years in my deal with Walt. He gave me a three-year sponsorship commitment. Tom, I'm not getting any younger, and I'm thinking about getting out of this after that agreement runs its course."

"Yeah, I can see that. Hard to work in the shop all day and then spend a few hours—or more—on the car, I suppose."

"Damn right. And this sport might be seeing some changes in the next few years, changes that wouldn't affect me right away, but eventually they will. It's that thing with C.J.... that car he won the 500 with this year."

· · · · ·

"Collect call from a Tom Lawton. Will you accept?" the long-distance operator said.

"Yes, I'll accept," Janet answered, groggily. "Hello, Tom?"

"Yeah, it's me, Jan. How you doin?"

"Not bad considering it's midnight."

"Mid…oh, right! I forgot. We're just pounding out the miles and I forgot all about the time difference. Sorry! We're gassing up in…uh…hey, Donny, where are we? Some place in New Mexico. Close to Gallup, he says."

"Are you stopping for the night?"

"Not sure. I've been the substitute for Donny and Chuck. I sleep until one of them gets tired, and then I take the wheel for one to rest."

"What if they both get tired at the same time, Tom? You guys thought about that?"

"That guy will have to wait to get tired!"

"You guys better stop! That doesn't sound like a great system."

"We might just try to drive it straight through, I'm not sure. Chuck did talk about stopping at a rest area and taking a nap, but we're okay so far. Anyway, how was your workday? Any problems?"

"No, boring. Missy was off today. She said she had 'stuff' to do, whatever that means. It was what I call a Moody Missy Day. I've known that girl since day one and I can see one of those moods coming. It'll take her over for two or three days, and that's when she's hard to get through to."

"Maybe it's just female—"

"No, Tom, not that. It's more…it's something else. And it's not Ray, either. She was like that, even in high school. Well, I don't know why I'm talking about Missy. She'll be okay. It happens to a lot of people."

"How was Tina today? School go okay?"

"She's fine. Said school was about as okay as school could be. Her words. She and James are on the front porch."

"On a school night?"

"James is helping her with her algebra."

"They've been pretty thick lately, haven't they?"

"Well, she says they're going steady."

"Huh? When did this happen?"

"Month or so ago. I thought you knew that. Course you've been gone a lot."

"Is that what that silver chain and class ring is all about? When I said goodbye to her yesterday, it slipped out of her shirt. It didn't register at the time. Huh. Steady boyfriend. James. Huh."

"Tom, sometimes you can't see what's right in front of you. I've got to get back to sleep. Next time maybe we can talk at a more reasonable hour."

"Right. Talk soon. Goodbye, Hon."

· · · · ·

Ascot Speedway in Gardena, California, was one of the truly great, half-mile dirt tracks in the country. In many ways it was like Terre Haute and some of the eastern tracks, such as Reading and Williams Grove, with longer straights and sharper, flat turns, unlike the banked, dirt ovals of New Bremen and Eldora. Night racing at Ascot made for superb traction—no hot, glaring sun to dry the dirt surface—and spectacular racing. A dedicated promoter and track staff ensured great competition and big crowds, especially when the stars of the Midwest made their annual, end-of-season visit. The West Coast stars looked forward to an opportunity to compete with their nationally known counterparts.

Adjacent to the freeway, Ascot was a busy track, offering stock cars, midgets, sprint cars, figure-eight races, and motorcycles. It had produced many drivers who'd moved on to the Midwest as preparation for a chance to race at Indianapolis. The western schedule also often included a championship race at Sacramento. As of Monday, Tom was only committed to the Saturday night Ascot race, though an opportunity to drive on Sunday was always possible. Chuck's driver, Carl Connors, had a ride in the Sacramento hundred-mile race as did Billy. Donny, Tom, and Chuck would start the return trip after the Sunday race.

· · · · ·

Twenty-three California cars took time trials late Saturday afternoon. Twelve cars from the Midwestern circuit made the trek out, including Billy Wallace with Cal Olsen's car. Billy qualified fastest— 23.21—of thirty-four cars. One car was damaged in hot laps and scratched for the night. Tom turned in third fastest time, 23.49, and Connors in Chuck's car qualified fifth fastest. Tom had a total of six hundred twenty points, and Billy had accumulated six hundred two points. If Billy won the race, Tom had to finish fifth or higher in the feature to ensure being named champion for the season. No other driver had a mathematical chance to earn that honor. It all came down to these two competitors, these two friends, this last race.

The first heat race with the six fastest cars lined up with Billy on the pole, a California car outside him; Tom was directly behind Billy, in third place; and Carl Connors in Chuck's other car was right behind Tom on the inside of row three.

After one false start by the car on Billy's right, last year's track champion, the green flag sent the field scrambling into turn one. Billy got into turn one and headed for the cushion, at this point in the evening's racing, a still-developing ridge of dirt fifteen feet from the outer guard rail. He held first place through turns one and two, down the backstretch, and through turns three and four. As Billy crossed the finish line to complete lap one, clouds of white steam erupted from the engine. Billy steered toward the inside of the track, driving over half-buried tires that marked the inside perimeter. He got out, looked at the oil dripping from the engine, took off his gloves, and threw them on the seat of the yellow racer. The race continued without him, the California car that started beside Billy winning. Tom ran a conservative race and placed second. Connors in Chuck's car finished third. When Tom pulled in after the race, Donny was waiting. "I can't be sure because Billy was in no mood to talk when he came walking by here, but it doesn't look good for car seven."

"Why? What you talkin' about? Just looked like a lot of steam. Water hose probably. Simple fix." Tom said as he unlatched his chin strap.

"Oil is pouring out of his engine. I think he's done for the night. Tom, you just became champion of the season. That car can't be fixed tonight!"

· · · · ·

"Sure, you can drive Connors' car, Wallace, but you know you go to the end of the starting order," the official told Billy.

"I know, but at least I have a chance to beat Lawton if I'm in the race. Sitting this out is giving up. I ain't giving up!"

Connors relinquished Chuck Williams' number twenty-two so Billy could have a fighting chance. Billy was back in the car he'd vacated in May to drive for Olsen, and he was racing to outpoint his friend. Both men were again in cars owned by Chuck Williams, the man who had brought Billy and Tom together last year. They were thirty laps, fifteen miles, from a resolution to the championship. Billy still had a chance, although it was a formidable one. He had to pass seventeen cars in thirty laps to win the race and hope that Tom finished no higher than fifth. Tom was in the first row, a great advantage. He just had to hold his own, drive "with his head, not his foot."

Billy walked to the first row of cars where Tom was

standing, helmet strapped on, his nose and mouth covered with a white cloth, staring toward turn one. His goggles hung down around his neck. Donny was squatted next to the left rear of the car, checking tire pressure. The red car was lined up second, outside of row one.

"Tom, good luck tonight."

Tom hadn't seen Billy approach and was mildly surprised to see his friend and rival. "Billy, what you doing up here? You better get back there with Chuck. He probably wants to give you some last-minute advice since you're sort of new to that car."

"A race car is a race car. Not much difference, at least in the good ones. I just wanted to say that I'm starting way back there, but I'm coming for you, Tom." His smile didn't hide his determination.

"I wouldn't expect anything less, Billy. We're all here to win. Good luck to you, too." Tom reached out, took Billy's hand, and shook it. "I know you can't see my mouth, kid, but I *am* smiling. See you later. These are the last thirty laps of the season, you know. See you when this is all settled!"

"Good luck, Pops!"

· · · · ·

Tom faded to third after twenty laps, driving as he'd told Janet he would. He could have contended for the lead, but the pole starter and another California driver used their home-field experience to great advantage, pulling out a ten-car length lead on Tom. Billy raced with the focus and determination he seemed to summon so easily. By lap twenty-one, he'd moved into fifth place and was able to see the red number eleven ahead. He still had an outside chance to pass Tom, but those two local hot dogs would be a challenge, to say the least. The leaders, Tom in fourth and Billy in fifth place, lapped slower cars. As they exited turn two and entered the back stretch, Billy was stunned to see Tom's car hit the outside guardrail, clear it, pinwheel in the track lights for a moment, then simply disappear into the darkness. Billy quickly glanced left, then right, threw up his hand to indicate he was slowing, pulled the car out of gear, steered toward the inside of the back stretch, stopped, and got out. The racing continued and the track lights stayed green. *What the hell? Throw the red flag!* He waited, looking for a gap in the speeding cars to run across the track. Finally, after that lap and another were completed, the track lights all went red. Billy ran across the track, hoping to find Tom's car upright and his friend safe.

* * * * *

Thirty minutes later, Billy walked back to Chuck's pit. Chuck was talking quietly with Carl Connors, who had given up Chuck's car for Billy.

"I'm done, Chuck. I can't race anymore tonight. Let's load up and go."

"You sure, Billy? You know what that would mean, don't you?" Chuck said. "I think Tom would want you to finish the race."

"That might be right, but I can't do that. That would

be…I'm not sure I can say what I think. But that would be one hell of a way to become champion. Is that the way Tom would do it? I don't think so. He wouldn't call himself a champion that way, and neither will I."

. . . . .

Epilogue

Weeks later, a different Tom Lawton came back from California. Treatment for severe concussion was rudimentary in the early 1960's. Therapy involved ice to reduce and control swelling, elevation of the head to avoid blood pooling, anti-inflammatory medications, reduction of stimulation by light and noise—all common treatment regimens of the time. Janet told the doctors this was Tom's second concussion, that she knew of for sure but Tom had been involved in high school sports, and getting one's "bell rung" was accepted as part of football, often laughed off by coaches and the young athletes themselves.

Doctors told her that Tom shouldn't fly home, that air pressure variations might cause more damage to his bruised tissues. She'd flown to Los Angeles on the earliest Sunday flight she could get and had asked Missy to stay with Tina until she and Tom were able to return. Janet had never flown but somehow made the flight arrangements on her own. Later she'd say, "I don't know what I did or how, but I got out there. I *had* to get there." Where she would stay, how long, how they would get home—those were questions she had not considered at the time.

Donny went to the hospital Saturday night, dirty as he was in his jeans and soiled white shirt. He sat in the emergency room waiting area until the ER doctor talked to him. He said that Tom's injury did not appear to be life-threatening but could have long-term consequences. That was as much as he'd say to non-family individuals, though he said he'd share more with Janet when she arrived.

Chuck, Billy, and Willy Caldwell, left the racetrack as soon as possible, skipping the usual post-race activities. They loaded the wrecked red number eleven onto its trailer before going to the hospital. The promoters locked the race cars into an equipment shed.

Janet got to the hospital in the early afternoon, California time. She'd been awake since a little after midnight in Ohio when Donny's call had woken her. Tom had been transferred to an intensive care unit. In the waiting area, she found Chuck, Donny, and Billy waiting, glum-faced, dirty, and tired—three men uncomfortable and out of place. There was nothing for anyone to do but wait.

Janet's "waiting" lasted nearly a week, time that allowed for arrangements to be made for her and Tom to get home. The racing community was also a fraternity, one that came together to help members in need. Cal Olsen seemed to have friends everywhere, and he contacted "a guy who owes me a favor." That favor was the use of an air-conditioned Cadillac for Janet to drive home. "Don't worry about it—it's just a car. I'll get it back to him," Olsen had said. So, over four long days, Janet and Carl Connors' wife took turns driving with Tom propped up in the back seat, dozing but comfortable, his eyes shaded with sunglasses and a washcloth.

· · · · ·

Tom would never drive a race car again, effectively. Attempts often found him spinning, missing the field due to slow qualifying times, or giving "the car doesn't feel right" explanations. He concluded that his skills were no longer sharp enough to make him competitive, even in Chuck's new car. He also knew that another, similar injury could have devastating results. His retirement from active racing did not remove him from the sport he loved and excelled at. He traveled with Donny and Chuck, helping with the car and serving as advisor to their drivers. That kept him busy during the racing season but didn't qualify as a job. "Jan, I need to find work. Something that will pay the bills."

Something found Tom. Roger Hicks stopped at Tom and Janet's house one day on his way home from Maxcell. He found Tom sitting on the front porch swing, sipping a beer.

"Tom, how you doing these days? Comin' along, okay? Relaxin' after a day of…whatever retired guys do."

"Relaxin', yes, but relaxin' don't pay the bills."

･ ･ ･ ･ ･

That visit led to Tom's employment at Maxcell. He did some production drill-press work, deburred and degreased parts from the machine shop, and was often fill-in man when extra help was needed for assembly jobs. His work enabled him to become part of the retirement and health insurance systems. Eventually, he got on the day shift and found it easier to travel with Chuck and Donny, helping with the number twenty-two race car. He enjoyed being close to the sport and competitors, both old friends and new drivers coming up. He especially liked watching Billy's steady improvement. Tina often accompanied her dad and the team for two summers. "It's fun, Dad. I really like it." She found it was a good way to keep an eye him, too. She also quickly learned how to deal with Donny Housman's good-natured taunting and goofy names for her: "short stuff," "kiddo," "girlie," and his personal favorite, "Gogeta" as in "Hey kiddo, go get a sandwich' or "go get a Coke."

･ ･ ･ ･ ･

Tina worked as an office helper for two summers at Maxcell. She was awarded the first ever Maxcell scholarship, which paid for two years of college. She earned an Ohio cadet teaching license, enabling her to get a position teaching English at Barton Junior High School. She completed her bachelor's degree in education at a nearby high school that served in a university extension capacity, offering night classes.

The track coach approached her in the school parking lot with an offer, not on the strength of athletic ability, but on her communication skills. "I need an extra hand, Tina. You want to be a track assistant?"

She chuckled and said, "Sure, Coach! I know *so much* about running! Whatever would I do?"

"I've seen you, talking with the kids. They love you and *listen* to you. You don't know how to run so much, but more important, I think you can make *them* want to run."

To her surprise, agreeing to "help out" as she called it—she never thought of herself as a coach, even though kids always called her that—was a good decision. After a meet one afternoon, she stopped at the concession stand for a snack. The visiting team was boarding their bus when she heard a girl say, "Well, Mr. Housman, didn't I tell you I'd whip these Barton girls in the mile?"

"Nice job, kiddo, nice job!" The tall, sandy-haired bus driver was standing by the open door of his bus. Tina, recognizing the man's voice and that "kiddo," turned around and saw Donny Housman, a man she had not seen for many years. The two old friends looked at each other in disbelief.

Tina hugged Donny and said, "*What are you doing here*?" at the same time Donny began to ask the same question. Some of the kids waiting to get on the bus poked their friends and smirked. One said, "Oooh, *Mr. Housman!*"

"Tina Lawton, little kiddo!" said Donny, using his pet name for the girl who'd often gone along with her dad when he'd worked as helper for Donny and Chuck. "I have a long and odd story to tell you. A story that involves Chuck Williams retiring, yours truly looking for a new job, a tip from a distant relative during a family reunion, and a newly consolidated school district in western Ohio looking for a bus mechanic. That school, Conway Consolidated, which today whipped your Barton Bulldogs, I'd like to remind you, took a chance on a race car mechanic. That mechanic—*again*, yours truly—filled in today for a sick bus driver. That's what brought me here. How about you?

That was how Tina renewed her friendship with Donny. And after several more years, Tina Lawton became Tina Housman. Long ago, Chuck Williams had said relationships sometimes best begin as friendships and the rest—romance—may occasionally "sneak up" later.

・・・・・

When the farm store acquired a similar retail outlet in a nearby town, Janet oversaw the expansion and eventually became "another something," her name for her new job. She was "just in charge of stuff" at two stores, as she described her new job. "I am manager/boss/number one bitch." I get called many things, that's okay. It pays the bills. *And* I get to work with my first baby girl/sort-of-sister/bookkeeper/friend, Missy Wilkins. What could be better?"

・・・・・

Janet was upstairs in the farmhouse she and Tom had lived in since they'd gotten married, over forty years ago. She wandered between bedrooms—hers and Tom's, Tina's, and an extra that had never been used a great deal, but became at various times a sewing room, the extra room (sleepovers) for Tina, then a catch-all room for many years of life, filled with horse show awards, old prom dresses, bridesmaid dresses, and unused furniture. And then there were Tom's trophies.

She walked around the room, looking at the ribbons from fairs and contests, Tina's show outfits, dresses hanging on a rack near the wall, the tarnished trophies, some broken, that Tom had won years ago. There was a box of photos: one picture of Tom, Tina, and herself before a high school prom; another of Tina and her beloved horse, Candy, in the field by the barn; a snapshot of Janet and Missy in the office at the farm store; Tom in his red number eleven race car with a push truck behind it; another picture of Tom, Chuck, and Donny after winning a race; a picture of Tom and James outside the Pine Street service station; one of a red race car close beside another at the Indianapolis finish line. Janet caressed each photo—with her eyes and her heart.

This was not going to be easy, but much had not been easy for her. It was time for this to happen, she had told herself often. It was something she, they, had to do. She went out to the hall, got an empty cardboard box, and started packing "horse stuff" in one, hoping that Tina would take some with her—she had planned to stop in with the kids sometime today. Janet mopped a tear with her shirt sleeve, smiled, and went ahead with her work, just as she had always done.

* * * * *

Tom sat on the porch swing, watching a neighbor on his tractor. He noted that the tractor didn't sound like the old "johnny-poppers" that he'd heard when he was a boy. It was a huge piece of equipment with dual rear wheels. He could see the little town of Barton was not quite so little now. A new development of homes was encroaching on farmland, and it was a distinct possibility that this small farm would be divided and filled with new homes one day. The field in which Tina trained Candy might someday be backyards with kids playing on swing sets.

He looked at the seat of the porch swing beside him. A pair of old, dry, and cracked leather gloves were on the seat. Tom knew the gloves were important, somehow.

Just then a car turned off the county road and drove down the lane, raising clouds of dust and crunching the gravel. The car stopped, and a forty-something woman got out. A boy and girl tumbled from the back seat, spatting with each other. The woman said, "You two, stop that, now," and walked toward the porch, limping slightly.

"Grandpa! Watcha doin'?"

"Grampy! Swingin' again?"

"That's about the best thing I've heard all day! Come on up here, I wanna hug you squirrels!" But the kids were already slamming through the screen door and probably headed to the cookie jar.

"Well, Daddy, we had a rare day with nothing scheduled so I thought I could help Mom some," Tina said as she sat beside Tom on the swing, squeezing her father's arm.

"That's sweet, hon. She's upstairs, I think, puttin' stuff in boxes."

"You can't pack boxes, Dad?"

"I started to, but after a while Mom said, 'If you're going to hold each and every thing for ten minutes and talk about when-where-how, maybe I should do this by myself, Tom.' I can take a hint. Right now, I can help by staying out of her way."

"That's funny, Dad."

"So, kids got nothing going on today, you say? Lizzy still all basketball crazy?"

"Now, but who knows? We let 'em try different things, so… who knows?"

"How about a horse? Isn't that a new idea?"

"Oh, Daddy, that would be nice. At least I know something

about that, but I think it's best if the idea comes from the kid," Tina mused.

"That's what a mom and dad that I know found out one time. And that turned out to be a very good thing." Tom looked at his daughter and smiled. "You know, kid, a young family, not so different than us at one time, came by to look at the place today. Mom came down while the realtor showed them around. We sat out here on the porch swing while they walked around, looking at the house."

"So, how did it go? Get any clues about what they thought?"

"No, they *seemed* interested, but who knows?"

Tina looked at her dad for a few seconds, looked down at her hands, and said, "Think I'll go inside, see what the munchkins are doing to disrupt Mom. Hey, what are these old gloves doin' here?"

"The gloves, yes! Billy stopped here today. Can you believe that? Billy Wallace! He wanted to show me his new award. Billy Wallace—the two-time 500 winner, and now he won this year as crew chief! Ain't that something? And I knew him when he was just a kid, too big for his britches."

"Remember that time over at Winchester? I must have been, what, thirteen or fourteen then, and he was tryin' to be all gentlemanly around Mom and Ernie and me? He had his arm in a cast."

"I remember that. Billy had never seen a high banked track before. That's the day Smitty tried to run me off the track. Eddie was there, too. Matter of fact, I introduced Billy to him."

"But these gloves, Dad. These things are all old, dry, and shriveled. They're not yours, are they?"

"Yes, the gloves! Billy said he was going through an old helmet bag, a *really* old one. Hadn't used that helmet in years. When he opened it up, he found a pair of driving goggles with a shattered lens and some dried blood stains. Then he looked in the helmet and found these gloves folded up in it."

"So, is there more to this story?"

"Those are the gloves I gave him back at Langhorne, when they had those twin fifties. That's the day he got a rock in his eye. He said he took them out of the helmet, said something to himself about 'old Tom', and thought I might have some good recollections of that day. He figured he'd take a chance and stop in, see if I was home."

"Billy's a pretty good guy, don't you think, Dad?"

"He is. I like that kid, well, he ain't a kid now. We didn't start out so great, but he grew up. I'm glad he didn't stay in it too long, you know? He drove a long time, and the longer you stay in, well, you know, things happen, even to the best. It's a lot safer twistin' wrenches than steerin' wheels! Say, he had that girlfriend for a while. I always wonder what happened to her, or to *them*. They quit seein' each other for some reason, and he married someone else."

"Yeah, and I'm like you, I think about her sometimes, too. Sweet girl. Rhonda…no, Roxie! That's her name. Mom had to take her out of the stands at Indianapolis…when there was that big wreck."

"Roxie Linton, no, Roxie…Lytell. That was her name, Tina."

"Donny has a story. I don't know if this means anything, but here's what he told me. He drove the track team to an early season meet, more like a scrimmage, over in Indiana a while back. He went up in the stands to watch and saw a woman. He looked at her and looked at her, thinking, 'Who is that? She looks so familiar.' But he could not put a name on the face. Then, he said there was this boy just tearing up the short distance events—hundred, two hundred, and he anchored the four by one hundred. When they announced the names of the winners in those events, it was a boy named

Billy Lytell. Then it clicked: was that Roxie? Was that boy her son? Donny didn't know Roxie too well, only saw her with Billy Wallace a few times, but he remembered that she was a beautiful woman. He looked for her after the meet but could never find her again."

"But Lytell? Why not some other name? She'd have to be married, right? Had a son."

"Maybe she wasn't married, Dad. Kept her own name."

"Huh. That *is* some story. Gotta wonder."

"Okay, Dad, I'm goin' inside to see what Mom's doing… *and, more important,* what my kids are doing."

"Now, wait! I just remembered something you'd like. That realtor. She brought that young couple to look at the house yesterday, and now get this, Tina. When they were leaving—they have a daughter, maybe twelve or thirteen years old. I can't judge ages good, you know. Well, that girl said, 'Look at that barn, Mommy! That would be a great barn for a horse!' "

"Oh, that was Candy's barn! And it *would* be a good place for a *girl and* her *horse.* I remember the time—well, there were so many times out there—the time James asked me to go out on a date with him. I was in the barn washing Candy, and he stopped in with his old car. He was a good boy, that James. I thought for a while we—you know—might have made a life together, but he went off to school, and we both took different directions. Where is he now, Daddy?"

"Not sure, he was up in Detroit working for one of the car companies. That's the last I know. I'd like to see him sometime. Oh, Eddie Spencer passed on. You might not remember him. He was a *real* old-timer. He helped Billy a whole bunch, getting' started at Indy. Some neighbor at his trailer park used to check on him every day. Found him on the sofa, TV on. Must have just slipped away. Just a tiny obit in the newspaper. Hardly even mentioned all the stuff he did."

"Donny wanted me to tell you about Chuck, Daddy."

"I don't like the sound of this."

"It's not *that* bad. He finally retired, sold the shop and house, but the buyer said he can stay in the house as long as he wants to. It'll be good for him, with Ernie gone now."

"I gotta wonder what he'll do now. He'll probably wander over to the shop, say something like, 'Got anything I can help with?' The new guys will name a few things, and he'll just smile, take a sip of coffee and walk out! A good man, Chuck Williams…*always* good to me. Speaking of good men, how's Donny? Not workin' too hard is he?"

"He's really busy, but things have settled down for him. The school consolidation finally got worked out. Most of the bugs are out of his end of it, at least. He's got a mechanic working for him, full-time. He does a lot of supervising work with the drivers, and bus routing, of course. They must have twenty-five buses, covering almost four hundred square miles. Not like the old days at Chuck's bus repair shop—five or six buses for, what, a fifty or sixty square mile district?

"Does he ever talk about our days racing, and all that?"

"All the time! We'll be watching TV and he'll see something—an old pick-up truck, a red race car, or a car numbered eleven—something like that. Then he'll say, 'Chuck had a truck just like that, same model year, same color.' Or he'll say, 'You know, Tom darn near won the 500 in a red car.' Then he goes off into what the kids call 'DonnyLand' with all his 'glory stories' and 'one time me and Tom and Chuck' reminiscences. The kids look at one another, roll their eyes, and yawn."

"No harm, girl, no harm. Those are good places to go sometimes."

"Oh, and listen to this! Some guy called a few days ago. Donny told me all about it. That surprised me, that he would even *tell* me about this. The guy said he'd set him up next year with a new race car, trailer, truck, and two years guaranteed sponsorship!"

"Oh, not sure about that. DonnyLand might be a better place, Tina."

"Yeah, DonnyLand *is* a good place. Here's another thing he's been workin' on. He thinks he tracked down your old number eleven. Chuck sold it out there in L.A., you remember, after the wreck. It was a mess, but somebody put it back together and ran it out there in California for a few years. It's been sittin' in a barn for a long time, but it's all there. Donny wants to buy it and restore it! He says they've got these things they call 'Old Timers' Days' when all the retired drivers and owners get together and talk about the old days. He says that would be a lot of fun!"

THE END

About the Author

Rich Gilberg was a teacher of history and language arts for forty years. He earned a bachelor's degree and master's degree from Wright State University. He taught in Graham Local Schools in Champaign County, Ohio. His long-time interest as a fan of open-wheel racing began in 1954 at age seven with a family trip to Winchester Speedway in Indiana, where he first saw the men who would become his heroes. Over many decades, he has seen nearly all the great men who chose to accept the risks and rewards of open-wheel racing. He is married to Beverly, his high school sweetheart, and now lives in Dayton Ohio. They have three children and nine grandchildren.

Printed in the USA
CPSIA information can be obtained
at www.ICGtesting.com
LVHW011312060324
773597LV00014B/440